THE

COMPLETE

DISCIPLE

A MODEL FOR CULTIVATING GOD'S IMAGE IN US

RONALD T. HABERMAS

An imprint of Cook Communications Ministries
Colorado Springs, Colorado

To my loving (and patient) wife
Mary
who has faithfully partnered with me
in marriage for 30 years.

Also, to our three wonderful daughters,
Elizabeth, Melissa, and Susan.
I am certain Fred MacMurray
(of "My Three Sons" TV fame)
never had it so good.

NexGen is an imprint of
Cook Communications Ministries, Colorado Springs, Colorado 80918
Cook Communications, Paris, Ontario
Kingsway Communications, Eastbourne, England

THE COMPLETE DISCIPLE
© 2003 by Ronald T. Habermas

First Printing, 2003
Printed in the United States of America

1 2 3 4 5 6 7 8 9 10 Printing/Year 07 06 05 04 03

Editor: Craig Bubeck
Cover Design: ImageStudios
Interior Design: ImageStudios

Unless otherwise noted, Scripture quotations are taken from the Holy Bible New International Version®. Copyright © 1973, 1978, 1984 by International Bible Society. Used by permission of Zondervan Publishing House. All rights reserved.

Library of Congress Cataloging-in-Publication Data

Habermas, Ronald T.
  The complete disciple / By Ronald T. Habermas.
    p. cm.
  ISBN 0-7814-3900-0
  1. Christian life. I. Title.
  BV4501.3 .H33 2003
  248.4--dc21

                                                        2003000031

Contents

—————◆—————

List of Figures and Tables

ACKNOWLEDGMENTS

Countless times over the past decade, my friend and colleague, Dr. David Brisben, and I have discussed this book's contents. Without exception, David's insights were "priceless." A couple years back, John Conaway (then at Cook) also helped to turn this literary dream into a reality. His early coaching skills were just what I needed. One of the unexpected pleasures of this project was a couple new friendships—those special "it-seems-I've-known-you-all-my-life" friendships: Rev. Paul Allen (Executive Editor of Rev. magazine) and I were finishing each other's sentences from the first day we met. Erin Healy offered her complementary gifts, as well, supplying keen editorial suggestions for this manuscript's formation.

I am further grateful for the many who prayed for this project and who offered timely encouragement: for fellow saints at John Brown University, for those at Fellowship Bible Church in Siloam Springs, for other friends, and for my extended family—but especially for my mother, Mrs. Roberta Habermas. I am so thankful for her persistent supplications to the Throne of God, on my behalf. Additional colleagues and friends in the greater "JBU family" deserve my heartfelt thanks, too: from Dr. J. Vernon McGee's Thru the Bible radio ministry (which generously endows the Chair I have been privileged to hold for ten years) to President Lee Balzer and Dr. Jim Worthington (Executive Vice President), who have regularly demonstrated their interest in resources on Christian discipleship.

It is difficult to even begin to fairly praise those who tirelessly invested "work in the trenches" for the sake of this book: Miss Sarah Blew, a part-time employee and full-time JBU student, has done much of this arduous duty. Also vested in this work are Mrs. Jerrell Ann Farmer and my daughter Melissa.

To the entire Cook team, I also say "thanks." I particularly appreciate Craig Bubeck, my editor, for his perseverance and leadership skills in sculpting this book. Likewise, thanks to Rev. Warren Wiersbe for his gracious pastoral advice.

Finally, I am indebted to my family: my wife, Mary, and our three daughters, Elizabeth, Melissa, and Susan. I don't know how to thank them enough: first, for their own personal testimonies in Christ and, second, for all that they sacrificed through the inordinate hours I spent on this task. Their lives have motivated me, inspired me, instructed me, and caused me to have a far greater admiration for the Family of God—what little I have experienced this side of heaven, as well as the tremendous anticipation for our celestial Home. Furthermore, I express my gratitude for Mary's superb skills in editing and proofing the manuscript. Her touch has made this a team effort.

Most importantly, I praise my Creator-Savior-Lord. I thank him for this difficult, yet satisfying journey—replete with the Sovereign mixture of pleasure and pain. My Father's rich blend of familiar truths and new insights about discipleship produced several epiphanies—some conflicting, some confirming—but all rewarding.

MORE PRACTICAL HELP FOR DISCIPLES

A great deal more materials were created for this complete model of discipleship, but they could not easily fit between these book covers. So additional resources are provided. Specifically, three of these Resources include:

- *Listing of Proven Resources*—An annotated list of dozens of best-selling resources for Christian living from Cook Communications Ministries.
- *Personal Growth Resource*—A practical tool to prepare for responsible Christian growth, consisting of both a how-to plan of growth and a series of reflective questions for each of this book's twelve chapters.
- *Supplemental Resource*—A useful tool that enables readers to go deeper in their study of biblical discipleship.

These resources are listed on the following website:

www.cookministries.com/completedisciple

Periodic information updates (such as additional, complementary products) may also be added to this website from time to time.

FOREWORD

I n recent years, the emphasis on discipleship has been very encouraging. Our churches desperately need maturing believers who can accept responsibility, give spiritual leadership, and train others to serve Jesus Christ. Our families need maturing parents who can guide their children into the best God has for them.

But there's a downside. When a healthy trend becomes a fad, so many books are published on the subject that people who are yearning for spiritual reality can easily become confused. What really is discipleship? Are there six steps to becoming an effective disciple or twelve steps? It depends on which book you read. How does discipleship fit into the total work of Jesus Christ and the total plan of God for my life? Most books on discipleship don't tell you.

This one does tell you just that. The most valuable contribution of this book is the way it integrates the truths of Scripture so that bits and pieces blend into an exciting pattern that makes sense.

It begins at the beginning—the creation of man and woman and their relationship to the God of Creation. It explains why God made us as he did and how in the experience of discipleship we can become all that he planned for us to be. As you read, reflect, and obey, you will not only learn more about God and his Word, but you will learn more about yourself and how being a faithful disciple can give you a life of fulfillment.

I commend this book to all thinking believers who are serious about learning and growing. It's not for religious hitchhikers who are looking for free rides to instant maturity. True discipleship is costly—but substandard Christian living is even more costly!

Take your choice.

—*Warren W. Wiersbe*

Introduction

✛

This book takes a fresh look at discipleship. It offers a comprehensive view of the Christian life, thus its title, *The Complete Disciple*. At the heart of the book is this message: All people bear the image of God because we were created in his image. The effects of the Fall severely distorted his image, but we never actually lost our priceless identity. The overarching purpose of discipleship—and it's a severely understated one—is to continuously restore the image of God within us. This is a lifelong task, and it obviously requires our Creator-Redeemer's power.

To accomplish this purpose, we disciples first return to Eden, but not in some nostalgic sense or in hope of finding Utopia. We figuratively return to the Garden to discover God's original intention for our lives. Once we reorient ourselves within Eden's homeland, we focus on subsequent acts of obedience; we specifically proclaim the Good News as we heed our Maker's voice to reflect his image to the world. We also look forward to our heavenly Home,[1] where we will one day be fully restored into Christlikeness. Why do we pursue this unconventional approach? Because Jesus first modeled this design: He adhered to the same Eden strategy through his incarnation as "the Last Adam" (1 Cor. 15:45). That deliberate Garden association, then, complemented his sacrifice on the cross. Our Lord's first connection demonstrated how we are to live, while his second connection enabled us to live again. Whenever we follow Christ within this two-part combination, we respectively make Jesus both our Lord and our Savior.

In order to communicate this comprehensive lifelong plan, I challenge traditional discipleship methods. This is not because these methods are inherently flawed, but because, individually, they do not represent the more complete goal of Christianity. I have no problem with conventional methods, products, or curricula. I would be dishonest if I did not admit I have benefited from such traditions, especially Scripture memory programs. However, I do have a problem when saints (laypersons and ministers alike) believe that, by completing a helpful course, by performing an important discipline, or by participating in a vital activity of faith—each a valued slice of discipleship—they have achieved Christian maturity.

I have found that there are two recurring obstacles for disciples, two sides of one coin. The first obstruction is not so much with actual discipleship methods. It is the uncritical practice of seeing methods as goals. For instance, a superb discipline like fasting may, over time, takes on such significance in a disciple's life that she transforms it into something it's not: an end in itself. I have met many believers in my thirty years of church ministry who fall into this thought pattern. Some of you reading this page may be saying to yourself, "I don't see myself falling into the trap of thinking that all of Christianity comes down to fasting." Fair enough. Not every saint gets tripped up by this first obstacle. But there is another larger and closely related challenge that's even more pertinent, since it affects everybody. As strange as it may sound, *there is no design for biblical discipleship* that includes the essential components of our faith. I don't mean a design that includes everything, since that's impossible. I mean there is no plan broad enough to identify the basic foundations *and* practices of what it means to fully "follow Jesus." There is no complete design that helps us understand what our Maker says he wants to do most: daily revitalize his image inside us.

People in the first group are prone to elevate some excellent discipleship methods into inappropriate goals because they eventually default to that position. Any method that isn't properly secured to its larger objective often takes on a life of its own. The people in the second group consciously avoid the methods-as-goal trap, but these participants end up at virtually the same point: They have no complete model of discipleship. They are left without a larger perspective of faith and life, a perspective that offers more potential, more responsibility, and much more satisfaction.

There are plenty of superb books about discipleship methods—like helpful ways to strengthen the believer's prayer life or how to evangelize more effectively. This book does not attempt to compete with those worthy resources. The contribution of this book is that it steps back and takes a look at the forest before it identifies some of the trees. It features a game plan for serious disciples.

(Note: download the *Supplemental Resource, Personal Growth Resource*, and an annotated *Listing of Proven Resources* from www.cookministries.com/completedisciple.)

A Preferred Phrase

I want to say a few things about vocabulary. This resource deliberately casts a vote for the term Christian "discipleship." This label has lost a good deal of its luster at the start of the third millennium. There are several reasons why this is so, but that particular investigation is beyond the scope of this project. Suffice it to say, I prefer the word "disciple" to the options in today's marketplace, for these key reasons:

- "Disciple" represents the most common term to describe Jesus' followers in all four Gospels and the book of Acts.[2] There's not even a close second.
- More than 260 citations of "disciple" surface throughout these first five New Testament books. That is a significant number of times.
- "Disciple" is almost exclusively derived from the Greek *matheetees*, which means "learner." The concept of disciple as learner:
  - complements Jesus' popular title of Rabbi or Master Teacher;
  - encourages the idea of discipleship as a lifelong learning process;
  - strengthens the promise that the disciple/learner will eventually become "like his teacher" (Matt. 10:25); and
  - accentuates the prominent command to "make disciples" by "teaching them," from Christ's Great Commission (Matt. 28:19-20).

It's time for the church to recommit itself to biblical "discipleship."[3]

A Primary Person

You've probably heard the following Sunday school joke about elementary-aged kids. There are different versions of the story, but only one punch line. I use the story here to emphasize the person who must be centrally featured in any discipleship model.

"What has four legs, a furry coat, and a tail?" Mrs. Howard asked her third-grade class.

Silence. Several children shot confused glances and made gestures at each other.

"Oh, come on!" the teacher prodded. "You know what I'm talking about! It's brown, lives in the trees, and gathers nuts for the winter."

Jessica, often the spokesperson for the class, took a risk. "Well, it sounds like you're describing a squirrel," the eight-year-old started slowly, as she scrutinized her classmates' faces for support. "But, to be on the safe side, I'll say the answer's 'Jesus'!"

On the one hand, too many question-and-answer times in church education unfortunately resemble this story—boring questions that require pat answers. On the other hand, the real answer to many faith questions *often is* God's Son. Since Jesus is the primary person in the disciple's life, each of this book's four sections hinges upon our Lord:

- Section I lays the foundation for biblical discipleship. It starts in the Garden of Eden—especially emphasizing the perfect creation of Adam and Eve in the image of God (*imago Dei*). It ends at the beginning of the New Testament. Jesus' title of "Alpha" connects us with this foundation, not only with Creation itself but precreation ("before the foundation of the world"). This first section provides us with our faith history, the *backward* look at discipleship.

- Section II focuses on the *inward* look of discipleship, as it explores a trio of mysteries from the Incarnation: Jesus' title of "Last Adam" shows us *who he was:* fully God and fully human. "Carpenter" and "Great Physician" feature *what he did:* attending to the holistic needs of people. Finally, his role as "Faithful Brother" enables us to see *how he responded to others.* Collectively, Jesus' powerful model of being (character), doing (calling), and relating (community) empowers the disciple to understand the purpose for living. He or she intimately encounters "the Jesus we wish we knew," because the full humanity of Christ is treasured.

- Section III specifically applies the contents of the previous section to contemporary disciples. Synthesizing Jesus' three key roles, we discover our message to the world: "The Jesus We Want Others to Know." This section values the richer, more inclusive testimony of our Lord. His focus on Character, Calling, and Community (each tied to Communion with God) provides the *outward* look of discipleship. It is the broader Good News of *shalom*, or holistic well-being. And so we proclaim the attractive message of this "Prince of Peace."

- Section IV takes the position of the disciple's *upward* look. We followers of Christ have some extraordinary privileges and responsibilities here on earth. Yet, at the same time, we long for our celestial Home. Jesus modeled this yearning for heaven and so did others (see 2 Cor. 5:6-9). This last section emphasizes "The Jesus We Will Fully Know." One day persevering saints will be like their Lord, fully restored through the same image we now possess. Jesus' "Omega" role leads the way, as we are ushered into eternity with Him.

A Predominant Purpose

As noted earlier, the disciple's predominant life purpose is image restoration. This doctrine is possibly the most underrated (if not ignored) in all Scripture. Some Christian leaders attempt to do justice to this topic, but many of us supply only token recognition. It is extremely rare to find a resource that features foundational insights as well as practical strategies to actually accomplish image restoration. Realigning this all-important objective with the four sections of the book, the doctrine of *imago Dei* is highlighted these ways:

- Section I (the Backward look) – Image Introduced (in history)
- Section II (the Inward look) – Image Incarnated (in Christ)
- Section III (the Outward look) – Image Imitated (by disciples)
- Section IV (the Upward look) – Image Immortalized (in heaven)

It helps to realize that the biblical account of Jesus' life was not merely centered on his final week, even though many of us often treat our Lord's last three years as "biding time 'til the Cross." What did the Father intend for Christ to learn during his first thirty years, as well as his last three, prior to Calvary? And what should we also learn? For instance, what does Jesus— through his image-bearing personality—teach us about discipleship issues for children and preteens, based upon his own experiences? The doctrine of *kenosis* holds a key to unlocking some of these vital questions. That is, Jesus' voluntary choice not to use his powers independently while he walked on earth (though he retained his nature as God) encourages us to appreciate his full humanity. As Hebrews 2:17 and 4:15 powerfully remind us, Jesus was both made like and tempted like us "in every way."

A Pertinent Set of Principles

I find myself on the horns of a dilemma when it comes to this next section. On the one hand, I am leery of reducing this book's comprehensive approach to discipleship to a series of rules or laws. In this sense, I share the legitimate concern that Warren W. Wiersbe raised in his foreword: Biblical discipleship can never be reduced to a series of six steps—or sixty-six steps, for that matter. On the other hand, there is value in providing explicit direction for would-be disciples. In light of this dilemma, I have adopted a compromise: I refuse to offer artificial, quick-fix steps. However, I will offer concise principles that convey the summative truths of each chapter, which form the foundation for a biblical model.

A Progressive Process

This book lastly features the disciple's ongoing process for becoming a faithful follower of Christ. After we affirm that "Jesus *is* the answer," and we accept the lifelong goal of daily restoration through his image in us—what do we do? How do we get there from here? Biblical process necessarily includes the familiar metaphor of pilgrimage that John Bunyan popularized in *Pilgrim's Progress*. His "King's Highway" metaphor complements the straight and narrow path paved by Jesus (from John 14:6). The early believers also took hold of that slogan, for their most common name in the book of Acts was "Followers of the Way."

Don't forget this solid-as-gold promise: You are not alone. Jesus personally guaranteed, "I am with you always, to the very end of the age" (Matt. 28:20). Your Beloved Brother is intimately near you. Jesus is closer to you than your breath.

It's a great journey. But it's also a lifelong trip. So pace yourself. And have confidence, for your loving Father planned your course "before the foundation of the world."

Enjoy the ride.

1 Paradise is labeled "home" for the disciple. Genesis 1–2 depict our Eden home, while Revelation 21–22 highlight our Home in heaven. To avoid confusion, lower and upper cases are respectively used for Eden and heaven in this book.

2 We don't need to be overly concerned that the word disciple is not found after these five books. Dallas Willard relates a personal experience that helps us understand one of the not-so-acceptable reasons behind current trends to devalue the term *discipleship*. It actually would be a humorous story, if it weren't so tragic. Dr. Willard shares, "I have actually heard it argued that because the word disciple does not occur after the Book of Acts, we are no longer supposed to teach or be disciples!" See *The Divine Conspiracy* (San Francisco: Harper San Francisco, 1998, page 414, endnote 3). Of course, if this "logic" persisted, we could no longer use other excellent words like evangelism, which can't be located anywhere in the Bible.

3 Other fine terms for discipleship include "spiritual formation," "Christian formation," and "Christian growth." I opt for a more thorough understanding of the concept of discipleship than is normally offered. I believe we must move beyond traditional and cultural uses of that term. So many popular interpretations of the word discipleship are purely cognitive or merely behavioral. A wider approach to discipleship must integrate features that are otherwise separated, such as those identified in Richard V. Peace's worthwhile contribution, "Spiritual Formation," in *The Complete Book of Everyday Christianity*, R. Banks & R. P. Stevens (eds.), Downers Grove, Ill: InterVarsity, 1997, pp. 938-943.

Chapter One

---+---

A New Way to Look at Discipleship

> *The door on which we have been knocking all*
> *our lives will open at last.*
>
> —C.S. LEWIS

The story is told about an elderly couple who lived in the sleepy town of Middleton. Their love for each other was surpassed only by their love for their Lord.

As their Maker would have it, one night Helen and Howard were both called Home in their sleep. The loss was great for those they left behind. Yet the news that they had passed away together was appropriate, for Helen and Howard (throughout their sixty-plus years of marriage) always did everything together. For example, the last decade of their lives found them enjoying good health, due to their mutual interest in healthful food and exercise.

When they reached the pearly gates, St. Peter himself personally escorted Helen and Howard to the Celestial Registry. There they received personalized robes with an everlasting warranty against wear, stains, and shrinkage. Likewise, each was given a special name[1] known only to himself or herself. It was blissful.

St. Peter then took them to their mansion decked out with a beautiful kitchen, a master bath suite, and a whirlpool. Their sprawling yard included a huge, lovely garden out back—much like the one they had enjoyed in Middleton, except for a couple of major differences. "Every flower, tree, and plant you ever knew on earth can be cultivated here," Peter promised. "But remember, up here it's all weed- and thorn-free. Also, there's a deluxe workshop area around the corner for you to continue your interests in building and inventing things like that."

The two newcomers "oohed" and "aahed," enraptured with what they experienced. As reason recaptured their emotions, however, Howard took Peter off to the side and quietly asked how much all this was going to cost them. "It's absolutely free," Peter replied. "This is heaven."

Next they went out to survey the championship golf course that ran along their property line. Peter told this elderly couple—slowly swapping their "aged" look for one of "agelessness"—they had daily golfing privileges, and each week the course layout automatically changed to represent one of the great golf courses on earth—only far better.

It was Helen's turn, this time, to ask the obvious: "What are the green fees?" Peter's reply was the same: "This is heaven! You play for free."

Then Peter took them to a neighborhood gathering. Of all the heavenly blessings received that day, this one was the most indescribable to earth-bound people. There, the now-ageless couple met beloved family again, as well as total strangers—who instantly became family. Helen claimed it was like the times, back on earth, when she met a person she didn't know, but after a few minutes she'd surprise herself by saying, "I feel as if I've known you all my life!" This particular experience was especially thrilling when it came time to gather old and new friends for community worship of the King.

Eventually Peter escorted the couple to the clubhouse, where they saw the lavish buffet lunch boasting all the cuisines of the world. "How much for people to eat?" questioned Howard, unable to forget their family's modest earthly budget. "Don't you understand yet?" Peter said for the third time with some firmness in his voice. "This is heaven, and it's all absolutely free!"

"Well, where are the low-fat and low-cholesterol foods?" Helen inquired. Peter explained, "That's the best part—you can eat as much as you like of whatever you like, whenever you like. You never get fat or sick. This is heaven!"

Both guests began to grow accustomed to the very pleasant pattern of Peter's answers to their questions. Finally, as all this too-good-to-be-true news sank in, Helen and Howard had no choice but to simply stare at each other. They shook their heads with synchronized disbelief, "We just don't get it. . . ."

"What's there not to 'get'?" Peter interrupted, using a more exasperated tone than ever. "What part of 'free' don't you get!?"

"No, no, no!" Helen said. "You misunderstand our confusion," she continued. "That's right," Howard echoed, not missing a beat. "We're both confused about the last ten years we spent on earth. With all these incredible blessings here, we've both been asking ourselves, 'Why did we ever waste our time riding exercise bikes and eating bran muffins?'"[2]

Heaven Can't Wait

In heaven, this godly couple eventually stumbled upon some truths that every disciple desperately needs to learn *today*. Waiting until we reach the pearly gates won't be nearly as satisfying without them.

Here are the life-changing truths we must embrace: Heaven is like the best of earth, yet it's far better. Whenever we experience any precious gift from God now—whether a nice home, a relaxing round of golf, satisfying work, meaningful service to others—we enjoy a little taste of heaven. This connection exists because that's how the Creator purposefully hardwired every person deep down inside. God linked us to these blessings through his image, grounded within our very first parents and handed down to us through the generations.

Every person inherits three particular legacies originally given to humanity in Eden. Those inheritances are our Family Name, our Family Business, and our Family Ties. In chapter 3 I'll explain how Helen and Howard became reacquainted with these legacies, which (since Eden) have been redemptively upgraded in Christ. As we contemporary believers follow the Bible for abundant living through those very same legacies, we likewise taste a bit of heaven. We increase our potential for experiencing heaven-right-now benefits because, in God's plans, our past and our future have always been connected with our present.

This teaching is not some wild-eyed fantasy or some new twist on prosperity theology. It certainly has nothing to do with salvation by good works, for we can never presume how, where, or even when God may bless our lives. Also, Scripture is clear: Good works cannot secure righteousness. And yet, humanly speaking, our chances of receiving heaven-can't-wait blessings grow immensely whenever we realign ourselves with the Creator's original patterns from Eden. Such realignment complies with the Creator's highest standards of personal fulfillment and contentment. That's precisely how he has chosen to work within his creation. His plan encourages us to recommit ourselves to the Garden's guidelines—guidelines that show us how to get the most out of life—as we travel God's highway (The *Supplemental Resource* offers more Scriptures concerning this highway in sidebar 1.1).

Breath of Heaven

The best (and the simplest) place to begin understanding biblical discipleship—which is vitally linked to the essential doctrine of image—is at Creation. In Genesis 1:26 the Triune God introduces plans to make people in his own likeness. The Genesis 2 version of this plan states, "The LORD God formed the man from the dust of the ground and breathed into his nostrils the breath of life, and the man became a living being" (v. 7).

Let's start with the primal word "breath" to explain the complex meanings of God's image. Breath represents a powerful, singular perspective of the human existence. Breath means God-given life. A study of the term "breath" provides as much sophistication or simplicity as the disciple may want. (Recall the Greek word for "disciple," *matheetees*, means "learner.") The primary term for breath in the Old Testament (*nephesh*) is comparable to its New Testament counterpart (*psyche*), meaning soul or core human personality. The respective Old and New Testament words for spirit (*ruah* and *pneuma*) also convey understandings of what it means to be human. Technically, soul refers to life (so even animals have souls). Our spirit is what is eternal—destined for heaven or hell. This is why Jesus (and others) asked God to receive his spirit at the end of his life (Luke 23:46; also see Ps. 31:5 and Acts 7:59). In a general sense, since all four Hebrew and Greek terms identify our immaterial qualities, these words may be used interchangeably.[3] Think about the English word "breath" as a basic synonym for life. Now insert that word back into the context of these familiar phrases, which depict the human life span:

- When a newborn is delivered from the womb, we say the birthing procedure is successful when the baby "starts breathing."
- When children learn to swim, we teach them to "hold their breath" whenever they submerge.
- After intense play or exercise, a person is said to be "out of breath" or "breathless."
- When a teen explains the jolt of her first love—exclaiming "it took my breath away"—she is describing what she believes is a totally unique encounter, using common, universal language.
- Honeymooners at Niagara Falls freely use phrases like "breath-taking" to describe their sightseeing experiences.
- As a person's age increases and health declines, this very same breath often provides clues to well-being. A comprehensive range from "labored breathing" to "breathing easily" may help gauge health.
- In due time every man, woman, and child will "breathe their last" or "take their last breath."

Our divinely given "breath of life," then—symbolizing God's image inside us—defines life for every individual. Stated in reverse, we have no life at all without this gracious gift from our Creator. Breath (as a life-giving symbol) coincides with a handful of foundational truths about our relationship to God's image. For instance, Adam and Eve shared their Maker's image and abundant life because they shared the one peculiar quality that distinguished them from all other creatures: God endowed them with something of Himself. They possessed the Breath of Heaven!

A Biblical Time Line of Breath

From time to time in the Bible, the three words "breath," "wind," and "spirit" overlap. They collectively provide the blueprint for biblical discipleship.

Consider only the last of these three words ("spirit") for a moment. Recall the numerous instances in which Scripture refers to spirit either as *Holy* Spirit or as *human* spirit. I've already pointed out verses that depict the Creation account of our "breath–life" linkage.[4] Biblical descriptions of righteous people, such as Caleb and Joshua, include references to their personal godly spirits.[5] In addition, we see God's Spirit at work with the human spirit to develop a powerful partnership; the stories of Gideon and Samson reflect this pattern.[6] King David, among others, implored God for a "pure heart" and a "steadfast spirit" following his sin with Bathsheba.[7] And the prophet Ezekiel predicted that the Holy Spirit would, one day, actually be put inside God's people.[8]

The Gospel of Matthew describes the Virgin Birth—the miracle that Mary's Child was conceived "through the Holy Spirit."[9] The Gospels also declare that the Spirit would baptize believers with fire, in contrast to John's water baptism. This promise anticipated the Holy Spirit's imminent and permanent indwelling of every saint, which was fulfilled at Pentecost.[10] Numerous times throughout Jesus' life we witness the Spirit's direct and purposeful leading of the Son. This same spirit will direct and lead Jesus' followers.[11]

The Original Nic-at-Night

In John 3, a handful of key verses bring particular significance to the overlapped meanings found in the three words *breath, wind*, and *spirit*. Nicodemus makes an appointment to visit Jesus in the late evening, perhaps choosing that time from a combination of curiosity and fear. Jesus deliberately moves their conversation to the fundamental need for all people to be "born again" (v. 3), yet this respected Pharisee doesn't follow what Jesus is saying. He suggests a bizarre picture of what he thinks Jesus is teaching: Nicodemus wonders out loud whether a person is supposed to crawl back into his mother's womb (v. 4)!

Jesus clarifies by describing two kinds of birth: one that is physical and one that is spiritual (v. 5–6). Nobody gets to heaven, the Lord concludes, unless the second criterion is met. Every heaven-bound individual must be twice born (v. 7). But Nicodemus still doesn't get it. So what does the Master Teacher do? He uses a related truth from nature, saying, "The wind blows wherever it pleases. You hear its sound, but you cannot tell where it comes from or where it is going." In essence Jesus asks Nicodemus: "Of course you believe in the wind, don't you? We witness its effects all around us every day. Yet even with something as natural and elementary as the wind, we still don't understand its origin and destination."

Then our Lord makes this brilliant connection: "So it is with everyone born of the Spirit" (v. 8b). What's so brilliant? For one thing, he ties the natural world of "wind" to the supernatural world of "Spirit." He links the known to the unknown—a standard educational tactic. But here's the genius part: For both "wind" and "Spirit," Jesus employs the same Greek word, *pneuma*, in verse 8. *Pneuma* means both "wind" and "Spirit." So our Lord intentionally teaches the subject of salvation, from the Bible's most-heralded chapter, using a pun (a play on words) to help Nicodemus link the natural world with the supernatural.

In sum, our first birth comes through the life-giving *breath* of the Creator. Our second birth of salvation comes by the life-giving *wind* of the Holy Spirit.[12] We must be "rebreathed," as it were, if we want to go to heaven.

More "Breath" to Come

Jesus continued to link this deliberate tie between breath, wind, and spirit at the end of his life too. He predicted that, after he left the disciples, the Holy Spirit would come upon them and "remind you of everything I have said to you" (John 14:26b).[13] During one of his postresurrection appearances—just after his prediction of the coming Holy Spirit, but just before the Spirit's arrival—Jesus displayed curious behavior. One Sunday the Lord met his disciples with the greeting "Peace be with you." He showed them the scars in his hands and side, then commissioned them. And "with that he breathed on them and said, 'Receive the Holy Spirit'" (John 20:22). This account testifies to one of the outstanding examples of transition between the Gospels and the book of Acts and between the second and third persons of the Trinity, since the words *breath* and *Spirit*, again, are interchangeable.[14]

The Conspiracy of Christlikeness

When we understand Christian faith by this illustration of breath as God's image, it is easy to see that serving Christ actually requires a conspiracy. I don't use that word in the traditional sense. Rather, I use that term in its most foundational sense, based upon the Latin *conspirare*, which literally translates "breathe together."[15] This chapter's opening illustration of Helen and Howard describes one couple who unknowingly breathed life together with Christ. They grew increasingly excited about what their new heavenly life offered, but they couldn't put their finger on the reason for their delight. What was the reason?

They found themselves unwittingly in unison with the Creator's unalterable views of healthful life and faith, first grounded in Eden. They experienced everything good and wholesome: beauty, orderliness, worship, work, relationships, service, personhood, and leisure. The growing evidences of their conspiracy—how each new experience in heaven surpassed even Eden's original design—eventually led to the couple's euphoric state. They became ecstatic, meaning they were driven outside of their senses. On earth we use the phrase "jumping out of our skin" to describe a condition of extreme fear. Heaven's newcomers also leap out of their skin, but for extreme joy.

Here's the amazing part: Every believer today is similarly invited to conspire with Jesus. God, in his unfailing mercy, welcomes each of us to breathe together with our Creator-Redeemer. These invitations to experience the breath of God's image come with various levels of challenge and corresponding reward. Here are some representative illustrations:

At an elementary level, whenever we experience the very best of this earthly life—from a brilliant, breathtaking sunset or rainbow to exhausting work that helps someone in desperate need, leaving us breathless—Jesus offers us the privilege of conspiracy.[16] This is how his invitation appears to us (in question form): "How do you see Me in this meaningful life experience? How do you sense My deliberate presence? How will you respond to My gift of life-breath inside you?"

At the next level, Jesus invites all members of his body into conspiracy through a couple of lifelong commitments: the dominion commitment to perpetuate the Cultural Mandate of Eden (I'll explain this further in chapter 3) and the redemption commitment to proclaim the Good News of Calvary. These restorative and redemptive commitments are complementary—the former challenges people to *seek* God, while the latter challenges people to *see* God.[17]

Compare these first two levels this way: The first conspiracy is generally a reactive one; most of us are caught off-guard by a stunning sunset or rainbow. Jesus' second invitation, however, ties into our daily thinking and plans. Our participation is usually more active.

At a third and more advanced level, Christ invites us into conspiracy by encouraging us to fully restore his image inside us. This conspiracy involves anticipating our eternal Home, in contrast to our temporal dwelling. Scripture metaphorically describes earth as a copy (at best) of heaven's original. At the start of his ministry, Jesus offered believers several invitations to join in this third conspiracy, which always links the "knowns" of earth with heaven's "unknowns." Remember the Master Teacher's instruction from Matthew 6?

- Jesus told us to pray that God's "will be done on earth as it is in heaven" (v. 10).
- We should invest in "treasures in heaven, where moth and rust do not destroy, and where thieves do not break in and steal" (v. 20).
- We should "seek first his kingdom and his righteousness, and [then] all these things [that people live for in this life] will be given to you as well" (v. 33).

At the end of his time on earth, Jesus continued to offer the third conspiracy invitation. He consistently linked this temporal world and our eternal Home—where he himself eagerly planned to return. For example (in contrast to our humble dwellings here), Jesus promised to build celestial mansions for us and then return to earth to take us back with him (John 14:1–3). In more simple language, this third conspiracy invites us disciples to visualize what Helen and Howard experienced. I don't mean we should live in some selfish fantasy world. But Jesus has encouraged us to anticipate our heavenly rewards as superior extensions of what we have on earth.

Christ calls us, then, to experience daily his presence through his indwelling image. His first call to conspiracy is mostly reactive; the second is proactive; and the third is restorative.

Consider this summary: Most of us have traditionally viewed discipleship as a "program," typically a series of lessons. Even with commendable curriculum, this traditional definition is far too limited. It lacks a broader historical and theologcal basis. If we want to be serious about discipleship, a biblical foundation of Creation must be initially laid. Consequently, this strategy leads us to the first of twelve foundational truths, which we earlier cited in this book's introduction:

> ## Truth 1
>
> God's model for discipleship is something of a conspiracy,
> since we intimately share our Maker's breath—
> evidence of the larger fact that we are created in God's image.

Applying "Breath" to "Life" Today

Breathing is an involuntary act. Just ask any junior high kid. Chances are he will tell you about the "science project" he did recently. No, not the one where an innocent volunteer unwittingly sticks his tongue to a frozen piece of metal. It's another experiment, the one in which a kid tries to see how long she can stop breathing and she briefly collapses into unconsciousness.

Brian is my asthmatic buddy. Several times a day—partly because of uncontrollable variables like weather or an array of allergies—Brian agonizingly gasps for breath. Unlike the aforementioned teenage scientists, Brian desperately hopes to remain conscious. You can imagine how painful it is to watch Brian's moment-by-moment struggle, especially when he has forgotten his inhaler. Whereas I have always been taught to pray, "Give us this day our daily bread," Brian implores heaven, "Give me this day my daily breath!" His labored inhale-exhale routine should remind us how we all take our effortless breathing for granted.

And what a gift it is! We receive this gift of life every second of the day. The following practical suggestions might enable us to value our "breathing together with Christ" even more. Biblical discipleship starts by prizing the partnership of life we share with the Creator: from his life-giving Eden breath inside us to his new life rebreathed into us by the Holy Spirit (at our salvation) to his gracious gifts of life and eternal life we now breathe several times every day.

So stop right now. Close your eyes and concentrate on your Maker's personal love for you—for you alone—expressed through these incredible gifts of life, new life, and abundant life. Consciously breathe deeply and slowly. Realize God's breath in yours. Realize God's breath is yours.

I know some readers may think this breathing exercise sounds too much like Eastern mysticism or New Age hocus-pocus. It does not need to be. Don't forget that we disciples are commanded to "take captive every thought to make it obedient to Christ" (2 Cor. 10:5b), and that directive certainly includes these truths about God's creation, salvation, and restoration.

So reaffirm your partnership with him in life and faith. You can be sure he is sincere when it comes to his desire to want the very best for you.

Breathe deeply again.

Thank God for being your faithful partner throughout life.

From time to time, create your own applications of this breath-conspiracy concept. For example, the next time you step into the crisp autumn air and you "see your breath," recall how intimately close Jesus is to you. Realize how very much a part of you he actually is. Or the next time you take a break from your schedule, you may consciously pause to "catch your breath." Give a purposeful sigh. Remember to praise your Maker—for it's his breath too.

Conclusion

Celebrate your first step of conspiracy. Celebrate your initial walk down God's highway toward abundant living. Rejoice in the humbling reality that he—the Author of all life—provides your moment-by-moment life-breath. Isn't that truth awesome? Each of us continues to share this secret of life with our Creator-God. And he can't wait to bless us more. He wants to transform our current lives into even more satisfying ones, through his indwelling image. He wants us to be like him.

We don't need to put our lives on hold—to wait like Helen and Howard—until we're eighty five or until we die. Christ invites us to conspire with him—without delay, to experience the beauty of breathing God's breath deeply, right now.[18] Anybody "twice born" has this immediate privilege: experiencing eternity now.[19]

Who wouldn't want to join such a conspiracy?

---

1 Revelation 2:17c.

2 This is a modified and expanded version of the illustration provided by Mikey's Funnies Website at www.YouthSpecialties.com on March 29, 2001. Used by permission.

3 I realize that, in a more technical sense, "soul" and "spirit" need to be distinguished, not blended. See Dallas Willard's *Renovation of the Heart* for a recent book that makes these helpful distinctions.

4 Two examples are found in Job 27:3 and Psalm 104:29.

5 Numbers 14:24 and 27:18.

6 Judges 6:34 and 14:6.

7 Psalm 51:10.

8 Ezekiel 37:14.

9 Matthew 1:18.

10 Compare Matthew 3:11 and Mark 1:8 with Acts 2:1-4. Note that the Spirit's fiery baptism at Pentecost is also described as "a sound like the blowing of a violent wind . . . from heaven" (Acts 2:2).

11 Compare Luke 4:1, 14, and 18 with Acts 2:4b; 4:8a, 31b; and 6:9b–10; 7:54–56, 59–60.

12 In light of the previous summary of how we use "breath" in contemporary references, we similarly use the word "wind." For example we have coined personal experience phrases like "get wind of," "take the wind out of one's sails," "get winded," and "to get the wind knocked out."

13 It's critical to note that one fulfillment of this divine recall is explicitly offered by Peter, when he explains to the Jewish-Christian leaders in Jerusalem why he took the Gospel to the Gentiles, namely to Cornelius's household: "As I began to speak, the Holy Spirit came on them as he had come on us at the beginning. Then I remembered what the Lord had said: 'John baptized with water, but you will be baptized with the Holy Spirit.' . . . Who was I to think that I could oppose God?" (Acts 11:15-17). Peter claimed Cornelius's household demonstrated the same evidence of the Spirit in their lives as the apostles' earlier Spirit experiences at Pentecost, fifty days after Jesus was raised from the dead.

14 It is, likewise, interesting to note that the divine inspiration of Scripture is said to be "God-breathed" in 2 Timothy 3:16. That Greek word (*theopneutos*) parallels the term in-spired (or in-breathed). That is also why "the word of God is living and active" and "sharper than any double-edged sword" (Heb. 4:12).

15 From the two words *com* ("together") and *spirare* ("breath"), as found in *The World Book Dictionary*, Volume One, A-K, (Chicago: World Book, Inc., 1990), p. 444.

16 With reference to these two specific examples of experiencing the beauty of God's Creation and the worthwhile pleasures of helping needy people, shaped in his image, note the "conspiracy" links to God from Psalm 19:1-4, as well as from Jeremiah 22:16 and Matthew 25:31-46.

17 I don't mean we literally "see" God. Rather, as we (first) perform the duties of Eden, we will be richly blessed. Yet we will desire something greater. Eden points to the cross, where God satisfies our soul and spirit. To restate it, our dominion commitment shows us how to live, while our redemption commitment shows us how to live again. I am indebted to Leland Ryken's complementary use of these two words from his chapter "Finding Heaven in Milton's *Paradise Lost*" in *Journey to the Celestial City*, ed. Wayne Martindale (Chicago: Moody, 1995), p. 75.

18 "Conspiring with Christ" doesn't need to be perceived as selfish, hedonistic, or worldly (certainly it can turn into that sinful pattern, however). Essentially, Christian living that completely satisfies is precisely what Jesus promised disciples in his "life . . . to the full" reference (in John 10:10b).

19 Many discipleship resources fail to identify two powerful truths: First, when we say yes to Jesus at salvation, we not only are assured of eternal life one day, but we immediately start living eternally! If you do a concordance study of the word "eternal," you will notice some verses that focus on our future salvation (like John 6:40), using terms like "will have" or "shall." Contrast those with other verses that speak in the present tense about our current gift of eternal life (e.g., John 3:36, John 5:24, 1 Tim. 1:16, and 1 John 5:11-13). I especially love how John 5:24 emphasizes this incredible fact from more than one angle: "I tell you the truth, whoever hears my word and believes him who sent me has eternal life and will not be condemned; he has crossed over from death to life."

Second, discipleship resources rarely talk about healthily enjoying life! We tend to forget teachings from God's perspective, such as those that claim he "richly provides us with everything for our enjoyment" (1 Tim. 6:17b). See chapter 10 for further discussion on this subject.

Section I

The Jesus Nobody Knows

Chapter Two

Our Way Back Home Through Eden

> *God Almighty first planted a garden. And,*
> *indeed, it is the purest of human pleasures.*
>
> — FRANCIS BACON
>
> *To the orthodox there must always be a case for*
> *revolution . . . a revolution is a restoration. At*
> *any moment you may strike a blow for perfection*
> *which no man has seen since Adam.*
>
> — G. K. CHESTERTON

I was completely speechless.

Although I had studied family behavior patterns professionally for some time, my research never prepared me for what I recently heard from one of my own children. Studies in family behavior show, for instance, that it is not unusual for an older child to confess to parents her earlier mischievous behaviors long after the fact. That's especially true for some kids blessed with accurate memories, sensitive consciences, and nurturing homes.

But those clinical realities offered no comfort the day I first heard an alarming tale from Melissa, my middle of three daughters. Her story was now more than ten years old and had remained secret until she attended college. At age eighteen, this is how she began her believe-it-or-not preschool account: "I used to crouch by myself in the ditch that ran between our house and the street. I was waiting for the traffic. I wanted to throw myself in front of a car."

As I said, I was in shock. So I'm not certain of the exact wording of Melissa's confession. I do recall my jaw dropped and then froze open. The one we have always called Missy read my startled look, and then she quickly added, "Oh, I wasn't depressed or unhappy. Nothing like that." She proceeded in her matter-of-fact style: "I just figured heaven was far better than earth. And since our family was heading there anyway, why wait? Why not get hit by a car so I could meet Jesus earlier than later? Why not go Home to heaven as soon as possible?"

Let's face it, the Apostle Paul drew his own conclusions—somewhat similar to my daughter's—when he shared this unprovoked confession as an adult: "To depart and be with Christ . . . is better by far [than to] . . . remain in the body" (Phil. 1:23).

Living with Jesus in our eternal Home easily beats all other options. No alternate thrill or blessing falls into the same category. No earthly experience comes even halfway close. There is no contest. It's safe to say that heaven will surpass our wildest dreams.

I am, of course, thankful Melissa never succeeded with her bizarre scheme as a five year old. But after mentally rewinding and replaying her tale more than once, I have come up with my own personal confession. As severely flawed as Missy's tactics were, deep down I must admit it: Her desire to be with Jesus was right on target. It doesn't get any better than going Home to be with Jesus—forever.

The Way Home Is Closer than We Think

In these reflective months that wrap around my fiftieth year of existence, I'm daily convinced that all *good* things in this present world actually mirror the *better* life we once had in Eden. Furthermore, those very same gifts are also promised to God's children—in their supremely upgraded *best* form—once we begin eternal life.

Let me rephrase that truism with a bit more detail: All beautiful, satisfying, and just gifts we saints encounter in this life are rooted in the original beauty, satisfaction, and justice we possessed in the Garden. To top it off, unmatched beauty, thorough contentment, and consistent justice await our arrival in heaven. So we must celebrate all ties between our temporal and our everlasting worlds. Why? If we miss those vital connections, we lose a couple of too-good-to-be-true mercies from God:

- First, we overlook incredible pictures of what heaven will be like.
- Second, we ignore a very desirable reward: with God's help, we can actually begin to enjoy some of heaven on earth right now!

We Can Go Back Home Again

Don't misunderstand me. We do not retreat to the Garden for lesser motives such as nostalgia, escapism, or other selfish sentiments. We should not be tempted to go back just to feel good. Rather, we return in order to grasp our Creator's perspective. We begin comprehending life and faith from the vantage point of the one who alone knows our human condition. Just like a person who is lost—and we are!—we must methodically retrace our steps. We return to our first ancestors' beginnings, in order to uncover our own theological and familial roots.

Landing in Eden offers us substantial blessings—not the least of which includes the inner peace and confidence that come from reacquainting ourselves with the familiar story of humanity's start. It's like finding the "You are here" logo on the directory of a new mall you have just entered. It provides assurance for the launching point of your life's journey. Besides peace and confidence to begin the journey, those who carefully study Scripture discover a less familiar reward: From within the Garden, we are sovereignly pointed forward to an even more satisfying future. In other words, Eden was never designed as our termination point. It has always been our point of departure to a heavenly land.

Pretend this excursion to the Garden starts when you borrow H. G. Wells's time machine. You set the instrument panel for "Creation." The moment you arrive at Eden you start receiving your God-given sense of history and destiny. All subsequent trips you make in Wells's invention go forward from that location. With Eden's perspective, you will gain the Creator's insights on sin, the Ten Commandments, Jesus' life, ministry, and sacrifice, the testimony of the early believers, and your personal tasks as a modern-day disciple—each subject representing specific stops in your time machine. Finally, you have the opportunity to fast-forward to heaven, as you anticipate your eternal Home.

Therefore we disciples are not meant to go home *to* Eden. We go Home *through* Eden. We set out on our charted course from that original locale. It is a course we must wholeheartedly pursue if we want to experience all the fullness of life our Maker wants for us. When we depart from Eden we are effectively launched toward an even better Home and Garden. We catch glimpses of our unbelievable celestial Eden as we start in the earliest chapters of Genesis and then set our sights on the conclusion of Revelation (see table 2.1). Almost daily, heaven's Home becomes clearer.

If we want to better know ourselves and God's divine plan for us, we begin in the Garden. There we start to understand who we really are within the broader scope of all humanity and the narrower span called the church.

God shows us we can go Home again—home to Eden and Home to heaven. If we want what's best, he says we must and we will.

TABLE 2.1

A Better Home and Garden: Eternal Eden

FIRST PERFECT GARDEN: *Eden (Gen 1-3)*

- Divine Creation: "In the beginning God created the heavens and the earth" (1:1).
- The first darkness: "God called . . . the darkness . . . 'night'" (1:5).
- The first light: "God made two great lights"—the sun and the moon (1:16).
- The first command:God's people are told to reign over all Creation (1:26, 28)
- The first pure water for temporal nourishment: "A river watering the Garden flowed from Eden" (2:10a).
- The privilege and reward of labor:work brings produce for people to eat (2:15-16).
- The first warning: "When you eat of [the forbidden tree] you will surely die" (2:17).
- The first holy marriage between people, initiated by the Creator (2:20b-25).
- The Creator walked with his people, before sin, but only at certain times of the day (inferred from 3:8).

POLLUTED GARDEN: *Eden (Gen 3)*

- Primary consequence of sin:The curse of death (3:3).
- Pollution enters Eden: A perfect garden becomes contaminated (3:6-7).
- Sin fractures the first family by guilt, shame, fear, blame, and conflict (3:7-12; 16b).
- Initial judgment of Satan: he is temporarily punished (3:14-15).
- Secondary result of sin: "I will greatly increase your pains" (3:16); "painful toil" (3:17).
- Disobedient and unholy people are dismissed from the first garden (3:23).
- Future access to the "tree of life" was denied to the rebellious first Adam and Eve (3:22-24).

LAST PERFECT GARDEN: *Heaven (Rev 20-22)*

- Divine Re-creation: "I saw a new heaven and a new earth" (21:1; 4c-5)(see Isaiah 65:17-25).
- No more darkness: "There will be no night there" (21:25).
- The one true Light: "The city does not need the sun or the moon" because of God's glory and the Lamb (21:23; 22:5b).
- The final condition: God's people will reign with their Lord (22:3b; 5c).
- God's pure (and "free") water of eternal nourishment: "water of life" flows from God's throne through the middle of Celestial Eden (22:1-2) for all who are thirsty (21:6; 22:17).
- The privilege & reward of labor continues, without the curse: fruit from the tree of life is regularly enjoyed (22:2-3a; see Isa. 65:17, 21-23).
- The final wonder: "There will be no more death" (21:4a).
- The final holy marriage between God and his people (21:2, 9; 22:17).
- "Now the dwelling of God is with men, and he will live with them. They will be his people, and God himself will be with them and be their God." (21:3).
- Primary consequence of salvation: "no longer will there be any curse" (22:3a).
- Pollution removed forever: Creation is perfectly restored, never contaminated again (21:27).
- Salvation reconciles God's people into new family ties as his children (21:7) and siblings (22:9).
- Eventual judgment of Satan: he is eternally punished (20:2-3, 7, and 10).
- Secondary result of salvation: "There will be no more death or mourning or crying or pain" (21:4).
- Obedient and holy people are welcomed back to the last garden, the "Holy City" (21:2,10, 27; 22:11,19).
- Future access to the "tree of life" is reopened to all who believe in the "Last Adam" (22:14).

Following Jesus Back Home

The only way to our Celestial Home is through the sacrificial gift of Jesus. All other proposed routes are false. Most Christians still believe the unique message of Calvary, yet, sadly, every year more and more appear to waver. Our Maker has graciously provided this objective (*external*) message of redemption to complement his reaffirming *internal* evidence inside each person, tied to the image of God. This outward-inward bond between the Messiah and his followers provides the indispensable means by which we journey to our Celestial Home.

Consider a favorite verse for many believers, Romans 8:28: "And we know that in all things God works for the good of those who love him, who have been called according to his purpose." That's a fantastic promise from our Heavenly Father. Yet I am constantly amazed that many people stop right there. The next two verses reveal both what God's purpose is and how he is going to accomplish it. Verse 29 says, "For those God foreknew he also predestined *to be conformed to the likeness of his Son*" (italics added). In a general sense we could say our purpose (through Jesus' salvation) is "becoming the person Adam and Eve used to be"—but even better, it's becoming like the Last Adam, Jesus. My paraphrase of Romans 8:30 concludes, "God predestined and chose his children, whom he also saved. Those same children are divinely helped to look a bit more like Jesus today than they did yesterday. In heaven, each child will finally become like him."

Constant image restoration, then, is what every believer should desire (see Phil. 3:12-21 and Col. 3:5-10). When understood in this comprehensive sense, disciples have no other larger, more inclusive life-long purpose than image restoration. Period.

Worship, evangelism, spiritual gifts, total obedience to God and his Word, stewardship, the Christian disciplines—everything fits under this larger umbrella of image restoration. Even the purpose of glorifying God goes hand in glove with this focus on image, which is precisely what 2 Corinthians 3:7–6:1 indicates. A summary verse from that passage describes this significant overlap between our mirrored image and God's glory, as it uses those nearly synonymous concepts interchangeably: "And we, who with unveiled faces *all reflect the Lord's glory, are being transformed into his likeness with ever-increasing glory*, which comes from the Lord, who is the Spirit" (2 Cor. 3:18, italics added).

Whenever any of my three daughters does something commendable in our small town—exhibiting signs of a maturing personality—here's what frequently happens: First, the person who has benefited from the girl's behavior pulls aside my wife or me and explains how one of our daughters pleasantly surprised him or her with some kindness or unexpected maturity. Then the person says something like, "Your daughter's behavior really reflects on you, too, as her parent!" That is exactly what happens to our Heavenly Parent, when we do what he asks us to do. When we grow— through restoration of his image inside us—others see our Godlike character and may exclaim, "That's God working" or "That's a God thing." Our faithful maturing process benefits us and concurrently glorifies our Father.

Obedient disciples figuratively follow their Lord—first to Eden's home, then to our eternal Home. Jesus, as "Alpha" (the Beginning), takes the lead. The prophet Isaiah lays the foundation with his powerful reminder: "This is what the LORD says—Israel's King and Redeemer, the LORD Almighty: I am the first and the last; apart from me there is no God" (Isa. 44:6; also Isa. 41:4; 48:12). The Apostle John picks up this same two-part theme, both in his fourth Gospel and in the book of Revelation. Specifically in his first book, John initially takes his readers back to pre-Creation with his familiar opening, "In the beginning was the Word, and the Word was with God, and the Word was God" (John 1:1). Then John 17:5 and 24 propose this same theme (using Jesus' words), saying that the Father and Son once shared an intimate bond "before the creation of the world."

If you are under the impression that Jesus' title of Alpha is interesting but it has no relevance for modern saints, consider Matthew 25. That passage, starting in verse 31, describes the future ("when the Son of Man comes in his glory") when the King will separate the sheep from the goats. Carefully read what King Jesus says to the righteous: "Come, you who are blessed by my Father; take your inheritance, the kingdom prepared for you since the creation of the world" (v. 34). Obedient discipleship has no other responsible choice but to return to Eden. All other options are inferior, and they will ultimately reveal their substandard quality.

Eden's Original Blessings

What was it like in the Garden? What was it we inherited? As I mentioned in the opening chapter, three extraordinary blessings—the Garden legacies—were once ours:

- The Creator's Family Name – Based upon our unique creation in the image of God (Gen. 1:26-27), initiated by his life-giving breath (Gen. 2:7), we were once innocent and holy.

- The Creator's Family Business – Based upon our unique purpose to rule over and to care for Creation, known as the Cultural Mandate, we once had no doubt what we were supposed to do with our lives (Gen. 1:28; 2:15).

- The Creator's Family Ties – Based upon our unique bonds of intimacy with God, which carried over into his institution of marriage (Gen. 2:18-25), we once understood the full contentment that all godly relationships brought.

In other words, within our once-perfect Eden residence we originally possessed the legacies of character (holy life and living with our Maker), calling (meaningful livelihood through partnership with our Maker), and community (deeply satisfying relationships from our loving tie with the Maker). These three legacies are as pertinent now as they ever were. And

I am convinced that anything that is important to any person today still has roots in these three categories of being, doing, and relating.

In specific post-Fall and Christian terms, this same rich heritage (now fully redeemed through Jesus) offers us all the necessary provisions for our lives: Our renewed holy name once again tells us *who we are*. Our restored business partnership with God regularly informs us of *what we do*. Our renovated ties tell us *how we relate to all people*.

Theologians have historically referred to our task of caring dominion over Creation as the "Cultural Mandate." I prefer to use that term in a fuller sense to describe the combination of all three legacies. The advantage of this fuller definition is that we get a better feel for everything we once had in Eden. That first mandate still includes our duty to carefully reign, but today it also sets God's initial Garden charge within the broader context of other blessings and obligations.

This comprehensive definition from Genesis matches up well with another comprehensive command from the Gospels, Jesus' Great Commission of "teaching them to obey everything I have commanded you" (Matt. 28:20a). Whereas the former mandate tells us how we can fully live, the latter tells us how we can live again.

A Tale of Golden Thread

Picture God's Word as a richly woven tapestry. Imagine that the entire Bible contains one vital hope for today's believer. This hope resembles a golden thread. It is a strand known as paradise (the Greek word *paradeisos*), and it connects the beginning of the New Testament with its end. *Paradeisos* is used only three times in the New Testament: First, Jesus promises the believer who hangs next to him (on his own cross), "today you will be with me in paradise" (Luke 23:43). Second, Paul refers to his heavenly vision where he was "caught up to paradise" (2 Cor. 12:4). Third, Jesus expresses these apocalyptic words to the church in Ephesus: "To him who overcomes, I will give the right to eat from the tree of life, which is in the paradise of God" (Rev. 2:7b).

The Septuagint (the Hebrew Old Testament translated into Greek before the life of Christ) also uses this Greek word, *paradeisos,* the first time Adam and Eve's home is described.[1] That Greek word for "paradise" was deliberately chosen when the Septuagint translation of Genesis 2:7 introduced the extraordinary phrase "Garden of Eden." The identical theological word, "paradise," then unites Genesis with the New Testament. Paradise couples God's Creation with the consummation of time recorded in Revelation. The entire Bible is woven together by this golden strand.

If we want to treasure the total meaning of paradise, here's another fact: The literal meaning for the full phrase "Garden of Eden" is actually a "hedging around delight."[2] (We will revisit this wonderful bequest from the Creator in chapter 10.)

An intriguing depiction of Eden is found in John Milton's *Paradise Lost.* As Ryken comments, "Milton's description of Paradise in Book 4 leaves us with the impression that it is the suburb of heaven."[3] C. S. Lewis claims as much, if we shift our imagination a bit.[4] In his preface to *The Great Divorce,* Lewis draws this contrast: "But what, you ask, of earth? . . . I think earth, if chosen instead of heaven, will turn out to have been, all along, only a region in hell: and earth, if put second to heaven, to have been from the beginning a part of heaven itself."[5]

Longing for Home

I want to express my gratitude and then make a confession. I have been wonderfully graced with an exceptional Christian family. That goes for both my immediate nuclear family and my extended family. We are certainly not perfect, yet the Lord went out of his way to bless us. And I thank him. I must also admit a related confession: What I have is not good enough. This confession does not contradict my opening point. For, in the past five years, I have been more thankful for my family than I have ever been. But I have come to the realization that as much as God has blessed us, I long for another home—my heavenly Home.

I used to think the believers' hope of heaven was meant either for the elderly or for those who were experiencing unbearable suffering. Certainly I still think of heaven as our genuine hope for something better, especially in troubled times. For years I used to think of heaven as an escape. Lately, however, I am convinced that the hope of our eternal Home is equally intended for the exact opposite audience: for the healthy, for the young, and for believers showered with all sorts of blessings. In some ways this latter group needs to be reminded of that hopeful message more than anyone. For instance, ask yourself: "When did Israel tend to forsake her Maker?" One simple answer is "Whenever they ignored their own history and, thus, grew independent from God." Judges 2:10-12a reports perhaps the most infamous incident in this regard: "After that whole generation had been gathered to their fathers, another generation grew up, who knew neither the LORD nor what he had done for Israel. Then the Israelites did evil in the eyes of the LORD and served the Baals. They forsook the LORD, the God of their fathers, who had brought them out of Egypt."

In our earlier years of the faith, plenty of temptations may move us far from God. We may erringly believe this world can meet all our needs—when exactly the opposite is true. Believers who have everything this world offers would be wise to heed the caution of Malcolm Muggeridge, who reminds believers that we are always strangers on this planet: "The only ultimate disaster that can befall us, I have come to realize, is to feel ourselves to be at home here on earth. As long as we are aliens, we cannot forget our true Homeland."[6]

More and more I gauge Christian maturity by how a saint approaches her own longings for heaven. (Sidebar 2.1, in the *Supplemental Resource*, offers numerous passages to remind us of our eternal Home and the pathway we must pursue to it.)

The Good Times, the Bad Times, and Christmastime

The funny thing about our longings for heaven's Home is that we feel these longings tug at us most when we least expect it. We may feel a heavenward tug when we're not even thinking about spiritual matters. These tugs normally connect with our legacies (our needs for being, for doing, and for relating). I have discovered I am as likely to be broadsided by heaven when things are going well as I am during times of discouragement or stress. Some Christian leaders attest[7] to this fact as the serendipitous pattern of God's plan for his people.[8]

It may especially happen to you—as I believe it does to thousands and thousands—at Christmastime. This holiday season is unlike any other. Christmas means many things to many people. Yet, for most of us, these rituals are annually repeated: we buy too much, we eat too much, we do too much, we give too much, and we get too much.

We engage this season's wonder and beauty through all our senses. We take time to reflect on some of our values and traditions. We constantly replay the historical stories of our faith, teaching them to others, and recommitting ourselves to them. In the middle of these delightful Yuletide moments, experience reminds us of one of the most bedrock messages of God's image inside us: Every *good* thing in this life was *better* in Eden and it will be *best* in our heavenly Home. Those reminders may cause both gladness and sadness.[9] They often lead to homesickness for heaven.

On a more disturbing note, counselors remind us of the thousands who respond to Christmas in unhealthy ways. They tell us that no other season of the year yields the same high incidence of substance abuse, familial abuse, and depression. They tell us that depression, especially, is a problem, and it affects Christians and nonbelievers alike. I realize there are many reasons for these cases of Yuletide depression, but I want to add one more reason, one that largely goes undetected. Yet it is as foundational to human nature as one can get. You probably guessed part of this syndrome already because it is based upon God's image in each person. I will state it simply, without intending it to be simplistic:

A Description of Post-Christmas Depression: During the Christmas season, many individuals taste delicious morsels of heaven (like peace, beauty, and intimacy). Then they realize how desperately they want more—and also want those sensations to last. But they soon arrive at the despairing conclusion that their deepest of heart's desires just won't happen.

Those morsels of heaven that set off this annual pattern of anticipation may include almost anything good or kind. Anything true. Anything special. It is often found in the most simple holiday experiences: a bright display of lights at night, glistening on freshly falling snow; the harmonious blend of a carol or hymn; or spontaneous acts of kindness, prompted by this season's tradition of sacrificial love and giving.

The Scrooge in each of us tends to deny my description as "hogwash." His "Bah! Humbug" attitude relegates every bittersweet Christmas encounter to either nostalgia or emotional mush. Some of that may certainly exist. But please don't miss this point: Beyond the tinsel—underneath all the wrapping and bows—God's quiet voice speaks to each of us. Noise and busyness may cover that voice for a little while. But if we disciples are still, and if we are teachable, we will experience his best present of all. He will remind us of Eden. Then his voice will preview what's in store for our future. He will softly whisper that it is almost time for our hearts to stop their longing. When we eventually arrive in our heavenly Home, nobody will have to tell us the party of all parties has begun. Our celebration will be spontaneous.

Obviously the dark side of life is not without God's voice too. For our Creator-Lover—"The Hound of Heaven"—pursues us unceasingly from every angle. Curtis and Eldridge remind us, "The Romance is even present in times of great personal suffering: the illness of a child, the loss of a marriage, the death of a friend. Something calls to us through experiences like these and rouses an inconsolable longing deep within our heart, wakening in us a yearning for intimacy, beauty, and adventure."[10]

Again, this view of God's person and intimate work does not need to be confused with mysticism or New Age rhetoric (though it holds those possibilities). The voice I know—not audible, but still clear—is firmly grounded in God's Word (i.e., never contradicts Scripture). That voice is also fused with meaningful history (Eden), yet it connects with us in private ways (through our individual consciences, gifts, intuitions, etc.). Here's how Curtis and Eldridge explain it: "This longing is the most powerful part of any human personality. It fuels our search for meaning, for wholeness, for a sense of being truly alive. However we may describe this deep desire, it is the most important thing about us, our heart of hearts, the passion of our life. And the voice that calls us in this place is none other than the voice of God. We cannot hear this voice if we have lost touch with our heart."[11] Or his. (Sidebar 2.2, in the *Supplemental Resource,* provides additional thoughts for reflection about God's voice calling us Home.)

In sum, there is a second principle (of twelve) that the faithful follower of Christ must embrace.

Truth 2

God's model for discipleship reminds us we can go Home— whenever we obey the Creator's directive of image restoration through our three Eden legacies.

Conclusion

Try as we like—or deny as we like—we can never get away from our loving Creator. King David was well aware of that truth, as Psalm 139:7-8 shows:

Where can I go from your Spirit?

Where can I flee from your presence?

If I go up to the heavens, you are there;

if I make my bed in the depths, you are there.

Whereas David's words are often used to reinforce the doctrine of omnipresence, this chapter stresses omnipresence through his image—omni-image, as it were. God has been with his people from the beginning of time. We cannot run away from our Maker, because he is literally inside us. Nobody can ever get Eden out of her breath! We are most genuine, then, when we are solidly reunited with the Garden, which ties us both to our real self and our journey Home. Let's remember that heaven is "not just a pleasant place but *our* place, not just a good place, but a *good place for us*. We fit there; we are fully human there."[12] That continuous image-restorative process—a nonnegotiable part of biblical discipleship—gradually renews us to our perfect state.

There will be no regrets, ultimately, when we adhere to God's plan. None whatsoever. Whoever accepts our Maker's out-of-this-world offer will regain every bit of Eden's paradise, and so much more. Eternity will be an exact fit.[13] And so we long for heaven. We desire our real Home. And that's not a bad thing. Our absence from heaven only makes our hearts grow fonder. One triumphal day we will shout in heaven, just as Jewel the Unicorn did when he entered the new Narnia and "summed up what everyone was feeling"—"'I have come home at last! This is my real country! I belong here. This is the land I have been looking for all my life, though I never knew it till now. The reason why we loved the old Narnia is that it sometimes looked a little like this.'"[14]

The Good News is that God delivers on his promise of a new Narnia for believers. Every lifelong dream will be relived. We will instantly recognize our surroundings. We will know we're Home.

And that is why even my five-year-old Melissa developed her naturally attractive—and thoroughly wrong—Home-going scheme.

Going Home appeals to just about everyone.

---

1 This translation began in Alexandria, Egypt, in the 200s B.C. It is the oldest known translation of the Hebrew Bible. Its title comes from the Latin word "seventy," alluding to the tradition that seventy Jewish scholars translated the first five books (the Pentateuch) in seventy days.

2 Two complementary phrases are used in Genesis 2: "a garden in the east, in Eden" (v. 8) and "Garden of Eden" (v. 15). Both employ the word "paradise," which is synonymous with the term "parkland."

3 Leland Ryken, "Finding Heaven in Milton's *Paradise Lost*" in *Journey to the Celestial City: Glimpses of Heaven from Great Literary Classics* (Chicago: Moody, 1995), p. 74.

4 C. S. Lewis, *The Great Divorce* (New York: Simon & Schuster, 1946), p. 11.

5 This promise of paradise is not reserved for Gentile believers alone. More than once Scripture predicts Jewish converts will one day be saved; at that time, their country's desolate land will produce fruit – following their "soon" return "home" – making it "like Eden" (Ezek. 36:8; 33-35; also Isa. 51:3).

6 From Malcolm Muggeridge, *Jesus Rediscovered* (New York: Doubleday, 1979) pp. 47-48.

7 I am especially indebted to two particular resources, at this juncture, for their influence upon my thinking: *The Sacred Romance* by Brent Curtis and John Eldridge (Nashville: Thomas Nelson, 1997) and *Heaven: The Heart's Deepest Longings* by Peter Kreeft (San Francisco: Ignatius, 1989).

8 Kreeft (1989), pp. 57-58, states it like this: "But it is precisely when life treats us best that the deepest dissatisfaction arises. As long as we lack worldly happiness, we can deceive ourselves with the 'if only' syndrome: If only I had this or that, I would be happy. But once we have all our thises and thats and are still unhappy, the deception is exposed. That's why rich and powerful modernity is not happier than previous cultures."

9 I'm convinced that some cases of atheism and agnosticism emerge from within people who are quite close to believing in God, even though they might not see it that way. I believe this reality is particularly true for people who possess deep wells of empathy and—because they have no answer for the world's pain and suffering—they opt for unfortunate conclusions.

10 Curtis and Eldredge, pp. 6-7.

11 Ibid., p. 7.

12 Kreeft (1989), p. 67.

13 C. S. Lewis, in *The Problem of Pain* (pp. 147-48) said, "Your soul has a curious shape because it is . . . a key to unlock one of the doors in the house with many mansions. . . . Your place in heaven will seem to be made for you and you alone, because you were made for it—made for it stitch by stitch as a glove is made for a hand."

14 From C. S. Lewis, *The Last Battle* (New York: Collier, 1956), p. 171.

Chapter Three

Making Way for God's Image

Deep inside every human being there is a private
sanctum, a sacred place where only God can
dwell. And that which makes him a human being
is not his body but his spirit, the place in which
the image of God was made to rest.

— A. W. TOZER

One can never consent to creep when one feels
an impulse to soar.

— HELEN KELLER

W hat would you do if you randomly got a check for $1.5 million? The next day you got another check. And the day after brought the identical gift. The next three days followed suit. A note was attached to the final check that first week: "You will receive $1.5 million daily for the rest of your life! You only have to sign and cash each check every day. Otherwise it becomes worthless paper in twenty-four hours."

What would be your first response? Would you be skeptical or ecstatic? Would you try to investigate the source of the gift, asking, "Who's behind this?" Would you be leery of strings attached? Imagine what you would do with all that money. After all, in less than two years, you'd be a billionaire!

Something like this fantasy tale actually happened in the true story of Yates's Pool.[1] The story is about an impoverished sheep rancher who was close to losing his property during the Depression. In desperation, Mr. Yates consented to a wildcat well drill on his West Texas property. Just below 1,000 feet, the drilling crew struck an oil reserve that yielded 80,000 barrels per day from only one well. Other drillings resulted in more than twice that yield. Three decades following the first drilling, reports still projected a potential 125,000 barrels of oil per day—again from only one well!

Mr. Yates, in a matter of hours one afternoon, was radically transformed from a very poor sheep rancher on government subsidy to a multibillionaire.

But the notable part of this story was not so much this rags-to-riches transformation. The remarkable part was that Mr. Yates had always been outrageously rich—and he didn't even know it! Mr. Yates came within a whisker of losing everything, and he never suspected his immense wealth. Yet he touched his immeasurable riches every time he walked on his property. Mr. Yates was clueless about his fortune.

This third chapter on discipleship uses this story as a metaphor for the Christian life. I have created the label "Yates's Syndrome" to describe a spiritual condition that strikes all Christians without exception. Some disciples show the effects of this malady only sporadically. But most of us battle it every single day. A syndrome is a collection of symptoms that characterize a disease or disorder. Yates's Syndrome is an accurate description of the universal disorder by which every saint fails to tap all heavenly riches at her disposal. This affliction causes a weakened spiritual immune system. We grow enfeebled. We're totally worn out. And we're completely clueless about the fact that we possess unbelievable wealth to empower us.

Therein lies the real tragedy, because we have each been given (according to 2 Peter 1:3) "everything we need" for our journey. That promise includes provisions for both our route back to Eden and the subsequent trip to our Celestial Home. We lack nothing (see sidebar 3.1 in the *Supplemental Resource*).

A Potent Prescription

Careful diagnosis of Yates's Syndrome reveals profound misunderstanding of who we are as image bearers. Two remedies await our use, each of which will begin our cure. I say "begin" since this restorative process is anything but a quick fix. Because of our fallen spiritual condition, we are required to take this prescription the rest of our lives—if we desire full health.

The first remedy involves what philosophers call an ontological fact, or a dead-serious reality: God's people are stamped with the tag of "gods" (John 10:34-39, which cites Ps. 82:6). Our Lord did not take this concept of god-likeness lightly. He did not associate it with some mythological Greek or Roman meaning. By quoting Psalm 82, Jesus affirmed the long-standing revelation that literally calls us *elohim*—a term reserved almost exclusively for Deity. The second remedy extends from the first one: Psalm 82 describes God's people as the highest members of Creation— even higher than angels! (See further analyses of both remedies in sidebars 3.2 and 3.3, respectively, in the *Supplemental Resource*.)

These two scriptural labels of *elohim* are not mentioned here to promote pride or boasting. The appropriate response to our special human nature, in every case, must always manifest itself in praise to our Maker. I point out these two remedies so every saint may begin imagining what image bearing functionally means.

Think about it: Even in our sinful condition, we still reflect the Maker of heaven and earth! We reflect the image of the one who intimately shares our breath! In this wonderful light, I'm certain we disciples consistently set the bar much too low. Our low view of people (which I will soon discuss) keeps our expectations and goals low. Then, modifying C. S. Lewis's well-worn phrase, when it comes to assessing our day—or our entire life—"we are far too easily pleased."

Rethinking Our Incredible Heritage

Recall this book's opening tale about Helen and Howard's "first day" in heaven. This elderly couple, who shed old age for agelessness, experientially discovered how all good things in this world reappear as best in that celestial world. Those déjà vu blessings include personal health and contentment. They comprise work, worship, and leisure. And every relationship (from friend to stranger) is also embraced. In other words, when we reclaim the unfathomable resources of God's image, we reconnect with Eden. From there we can envision heaven's Home.

Helen and Howard experienced all of the Garden legacies. Their core communion with the Creator was purposefully linked with their:

- Family Name (Character)
- Family Business (Calling)
- Family Ties (Community)

Again, I call these Garden legacies because every person inherits these comprehensive blessings.[2] Each legacy is attached to God's image inside us, and each is linked to his life-giving breath we breathe. Another way to contemplate our legacies is as a three-way communion with the Creator (see figure 3.1).

Markers that Point Us Home

Scripture explains each legacy in terms of three supportive gifts.

FIGURE 3.1

Legacies and Partnerships

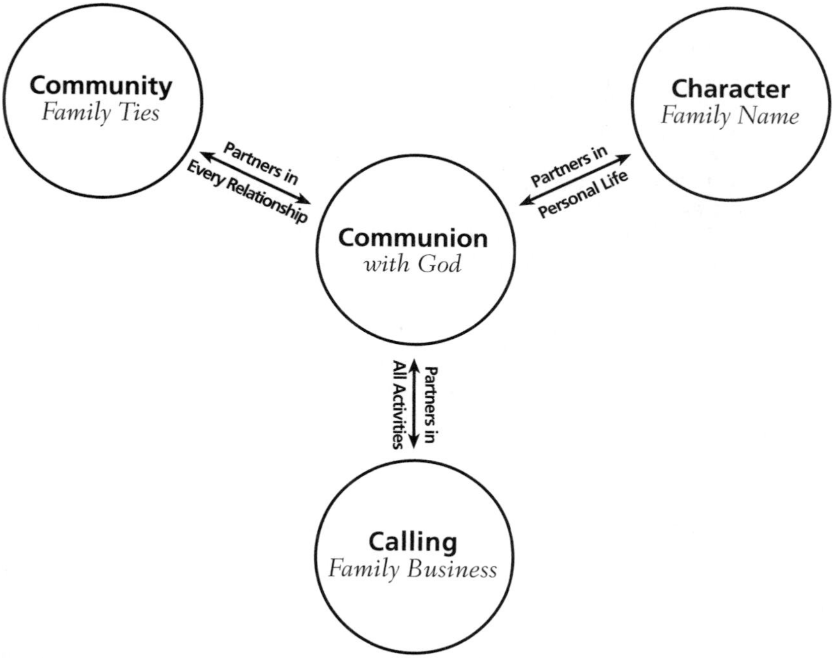

When organized through the metaphor of pilgrimage, these nine gifts—what I call the Super Nine—represent the Creator's internal road markers for our journey Home. Far more accurate (and intimate) than any Global Positioning System, our Maker's internal markers feature nine powerful homing devices. The Super Nine gifts are practical expressions of how the Creator's likeness is revealed in us. It is foolish to think these nine traits exhaust what *imago Dei* (image of God) means, yet they do portray substantial attributes of all image bearers (see Gen. 1–2). In one sense, the basic categories are the same for every person (e.g., all people need to love and be loved). In another sense, every person expresses these nine gifts uniquely. The Super Nine, to repeat, describe the internal evidence of our authenticity. They are what make us human. These gifts symbolize the facts that we all were once:

1. Godlike Physiques
2. Passionate Thinkers } Character
3. Sensory Learners

4. Kind Rulers
5. Worshipful Workers } Calling
6. Artists and Scientists

7. Intimate Families
8. Good Neighbors } Community
9. Responsible Citizens

Whenever we think about *any* person—Christian or not—in anything less than these nine inheritances, we underestimate and disrespect God's image. We dismiss how our Maker still works through his Creation. In short, we settle for a second-rate portrait of humans.

We should not be surprised that the Super Nine lay the necessary theological foundation for biblical discipleship. One of the foundational elements of the Super Nine is that each gift is quite complex. Each is rich in meaning. Consequently, I will describe each gift below with respect for its comprehensiveness and richness.

Furthermore, respect for these complex qualities is illustrated by framing our gifts within tensioned sets of traits. (Following each of the three subsequent sections on our gifts, a table of "breathing exercises" offers reflective questions for personal or small-group application.) Perhaps the best way to understand what I mean by "tensioned sets of traits" is to think of the word "paradox"—seemingly contradictory words that appear to work against each other. We find paradoxes throughout our culture in phrases like "jumbo shrimp," "deafening silence," and "bittersweet." We also find paradoxes within Jesus' teaching, when he used phrases such as "the first will be last" and "the greatest will serve the least." Whenever we respect these tensions within our Creator's nine

Gifts we value their rich complexity from the Garden. The Super Nine are anything but static. These lively, kaleidoscopic qualities of our inheritance faithfully mirror the light of our Maker. Our gifts embrace complementary attributes—even those that seem contradictory.

The First Legacy of Family Name

When we were very young, my older brother Gary and I spent a considerable amount of time at my grandparents' house. Gary and my great-grandmother "Granny" (who resided with my grandparents) really hit it off. They had an extraordinary relationship. They had secret meetings together. They even had secret names. Their exceptional relationship stirred up jealous feelings inside me. This, in turn, caused my grandmother (whom we kids called "Nin") to take me aside. In her best attempts at justice, Nin suggested she and I create our own secret club. (Don't try to overanalyze this strategy!) Nin subsequently bestowed upon me the affectionate nickname of "E. S." I could not have been more delighted. Of course, Gary didn't take too long to figure out those initials meant "Extra Special." When he confronted me rather boastfully with his discovery, I also experienced my first recollection of lying when I told him he was wrong.

I tell this story to emphasize that there is tremendous power in a personal name. To have my own secret name, as Gary did, was exhilarating. Furthermore, it greatly helped to have my unique title come from someone I dearly loved. "Extra Special" represented an enormous emotional treasure trove for me.

Names are God's relational trademarks. That's a rule almost without exception in Scripture. From Adam and Eve's names to Israel's tribal labels, and from the Holy Land's sites (like trees and wells) to memorial altars, the Creator used names to describe his relationship with his children. (Sidebar 3.4, in the *Supplemental Resource*, provides more insights into the power of Bible names.)

The next section details the first three gifts that aid us in our task of lifelong discipleship. This threesome combine to form our character.

Gift 1: Godlike Physiques

We are spiritual yet physical people. We humans possess bodies as well as an inseparable bond with the Creator. Genesis 2:7 says our Maker fashioned man by breathing life into him, resulting in a "living being."

One of the most disregarded characteristics of image is that God's creation of humans means we received not just a spirit but also a body. This fact is critical for the believer—in terms of who we were before sin, who we were after sin, and who we are now in Christ. For example, Christians should never fall into the common trap of conceptualizing people as "immaterial" (spiritual) versus "material" (physical). We ought to value *both* sides of this paradox. When we don't, we almost always esteem this gift's first trait and devalue its second.[3]

First Corinthians 15 indicates that there is a world of difference between what we inherited "in Adam" and what we received "in Christ." For instance, nothing that's merely physical and perishable will enter heaven. But Scripture also discloses that "body" also describes our nature—both now and for eternity (see chart 3.1 in the *Supplemental Resource*). We are sure that everything associated with "flesh and blood" and "mortality" will be left behind in this world. But we are likewise told we will inherit a new body like Jesus' resurrected body. That's why our fully restored, integrated "spiritual body" sounds so oxymoronic. It may sound contradictory to us, but not to our Maker.

This is not an easy concept to grasp. We have never experienced this type of body before. So it is helpful to focus on a few familiar "body" traits we have experienced—traits that continue throughout eternity—such as the abilities to recognize others and to use our human senses.[4] Let's not forget that all people, even in this life, are much more than physical. We are also spiritual and eternal, because we are the only creatures who share the Maker's breath. We have never-ending existence.

Gift 2: Passionate Thinkers

We are emotional yet rational people. Individuals possess the capacities to be lonely and to love (Gen. 2:18, 23-25). We also have the ability to discern and to choose (Gen. 2:16-17). Again, these two traits must never be set at odds against each other. Feelings should complement thinking. If we diminish either trait, we see people as less than fully human.

Both qualities are also found in the Trinity's witness throughout the Creation account. Intellectual abilities are repeatedly seen in God's wisdom, knowledge, and communication skills. God's passion is found in his loving plan to bring Adam a "suitable helper" in Eve. Following Creation (among other passages that acknowledge our Maker's emotions) Scripture records God's grief, which arises from increased wickedness in people (Gen. 5:10).

Gift 3: Sensory Learners

We are experiential people. The human senses of sight, taste, smell, and touch are explicitly noted in Genesis 2:9b, 2:9c, 2:12b, and 3:3. Hearing is noted in Genesis 3:8. Two of the most unfamiliar yet important verses in the Creation account emphasize the place of purposeful beauty in God's grand design. (Recall that the literal meaning of the "Garden" of Eden is a "hedging around delight.") This beauty was intended for enjoyment through the human senses. Genesis 2 records that God not only fashioned trees "for food" but he also sculpted "trees that were pleasing to the eye" (v. 9a). Besides the fine gold in Eden, "aromatic resin" appealed to our sense of smell (v. 12b).

TABLE 3.1
Breathing Exercises for Character
(Reflection Questions for Character Legacy of Family Name)

I. Questions for Gift 1 (Godlike Physiques):
   Review the first pair of *physical* and *spiritual* attributes from our Garden Legacies.
   A. What are your initial impressions of the image of God as "*physical*"? What personal responsibilities did this first inheritance bring to Adam and Eve? Make a list of three obligations that come to your mind—such as taking care of personal health needs.
   B. Stop for a second and ask yourself: "How does the eternal *spiritual* characteristic of people affect the way I now think about the Christian life?" In particular, answer these two subthemes: How does this reality shape my need to personally grow as a disciple? How does this influence my personal need to evangelize?

II. Questions for Gift 2 (Passionate Thinkers):
   A. What are some illustrations of how you could blend *emotions* and *thoughts*, honoring your Maker in the process?
   B. What does Mark 12:28-31 tell you about this blended second gift—both from historical Jewish tradition and from Jesus' perspective?

III. Questions for Gift 3 (Sensory Learners):
   A. One sweeping application of this sensory potential features our vast capacities to participate in experimental learning all around us—from music appreciation to rock climbing, from art exhibits to browsing a scented candle shop, and from enjoying pasta delicacies with homemade garlic bread to watching a fireworks display. From the list below, provide at least one example (for *each* sense) that could consciously be used to glorify God:

Sense of *Sight* —
Sense of *Smell* —
Sense of *Hearing* —
Sense of *Taste* —
Sense of *Touch* —

B. Select one of the five sensory areas. Brainstorm at least three specific ways an obedient disciple could "recapture Eden" (in your selected sense) as he or she consciously connects with the ultimate aim of image formation. Using your selected sense, also identify several temptations that may arise for the follower of Christ, potentially causing image *de*formation. For instance, what negative experiences could result from using your senses selfishly?

The Second Legacy of Family Business

Family Business likewise incorporates three subsets. Each gift pertains to what we were made to do from the start of time. By way of preview, Gift 4 pinpoints our position (our role as rulers): who we are in the Creator's business plans. Gift 5 highlights our posture (our humble worship and service): why we do our business. And Gift 6 features our practices (our range of skills): how we encounter the privileges and challenges of God's business.

One of the most brilliant insights that C. S. Lewis makes regarding human depravity is found in his introduction to *The Great Divorce*. It's a reversal of the Garden's second legacy. The worst of earth—technically what hell is like—is described as having so much abundance that people have no needs whatsoever. They get everything they want by just imagining it! There is no toil or commitment to work. Certainly no allegiance to their Maker is anywhere in sight. There is also one major drawback: What they possess is inferior—their belongings are nothing like the "real commodities" of heaven.[5] In short, Lewis's worst-case scenario is that

Cultural Mandate is all but abandoned, since "Family Business" is disregarded. The reality of life today is, sadly, not too far from his fiction (see sidebar 3.5 in the *Supplemental Resource*).

Family Business all comes down to our calling—what we were created to do.

Gift 4: Kind Rulers

We are reigning leaders yet caring servants. Adam and Eve were commanded to "subdue" and "rule over" the Garden (Gen. 1:28) and we continue in that role, a role that entails three tasks. First, we are regal people. Through our image reflection of the Trinity, we are formed to exercise dominion—to have mastery over—all life on this planet. But with our regal rule comes the second duty, "to work" the Garden (Gen. 2:15b), and the third task to "take care of it" (Gen. 2:15c). The last two tasks balance the first, as concepts such as ecology, stewardship, and service complement our traditional understandings of dominion and leadership.

Gift 5: Worshipful Workers

We are working yet resting, worshiping people. Humans obediently emulate their Maker by first laboring (Gen. 2:15), then, by implication, resting as God did (Gen. 2:2-8). Exodus 20:8-11 provides the first explicit command for Sabbath rest.

We are fundamentally vocational people. We partner in our Family Business with our Maker. We may be faithful partners or slackers. But we always retain our partnership because his image is permanently stamped inside us. Part of the reason why we don't pick up on the importance of this fifth gift is that we misinterpret its primary reference (Gen. 2:15): "The LORD God took the man and put him in the Garden of Eden to work it and take care of it." John H. Sailhamer makes a provocative case for saying that "working" and "keeping" the Garden should actually have an alternate set of words: "a more suitable translation of the Hebrew text would be 'to worship and obey'."[6] This perspective sees the key ingredients of working, worshiping, and obeying as harmonious, almost synonymous. Therefore, to work is to worship is to obey. And that is exactly why any person can experience an "emotional high" from an honest day's work. Whether he knows it or not, he is reconnecting with the Garden of Delight (see Paul's discussion of this topic from passages like Eph. 6:5-7 and 2 Thess. 3:6-10).

Gift 6: Artists and Scientists

We are creative yet orderly in our problem-solving challenges of life.[7] When Adam names the animals, the first man uses his capacities of curiosity and imagination, along with his skills of structure and logic (Gen. 2:19-20). It is the best of right-brain and left-brain operations.

Bringing Eve to life occurs as an extension of Adam's Garden assignment to name the animals. It's a plan undergirded by curiosity and creativity—starting with God Himself and running through to his human creatures. The Maker wanted man, as he named the animals, to experientially realize his need for the woman. When Adam discovers "no suitable helper" for himself (Gen. 2:20b), the Creator reveals an interesting characteristic about his own personality: God is *curious* "to see what [Adam] would name [the animals]," according to Genesis 2:19b. People still possess this reflected trait of curiosity as image bearers. We also possess both the creativity and the organizational ability of Adam. Our abilities as artists and scientists are expressed through many related skills like imagination, observation, wonder, reason, deduction, the taking of divergent perspectives, and troubleshooting.

The Third Legacy of Family Ties

A joke currently circulating goes something like this: Three best friends

---

TABLE 3.2

Breathing Exercises for Calling
(Reflection Questions for Calling Legacy of Family Business)

I. <u>Questions for Gift 4 (Kind Rulers):</u>
   A. Stop and ask yourself, "How has this fourth privilege of Eden been abused by people since the Fall?" What are some historical or recent examples of that abuse, that first come to your mind?
   B. If Christians took this Garden blessing seriously—in light of our larger discipleship objective of image restoration—what particular expressions of godly rule and care could you identify? For starters, recall the conclusion from C. S. Lewis's *The Lion, the Witch, and the Wardrobe*: The four hero and heroine children (now adult kings and queens of Narnia) demonstrated their godly reign when "they made good laws and kept the peace and saved good trees from being unnecessarily cut down."[1] What could you add to these virtues?
   C. As you picture the personal responsibilities you have been (regionally) given within God's (universal) kingdom, suggest a few healthy signs of your own conscious attempts at "caring dominion" on this earth.

II. <u>Questions for Gift 5 (Worshipful Workers):</u>
   A. Select a couple of personal experiences in which you derived satisfaction from your work. List at least two tangible and two intangible rewards.
   B. Also, identify a handful of specific ways you observe that work has generally been distorted by sin (e.g., the temptation toward "workaholism").
   C. How might these two lists influence you as you, again, prepare for the work week? What do these lists say about your holistic faith walk?

III. Questions for Gift 6 (Artists and Scientists):

A. Contemplate the past week or so and ask yourself where you have observed any creativity or orderliness (from this Gift) whether in your life or someone else's. Your observations may be complex or simple—like elementary illustrations of problem solving, a new approach to balancing your checkbook, doing daily routines more efficiently, or discovering a better way to travel to work.

B. Make at least one statement of life application this Gift's contribution might have on modern-day disciples who are teachable.

---

1 *The Lion, the Witch, and the Wardrobe* (New York: Macmillan, 1950), p. 180.

were marooned on an island. While looking for food they discovered a magic lantern, and its genie granted each man a wish. The first said, "I'd sure love to get back to New York for a Yankees' baseball game."

Poof! Instantly, he found himself behind the home team dugout at Yankee Stadium for a doubleheader with the Red Sox.

The second man said, "Ya know, I always wanted to cruise Route 66 in a brand-new Corvette."

Poof! He was last seen traveling west on a gorgeous day—not a care in the world—in his new, red convertible.

The third man, the quietest of the three, realized his buddies had each gotten their wish. They were long gone. His face grew somber. "What's wrong?" asked the wish granter. "You still have your one request."

"Yeah, I know," the third man said. "But it's hard to think straight when your best friends are gone. I'm so lonely. I wish they were here."

Poof!

We all need other people (figure 3.2, on the opposite page, illustrates how the last three gifts pertain to relationships). The Creator's first (and negative) critique of his own perfect Creation—"It is not good for the man to be alone" (Gen. 2:18a)—primarily refers to the need for both genders, for humanity to be complete. But secondarily it means "people need people." (Sidebar 3.6 supplies further introduction to this final legacy, in the *Supplemental Resource*.)

Gift 7: Intimate Families

We are individual yet relational people. The covenant faithfulness between Yahweh and individuals, found in Genesis 2:4, begins here. The creation of male and female (Gen. 1:27) is based upon the fact that it was "not good for man to be alone" (Gen. 2:18): Every person—as valuable as he or she is, individually—needs other people.

The point is that image is male and female combined. Each individual (besides his or her dependency upon the Creator) needs others to be complete. We are familial people. When the three Persons of the Godhead convened their first meeting to discuss the creation of humans, their plural presence was apparent: "Let *us* make man in *our* image, in *our* likeness . . ." (Gen. 1:26a, italics added).[8] Human nature, in its broadest sense, reflects that plural nature of God. In other words, because of the three-in-one Maker's makeup—which we mirror—this seventh gift reminds us of the truth that we will always need other humans. In the words of poet John Donne, no person is an island.

Gift 8: Good Neighbors

We are moral people, yet we have potential for immorality. The command to not eat from "the tree of the knowledge of good and evil" (Gen. 2:9, 17) implies the duty of continuous moral choice. It also implies the capacity people have to embrace "the dark side." Personal choice links these two tensions. (Of all the Super Nine, this is the only gift that does not completely reflect the Creator. Since the nature of God is good, he never

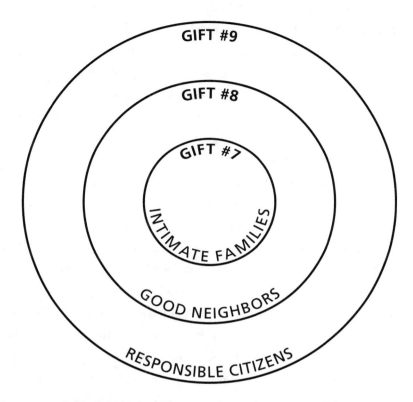

FIGURE 3.2

Concentric Ring Summary of Three Family Ties

GIFT #9

GIFT #8

GIFT #7

INTIMATE FAMILIES

GOOD NEIGHBORS

RESPONSIBLE CITIZENS

chooses evil. God does, however, express volition, or will.)

Unfortunately Adam and Eve chose to defy God's moral standard, bringing instant unrighteousness. Their decision also brought personal bondage through a new master called sin. A pair of related concepts emerges from this eighth gift: God's two-part command to Adam in Genesis 2:16-17 links human autonomy ("You are free to eat of any tree . . .") with divinely sanctioned borders (" . . . but you must not eat . . ."). Independence (and disobedience) is offset by a dependence (or obedience) the Creator purposefully shaped into his perfect Garden children. Again, human volition connects these two concepts. People have always had the capacity to reason, to understand consequences, and to make personal choices.

As it was noted in the introduction to this section, Gift 8 represents implied moral obligations to our neighbor. We daily choose—just like Eve and Adam—to do good toward others or not. As chapter 5 shows, this is not choosing goodness for goodness' sake. We choose goodness toward our neighbor because there is a direct correlation with God's image. That is, as we treat human creatures, so we treat our Creator.

Gift 9: Responsible Citizens

We are cultural people yet heavenly citizens. The mandate for people to rule and to care for the earth is held in tension by our ultimate service to God in heaven. God's ordination of marriage, which calls for man and woman to each leave their respective homes and "become one flesh" (Gen. 2:24), implies the eventual proliferation of many homes, in a human civilization populated by responsible citizens.

As I noted earlier (and referenced in sidebar 3.6 in the *Supplemental Resource*), this last gift is a catchall for every remaining cultural obligation. A whole host of subjects pertains—from time management to fashion, and from computer technology to global cleanup projects. Even baseball fits within a comprehensive Christian worldview, because our national pastime affirms our Creator's initial intention for us to enjoy life.[9] We revalue the proper place of entertainment and pleasure, since he is the one who introduced us to the Garden of Delight. Moreover, he hardwired our image so that pleasure is as natural as breathing. Like a gracious parent, he delights when we obediently delight. These ordinary activities of Gift 9 fit well into the Lord's Prayer, whose opening petition covers everything under the sun, while it holds our dual citizenship in tension: "Your will be done on earth as it is in heaven."

Biblical discipleship could powerfully impact human civilization if we took Jesus' lordship seriously—whether onto the trading floor of the New York Stock Exchange or into the rain forests of Brazil.

TABLE 3.3

Breathing Exercises for Community
(Reflection Questions for Community Legacy of Family Ties)

I. Questions for Gift 7 (Intimate Families):

  A. Think about the value of this seventh Eden blessing from a reverse angle: What if this relational theme was *never* mentioned in our Garden Gifts? What if Scripture implied that we were supposed to live isolated lives, even though we were created with relational needs? List your initial reactions.

  B. Continuing this same scenario, what sections of Scripture would necessarily need to be omitted or drastically modified? What biblical directives (along with their rewards) would be lost? How would our homes, churches, and local communities look?

  C. Reread Galatians 6:10 and 1 Timothy 5:4b, then provide one principle you would like to share with every saint.

II. Questions for Gift 8 (Good Neighbors):

  A. Contemplate Bible verses that recognize the superior human (versus animal) capacity to reason and to choose. Without any help, list at least a half dozen references or phrases on this topic that first come to your mind.

  B. Study Joshua's well-known challenge in Joshua 24:15 and Paul's familiar charge in Romans 12:2. What do these two passages tell you about the Creator in terms of Gift 8? What do these verses say about people?

III. Questions for Gift 9 (Responsible Citizens):

A. Genesis 2:20 concludes Adam's naming assignment by identifying three basic animal groups that were affected: livestock, birds, and wild animals. These terms portray representative ways humans employ categorizing skills, including the capacity to compare (and to contrast) entries from within a larger group—"animals" in this case. How would you respond to a cynic of Christian discipleship who, upon reading this section, says, "So what? How does this ninth gift practically affect human civilization?" In two or three sentences, what would you say?

B. Ideally speaking, what should disciples be able to offer their culture? Select one cultural area of concern or interest you have (e.g., politics, education, entertainment), and then write out one paragraph that summarizes the potential that believers bring to this final Gift.

In sum, the third of the twelve principles that mature believers must claim is this:

Truth 3

God's model for discipleship contains "everything we need" for our lifelong pilgrim journey—employing the Maker's Super Nine Gifts (from his image) helps us become all we were created to become.

Respecting the Gift Giver

We have all received presents that have embarrassed or disappointed us—like clothing three sizes too large or too small, or an appliance (or gadget of any sort) that solely benefits the giver of the gift.

We affectionately name these exasperating gifts "white elephants." But there's one attribute that all white elephants have in common. No, it's not their worthlessness. Neither is it the way they are refunded, discarded, or set out in the next garage sale. What's common is that—as useless as they might soon become—they're always opened. Why? There are usually three reasons. First, we typically don't know we've been given a white elephant until we take the effort to unwrap it. Second, we usually have some kind of appreciation for the gift giver. Third, our name is on the package.

Think about those facts for a minute, then ask yourself: When it comes to our nine phenomenal Gifts, why do we often ignore those presents without unwrapping them? That analogy might sound silly, but I believe the comparison is fair. Actually, when this does happen, I suspect we might look silly to the ultimate Gift Giver.

Not only do we frequently dishonor the Gift Giver (by not pulling off the wrapping) but we regularly forget that:

- God has customized his gifts precisely to our particular size.
- We (not him) are the primary ones to benefit from those riches.
- He put incredible thought and sentiment into each gift—literally from the foundation of the world!

Those multiple Eden Gifts became ours when we were uniquely fashioned out of the dust of the earth and from the breath of God (Gen. 2:7). That act was an epic event. And it brought the stamp of approval from the Creator who proclaimed everything "very good" as he stepped back to assess his completed work. This aspect of human creation prompted Francis Schaeffer and C. Everett Koop to exclaim a quarter century ago, "The Bible tells us who we are. . . . We do not need to be confused, as is much of modern mankind, about people's distinction from both animal life and . . . complicated machines. . . . Suddenly people have unique value."[10] These two Christian leaders clearly understood the rudimentary implications of people as image bearers[11]—both in the descriptive and prescriptive senses. And it all starts in Eden.[12]

Table 3.4 offers a chapter summary of our Garden inheritance. Whether we understand these gifts to total nine or ninety-nine, biblical discipleship must proceed from this foundation.

Conclusion

It does not take a lot of Bible study to realize the Creator has a much more expansive view of people than most Christians do. If we choose to show our disobedience, our ignorance, or our ungratefulness toward his design (by holding self-limiting views of humankind), we arrive at this stagnant end point: shallow and shrunken views of men and women. But the moment we acknowledge God's magnificent "Super Nine" potential in all people, we begin to swap our puny, locket-sized, black-and-white snapshots of humans for the Creator's breathtaking, individually customized mural masterpieces.

The simplest way I can apply this chapter's principles on image—at the progressively increasing levels of human experience I introduced in chapter 1—is to say this: Whenever anybody engages any of the Super Nine, even subconsciously, he automatically taps the essence of our true humanity. Whenever anybody encounters one of these gifts, with thanksgiving, he starts to brush up against the supernatural. And whenever a Christian implements any Super Nine gift with the intention of restoration, she becomes more like the Creator—more Godlike, more like our original image from Eden. At the same time, she grows more thoroughly human.

Christ's disciples, then, don't need to succumb to Yates's Syndrome. We don't need to live like impoverished sheep ranchers when we actually possess immeasurable wealth from God's rich resources. We have been graciously given "everything we need." Everything.

So don't wait a second longer. Don't dishonor our Gift Giver. Take hold of his presents, postmarked in heaven from the foundation of the world.

Rip open your gifts! After all, each one has your name on it.

TABLE 3.4

Image and Super Nine Gifts

	Complementary Descriptions of the Super Nine	Super Nine References from Creation in Genesis	Attributes of God that People Mirror in His Image
1. Godlike Physiques	We are *Physical* and *Spiritual* People	• (2:7b) People were *specially created* (from God's breath) to become "*living beings*" • (2:9c) Trees were "*good for food*" (implies need for *nutrition and growth*)	• The *spirituality* of God (John 4:24) refers to his *immaterial nature*; people partially reflect the Maker by their *immaterial nature* (Gen. 2:7; 1 Thess. 5:23) • Yet God is *also something more than spirit*—he "*breathed*" (Gen. 2:7) and *walked* in Eden (3:8; see 2 Sam. 22:9a, 9b, 10, 14, 16)
2. Passionate Thinkers	We are *Emotional* and *Rational* People	• (2:16-17) There was potential to discern and *to choose* • (2:18; 23-25) There was also potential to be *lonely* and *loving* • (3:10) *Fear* resulted from sin	• *Intellectual* abilities of God (*knowledge* and *wisdom*) are seen throughout Creation • God's *passion* for Adam to have a "*helper*" (Gen. 2:18); also, God's *grief* arises from increasing wickedness (Gen. 6:6)
3. Sensory Learners	We are *Sensory Experience* People	• "Garden of Eden" literally means "hedging around delight" • (2:9b) Trees were created as "pleasing to the eye" (*sight*) • (2:9c) And "good for food" (*taste*) • (2:12b) There was "aromatic resin" (*smell*) • (3:3; 8) Post-sin references are made to *touch* and to *hearing*	• Creator "*saw*" that his Creation was "*good*" (Gen. 1:4, 10, 12, 18, 25, and 31) • Creator God uses certain forms of senses (See 2 Sam. 22:1-17; esp. v. 7, 9a; 17; Ps 94:9) Also Eph. 5:2–Jesus was a "*fragrant* offering to God"
4. Kind Rulers	We are *Regal* and *Ecological* People	• (1:28b) People were commanded to "*subdue*" and to "*rule*" over the Garden • (2:15b) People were also commanded to "*take care*" of the Garden	• El-Shaddai values God's *power* and *faithfulness* to his people, through his *consistent blessings and comfort* (see Gen. 17:1; 28:3; Exod. 6:2-3)

5. Worshipful Workers	We are *Laboring* and *Restfully-Worshiping* People	• (2:2-3) There was an implied command *to rest* as the Creator did (compare Exod. 20:8-11) • (2:15a) People were commanded *to "work"* the Garden	• The Creator modeled his *commendable work pattern* through his Creation (Gen. 1:1-31) • The Creator *rested* on the seventh day, making it *holy* (Gen. 2:2)
6. Artists and Scientists	We are *Creative* and *Orderly* People	• (2:19-20) *Multiple capacities for* curiosity, adventure, and organization for creative problem solving were given to people • (3:1-6) This *same potential* within people was found in the very first sin	• (Gen. 2:19b) The Creator shows personal *"curiosity"*: He personally "brought [the animals] to the man *to see* what *he would name* them"— then *God made woman* (v. 21-22). In Ps. 147:4 God similarly *names the stars* • The *orderliness* of God is displayed in Creation (Gen. 1:1-31); a *parallel order* is to be found in church (see 1 Cor. 14:33; 40)
7. Intimate Families	We are *Individual* and *Relational* People	• (1:27) God created people as *"male* and *female"* • (2:18) Before sin, God determined it was *"not good* for the man to be *alone"* • (2:20-25) The woman was created *for* man	• Yahweh features the *covenant faithfulness* of God (Gen. 2:4b; Exod. 3:12-16; 6:2-3) • *Relational* references to God (*plural* pronouns "us" and "we") refer to the *communitarian* (or fellowship) attribute of the Trinity (Gen. 1:26; 3:22)
8. Good Neighbors	We are *Morally Helpful* People	• (2:9, 17) The "tree of the knowledge of *good and evil"* implied moral potential • (2:20-24) Eve was created as Adam's *"suitable helper"* • (3:7-8) Moral *shame* resulted from the first human choice to sin	• The *holiness* of God is witnessed in *Creation*, related to the *Sabbath* (Gen. 2:2-3) and continues to the end of the Scriptures (Rev. 4:8; 21:2, 27; 22:19) • God's *holiness* causes him to evict unholy Adam and Eve from the Garden (Gen. 3:22-24)
9. Responsible Citizens	We are *Broadly Cultural* People	• (1:28a) God commanded people to "be *fruitful* and *increase* . . . and subdue" (*Cultural Mandate*) • (3:1-6) The human capacity to *communicate* and *work together* was demonstrated, even for the purposes of evil	• The positive *cultural* traits of God—modeled by his own attributes of *communication* and *cooperation*—are constantly evident within the Trinity (Gen. 1:1-2 and 3:22)

1 See *How You Can Be Filled with the Holy Spirit* by Bill Bright (Orlando, Fla.: New Life Publications, 1971), pp. 21-22.

2 Walter Wangerin (in his *Mourning into Dancing* [Grand Rapids, Mich.: Zondervan, 1992], p. 44) offers a parallel model to my "four Cs" design: Wangerin calls our *Communion* with God our "Primal Relationship"; Family Business (*Calling*) is labeled "the Natural Relationship"; Family Ties (*Community*) is identified as "the Communal"; and Family Name (*Character*) is comparable to Wangerin's "the Internal."

3 One common example of the compartmentalization in discipleship is the unfortunate use of the dichotomous phrase "saving souls" in evangelism. A much better way to integrate these two domains is to prize the health of both parts of our lives, as the Apostle John does in 3 John 2: "Dear friend, I pray that you may *enjoy good health* and that all may go well with you, *even as your soul* is getting along well."

4 Christian philosopher Peter Kreeft helps us understand this topic a bit more when he contrasts other philosophies and religions, then concludes: "*Only Christianity truly glorifies the senses.*" Kreeft continues offering helpful understanding about human senses as he deliberately ties them to *imago Dei*. Finally, he raises the question many readers are thinking: "*Does this mean God has some sort of body Himself?*"

> Therefore, something like them [senses] must be in God. Rather (we have it backwards again) they must be like something in God. For God is the source and model of all pluses, all perfections, all that it is better to be than not to be. We usually think of God in Cartesian rather than biblical terms, as the model only of spiritual things, and as Himself spiritual in the Cartesian sense, that is, negatively spiritual, spiritual not only because of something he has (mind) but also because of something he lacks (body and senses). God does *not* have a physical body or senses, *but he does not lack them either.* Just *how* God "sees," "hears," "feels," "tastes," and "smells" is *not clear.*

> From *Everything You Ever Wanted to Know About Heaven . . . but Never Dreamed of Asking* (San Francisco: Ignatius, 1990), pp. 91-92. Italics are mine.

5 From *The Great Divorce* (New York: Macmillan, 1946), pp. 21-22.

6 Sailhamer in *The Pentateuch as Narrative* (Grand Rapids, Mich.: Zondervan, 1992), pp. 100-01.

7 C. S. Lewis (in *The Problem of Pain*, p. 150) used these words to summarize Gift 6 from Eden: "For doubtless the continually successful, yet never complete, attempt by each Soul to communicate its unique vision to all others (and that by means whereof earthly art and philosophy are but clumsy imitations) is also among the ends for which the individual was created."

8 Whereas other creatures were also fashioned to reproduce "according to its kind" (Gen. 1:24-25), only people were supernaturally endowed to pass on God's image to their children. Adam bequeathed to his son Seth "his *own* likeness, in his *own* image" (Gen. 5:3), so the inference is that the human components of divine "likeness/image" were transferable from the beginning. Yet the inquisitive mind will ask: "But given the sinful Fall in Genesis 3, did Adam and Eve *fully retain the image* they *originally* received?" The simple answer is no, but the complex response offers more hope. Genesis 9:6 and James 3:9 substantiate the fact that all post-Fall people continue to possess some semblance of God's image—and pass it on to their family—even though it's been severely distorted. We still serve as the Creator's sole ambassadors.

9 Reviewing a recent book by Richard J. Mouw (*He Shines in All That's Fair*), David Neff raises the significant topic of God's common grace. He contrasts Mouw with other theological voices, which respond to every question on the Creator's purposes with some answer involving salvation, saying, "But theologians like Mouw allow for God *to desire* things (and *to delight* in things) that have no direct connections to salvation. Mouw believes that *God can take just as much delight in what he makes as in what he saves*. Could God not enjoy a baseball game for reasons that 'stand alongside of, rather than be subservient to, the goal of bringing about election and reprobation'?"

Then Neff concludes, "That is not trivial or sacrilegious. It is a way of affirming the Bible's first picture of God: the Maker of Heaven and Earth. And it *recognizes that God's act of creating people contained the flowering of human culture that was to come, including baseball*." From "Why God Enjoys Baseball" in *Christianity Today* (July 8, 2002), pp. 49-52.

10 *Whatever Happened to the Human Race?* by Francis A. Schaeffer and C. Everett Koop (Old Tappan, N.J.: Fleming H. Revell, 1979, p. 158).

11 Schaeffer and Koop (p. 195) add: "*People are special* and *human life is sacred*, whether or not we admit it. Every life is precious and worthwhile in itself—not only to us human beings but also to God. *Every person is worth fighting for*, regardless of whether he is young or old, sick or well, child or adult, born or unborn, or brown, red, yellow, black or white." Italics mine.

12 Leland Ryken (in "Finding Heaven in Milton's *Paradise Lost*" in *Journey to the Celestial City: Glimpses of Heaven from Great Literary Classics*, [Chicago: Moody, 1995], p. 74, italics are mine), likewise, chooses his words carefully when he provides this pertinent summary of John Milton's *Paradise Lost*:

> Furthermore, Milton's portrayal of life in Paradise is in effect his pattern of the pilgrim's life for all who seek heaven. *How does God intend human life to be lived?* Basing our answer on Milton's picture of life in Paradise, several answers are obvious: in continuous communion with God and worship of Him; in harmony with nature; in companionship with one's fellow humans; with every human appetite (including the sexual) satisfied; with work to give life meaning; in contentment and joy; in reliance on God's perfect provision. An implied message is that *if we wish to attain heaven, we should live as Adam and Eve lived before the Fall.*

Chapter Four

The Way Out of Paradise

> *The whole range of human miseries, from restlessness and estrangement through shame and guilt to the agonies of daytime television—all of them tell us that things in human life are not as they ought to be.*
>
> —CORNELIUS PLANTINGA JR.

S omething was wrong, terribly wrong. Birds and crickets stopped their chirping. Majestic cedars bowed in shame. A colony of ants abandoned their collaborative activity and scattered. Clouds blackened the blue sky as if to protest.

Eve said no to her Maker.

Lengthy walks with the kind Creator abruptly halted—rudely replaced by not-so-fun diversions of hide-and-seek. Harmony no longer existed between the animals. Or between people.

No more contentment. No more purity. No more innocence.

Adam also said no.

For the first time, humble lambs wouldn't dare rest beside a pride of lions. Dandelions and earthquakes made their annoying and frightening arrivals known. Angry looks, evil thoughts, wicked deeds—and clothing—all made their debut.

The belated eighth day of Creation arrived, full of all things hideous and perverted, crashing the perfect party of Eden. Pandora's original box opened. Every subsequent display of beauty, truth, and goodness was shadowed at its birth.

Actually this was not the first rebellion but the second. So the unfallen angels cried, once again, having twice witnessed blatant disobedience toward the Maker.

It was the day all Creation died.

The Real Problem in Eden

I've heard some preachers make a great deal out of the fact that—when confronted by the serpent—Eve said more about God's prohibitions in Eden than God Himself ever did. That is, she accurately reported the Tree of Knowledge's fruit off-limits, then errantly declared that the entire tree was untouchable.

But that wasn't Eve's most serious flaw. The real problem lay much deeper.

Eve's fundamental error (and Adam's as well) was that *she undervalued what she already had*. I don't mean that she was ungrateful for all the other fruit trees, or that she was ungrateful for living in such a wonderful place called paradise. Eve's transgression was even more foundational. Remember the heart of the serpent's temptation: "You will be like God" (Gen. 3:5b). Eve and Adam largely disobeyed their Maker because they didn't fully appreciate that they already were like God. Not in terms of possessions, but in terms of personhood. They already were the highest among the Creator's Creation. They already fully reflected their Maker, uniquely formed in his image.

Most of us repeat Adam and Eve's sin daily: We likewise yearn to be Godlike, although our yearnings are now mistakenly directed at fame, power, and fortune. We are also discontent, ignoring our image-bearing privileges. We forget who we are.

The day Eve and Adam sinned—the day Creation died—was the darkest period in Earth's short life span. Sin's touch killed everything. Sin was the original equal opportunity employer, embracing every gender, race, religion, and nationality without bias. More accurately, sin was our equal opportunity destroyer. Dan Millman reminds us, in his poignant tale of human nature, that even preschoolers long for a sin-free world:

> Soon after her brother was born, little Sachi began to ask her parents to leave her alone with the new baby. They worried that like most four year olds, she might feel jealous and want to hit or shake him, so they said no. But she showed no signs of jealousy. She treated the baby with kindness and her pleas to be left alone with him became more urgent. They decided to allow it.
>
> Elated, she went into the baby's room and shut the door, but it opened a crack—enough for her curious parents to peek in and listen. They saw little Sachi walk quietly up to her baby brother, put her face close to his and say quietly, "Baby, tell me what God feels like. I'm starting to forget."[1]

On a lighter note, little Sachi's sin predicament parallels that of Charlie Brown (from Charles Schulz's *Peanuts*). From time to time Charlie Brown was known to lapse into a reflective mode of thought, pondering the larger questions of life and faith. On one particular occasion the issue of personal accountability surfaced. Here's how the sequence of comic frames unfolded for that meditation: "Sometimes I lie awake at night, and I ask, 'Where have I gone wrong?' Then a voice says to me, 'This is going to take more than one night.'" (See sidebar 4.1 in the *Supplemental Resource* for a humorous look at the truth about sin.)

Understanding Sin

The contamination of sin runs so deeply inside each of us that it is fair to say that, though all of us are aware of sin, none of us fully realizes the extent of sin's devastation. Extending Charlie Brown's wisdom, it takes a lifetime to begin comprehending sin's tragic complexities. We intuitively know this to be true. Throughout our lives we have confessed, "Why did I think that?" or, "I really didn't want to do that!" We repeatedly validate the Apostle Paul's confession from Romans 7:15-19: "I do not understand what I do. . . . I have the desire to do what is good, but I cannot carry it out. For what I do is not the good I want to do; no, the evil I do not want to do—this I keep on doing."

As someone once said, "Everyone seems perfect—until you get to know them."

We are so thoroughly sinful (even after we say yes to Jesus as Savior) that we sometimes don't feel comfortable within the body of Christ. And, as we already know, believers should have nothing to do with this world, for Scripture reminds us we are "aliens and strangers" in this life (1 Pet. 2:11). And so we feel trapped. We feel like citizens without any country at all. Put more graphically, at times we don't even feel at home in our own skin![2]

Perhaps I am getting ahead of myself. We need to rewind the tape and start at the beginning. We need to first pursue some foundational descriptions of sin. Plantinga clarifies, "All sin has first and finally a Godward force."[3] The original transgression began with an attack by human creatures upon their Creator. It wasn't enough for us to be like God.

We yearned to be God! Every subsequent sin essentially follows that same rebellion. Sins may include anything unholy: dispositions, thoughts, emotions, words, or behaviors. They consist of both overt premeditated sins and implicit sins of neglect or omission. The result (theologically speaking) is death: Instant spiritual death separates us from God, others, ourselves, and the rest of Creation. Eventual physical death also occurs. Finally, if we do not claim God's sole provision for salvation in Jesus Christ, the effect is eternal separation.

In addition to these descriptions of sin, I have found it useful to understand sin as it directly pertains to the image of God. I have organized the effects of sin upon image into a time line of human history for believers:

- Precedent Condition of People—What we once had in Eden
- Consequent Condition of People—What we now have since Eden
- Subsequent Condition of People—What we will have in Christ

Since we experience only the Consequent phase of life after Eden, the next section mainly features that second topic, focusing on the results of the Fall. But we must start our study of sin inside the Garden itself.

What We Once Had in Eden

We saw in chapter 3 that believers stand a much better chance of fulfilling God's complete purpose when we acknowledge our full heritage—who we were before sin. If we don't begin our investigation with created life before the Fall, we skew our entire study of people in relationship to God. I can't emphasize this point enough: We must always begin the subject of discipleship with Adam and Eve.

It is helpful to review the pre-Fall state of our image-bearing condition. I suggested that three legacies clarify our sinless humanity. That is (as noted in figure 3.1), our core relationship with our loving Creator (communion) is purposefully linked with:

79

- Family Name (character);
- Family Business (calling); and
- Family Ties (community).

Furthermore, each of the three legacies carries three supportive Gifts (comprising the Super Nine). Adam and Eve were human beings who could be described as:

- having Godlike physiques
- passionate thinkers
- sensory learners
- kind rulers
- worshipful workers
- artists and scientists
- intimate family members
- good neighbors
- responsible citizens

This original state of humanity lays a critical foundation for what it means to be human. It provides us with our historical footings. Employing another metaphor, our Garden heritage offers a plumb line of authenticity. It supplies an objective reference that marks our original, total well-being.

What We Now Have Since Eden

From the human vantage point, everything that happened since our Garden rebellion causes us to be less than human. Plantinga is right when he concludes, "We must see the fall as anti-creation."[4] Just as creation equals what it means to be fully human, the consequences of the Fall are largely synonymous with all that is unhuman. And sin still continues unraveling our humanity. Specifically, sin unravels God's image inside us. George Macdonald framed it this way:

The awful verity, that we make our fate in unmaking ourselves; that men, in defacing the image of God in themselves, construct for themselves a world of horror and dismay; that of the outer darkness our own deeds and character are the informing or inwardly creating cause; that if a man will not have God, he never can be rid of his weary and hateful self.[5]

This sequential movement from created image to sin to human deformation is automatic. Sin's unraveling effects are certain. That fact can be trusted more than the trust we place in the law of gravity. We might call sin the law of inauthenticity. Whenever we sin, we become less authentic, less of the person we were before that transgression. The term "authentic" (from the Latin word *auctor* and the Greek root *authentes*) means "from the author, the original creator." So inauthenticity is the end result of sin, since sin distorts every genuine tie we had with our Author-Maker.

Many of us have seen the television program *Antiques Roadshow*. The show centers on people living in the vicinity who bring in various personal possessions to have each item's value estimated. Whenever guests are told that their belongings are inauthentic, they are being told they own a fake. The reputable artist whom they thought created their valued possession did not. I recently saw an episode in which one leg on a very expensive piece of furniture had been replaced. It had neither come from the creator's thoughts nor from his hands. Consequently, several thousand dollars were deducted from the "fully authentic" original.

We learn the very same lesson through our personal transgressions. Sin consistently devalues us. There are absolutely no exceptions to this rule. Sin continues to make us less and less what we originally were in Eden. We are greatly diminished from what our Author first created. Whenever we surrender to any kind of sin—even as attractive as it may appear—we increasingly unravel. The Bible describes our inauthenticity, and how we need the once-for-all rebirth from our Savior. But we also need the constant, healing touch of the Great Physician. When Jesus forgives our daily sins, he not only removes the legal blockage between our Maker and us, reactivating our fellowship with him, but also begins sin's reversal of image deformation. His daily forgiveness restores us to become more and more like him.

There is both "good news" and "bad news" from the Fall, if we can use those trite phrases. The "good news" is that we humans never fully lost the image of God from Eden. But everything else is "bad news." God's image became severely twisted and distorted by the first sin.[6] The image all humans now possess, after the Fall, is something like a distorted amusement park mirror. It still reflects the person in front of it, but it is not even close to the perfect mirroring from the Garden. That's how all unredeemed creatures now reflect their Creator. The rest of the "bad news" is that the one quality we did lose from our original image was significant: holiness. That loss was enormous. It was (and is) central to all that we are. Our holiness was replaced by profanity, instantly corrupting the core of our communion with God.

Humans have always had the ability to choose. But, since Eden, our choices are misguided. To use a computer analogy, after the Garden we now possess a new software that is infected with sin. We think impure thoughts. We use relationships for personal gain. We often approach responsibilities selfishly. And we will never completely delete that infected software while on earth. We now choose to sin. When we don't, it is because God's grace is working overtime through his image in us. (See sidebar 4.2 in the *Supplemental Resource*, for more biblical examples of sin's unraveling.)

Because we have not actually lost the Creator's image, the Super Nine Gifts remain within all people. Like the earlier amusement park mirror illustration, these gifts are severely distorted yet they remain in operable condition. That's precisely why a nonbeliever can do something better than a believer. I am not talking about doing good works to earn salvation, because nobody does that (see Isa. 64:6). I am referring to areas like competence and excellence. So saints must recognize God's image within all people. We are also obliged to praise the Creator whenever any person does anything commendable. King David models this in Psalm 8. His nine-verse praise deliberately thanks the Lord at the start and the end (vv. 1, 9), sandwiching in acclaim for all people. I call this the "Sandwich Psalm." David's praise is partially based on the reality that all humans are still hardwired with God's image—created "a little lower than *elohim*" (v. 5; review sidebar 3.2 in the *Supplemental Resource*).

Even More Unraveling

We have established that our inner communion with God was immediately perverted by original sin and that current sinful behavior continues to unravel us. C. S. Lewis's *The Great Divorce* provides a provocative expression of this disturbing outcome of human disobedience. His novel describes how a celestial-bound busload of earthlings encounters heaven. The reader doesn't venture too far before realizing that traditional pictures of earth and heaven are flip-flopped. Instead of describing an eternal world of fluffy clouds and semitransparent angels, Lewis portrays heavenly people as "solid" and features the bus travelers as "ghostly." Lewis makes heaven more real and more complete than earth. Playing out his inverted portrait, this gifted storyteller makes certain the smallest details coincide. For example, even the solid grass of heaven hurts the delicate feet of the less-than-fully-solid earthlings.

In short, Lewis does his best to report a major consequence of the Fall: Sin continues to undo us. We become more unhuman as we give in to sin's diminishing prospects. We are mere shadows of who we were in Eden.[7]

Several other consequences of sin could be cited.[8] Sin so badly distorts our image that it causes us to be:

- Uninformed—We ignorantly search for meaning in life after we ironically reject the truth.[9]
- Undirected—We "mysteriously live against the purpose of [our] existence."[10]
- Unreliable—We are so consistently inconsistent we are characterized as "a set of walking contradictions."[11]
- Unhappy—We are frequently fooled into believing that Christians are supposed to be happy, which is actually "the silliest and surest way to unhappiness."[12]
- Unsettled—We long for our Homeland in heaven, experiencing loneliness and dissatisfaction until that time of reunion.[13]

This last point—our unsettledness—says it all. It lies at the core of our restless wanderings (see sidebar 4.3 in the *Supplemental Resource*, regarding God's way and our waywardness). It causes us to ache for heaven.

In part, this sensation is what the reformer John Calvin called *sensus divinitatis*, or a "sense of the divine." No image-bearing person will ever forget her Maker. Nobody will ever be able to fully dismiss Eden in their heart. And that is because our Father-Creator refuses to give up on us children. To our dying days, he consistently pleads for us to come back Home. He faithfully pursues us as Lover. (See table 4.1—"Our Early History of Homelessness Through Cain"). One way to summarize the Precedent and the Consequent conditions of God's people is found in table 4.2. Contrasts are drawn between the ideal Super Nine and distortions from the Fall.

What We Will Have in Christ

Since the Precedent condition of God's people portrays what we once had and the Consequent position shows what we now have, then the

TABLE 4.1

Our Early History of Homelessness Through Cain

All at once, all that we once had—at this nearly breathless height of Creation—came crashing down into despairing depths. Our own rebellion caused it all. Furthermore, our three inherited legacies were instantly and thoroughly distorted.

Adam's and Eve's holy lives (Family Name) corroded into ungodliness and death, just as the Creator promised any who would defy his lone directive (Gen. 2:17). They had instituted their own rebellious plan for Garden life by eating forbidden fruit.

That instant deformation of their inner human lives also promptly distorted the other two legacies: our immensely fulfilling livelihood (as partners in the Family Business) was traded for painful and directionless labor. And our satisfying intimacy with people (Family Ties) was quickly swapped for shame, blame, and selfishness.

It wouldn't take but one short generation later for humankind to display the absolute reversal of everything that initially graced them in Eden. Genesis 4:13-14 says it all. On the heels of the Bible's first murder, after hearing his Maker's swift and fair judgment upon him, Cain complains: "My punishment is more than I can bear. Today you are driving me out from the land, and I will be hidden from your presence; I will be a restless wanderer on the earth." Paraphrasing his cry according to this trio of legacies, Cain confesses three aspects of his personal sin:

- "I've rejected the Family Name" (Consider his despairing results of being "hidden from [God's] presence," in contrast to his parents' earlier fellowship in Eden, from Genesis 4:14 and 16.)
- "I've closed the Family Business" (Notice his own restlessness and dissatisfaction. Later, the next generation of Cain's family expresses this same vocational alienation by their shift to nomadic herding—a good example of literal "wandering" that results from sin—in Genesis 4:12-14 and 20.)
- "I've broken all Family Ties" (Contrast how the once-intimate family of Eden has now been torn apart by extreme hatred and a pattern of murder, identified in Genesis 4:5, 8, and 23.)

Ironically, the first human transgression took the first mandate of dominion over Creation and caused the first people (and everyone thereafter) to be ruled by sin. And this, all because humans, uniquely shaped in the image of God, said "no" to the One they once perfectly reflected.

Overnight, the first sin caused us to be homeless—driven from Paradise.

TABLE 4.2

Super Nine and Sin

A Combination of Image Precedent and Consequent Conditions

The IDEAL	The REAL
(*Image Precedent* from Eden's Super Nine)	(*Image Consequences* of the Fall)
Godlike Physiques . . .	. . . deformed the Creator's design, through idolatry and physical distortions (e.g., gluttony)
Passionate Thinkers . . .	. . . abused their personal passion and thought, by substituting lust, greed, and pride
Sensory Learners . . .	. . . degenerated into sensual learners, as their ungodly personal appetites were fed
Kind Rulers . . .	. . . shifted to unruly, power-hungry leaders "lording it over" others
Worshipful Workers . . .	. . . were dehumanized by imprudence and undisciplined life, as laborers and as idolaters
Artists and Scientists . . .	. . . wasted their skills, turning their focus of worship and service away from Creator—toward Creation and self
Intimate Families . . .	. . . became unfaithful in home obligations, causing dysfunctional ties and abuse
Good Neighbors . . .	. . . unraveled their moral duties, becoming increasingly immoral and unjust
Responsible Citizens . . .	. . . spiraled consistently downward into incivility and inhuman signs of governance

Subsequent view depicts our final, heavenly Home. It is the realized eternal rewards for God's people. This third phrase (super)naturally builds upon the previous two phrases, as it emphasizes total restoration. All the great blessings our first parents experienced in Eden will one day become our blessings to enjoy, upgraded to their maximum levels.

Our present dehumanizing bent toward sin will no longer be an option in heaven. Leonard Verduin comes to that conclusion as he offers a helpful review of the believer's four-part history (pre-Fall; post-Fall; Christian life; and eternity).[14] Kreeft also arrives at that conclusion, showing how heavenly saints are "not able to sin." Through a series of logical constructs, Kreeft answers his question, "Will we be free to sin in heaven?" saying, "Sin is inauthenticity and freedom is authenticity; sin is our false self and freedom is our true self."[15] When we become fully reflecting image bearers in heaven, we will attain our true, authentic selves. We will have no desire to settle for the inferior option of rebellion. We will be completely content—totally satisfied in Christ.

One word that describes all we had in the Garden—our perfect communion with the Creator, all three legacies, and all nine gifts—is *shalom*. Our English equivalent is the word "peace." But we should not be fooled into thinking this Hebrew word merely means the absence of conflict or soothing music in the car on the way home from a hard day's work. It's not a superficial state of "peace and quiet." *Shalom* means total well-being. It is a holistic harmony with God, self, others, and all of life. At Creation, Adam and Eve possessed *shalom*. Our Creator has always wanted his children to enjoy deep-seated peace. Plantinga describes this ideal with the everyday language of "the way things ought to be."[16]

All transgression runs contrary to *shalom*. Sin is inauthentic to our original state. That's why we are all restless and homesick. To restate it: "Sin is never normal." The sinful life is best described as "a ludicrous caricature of genuine human life."[17] Our anticipated hope in the "new heavens and earth," then, is that the Creator-Savior-Judge will restore all things to their right (and rightful) condition. *Shalom* will reflect God's light throughout every nook of paradise.

But we don't need to wait for eternity to start enjoying these other-worldly pleasures. Since *shalom* represents both the "oughtness" of what we once had, as well as the total contentedness we will have, our current state emerges from a combination of these two realities. Saints are enabled to daily taste a little bit of heaven. We are called to cooperate with the Creator's restorative processes each day. Restating a key point from chapter 1: All *good* things here and now were *better* in Eden and will be *best* in heaven. So God's *re-shalom* project is now at work within us and we can observe the interplay between what we once had and what we will have.[18]

This third Subsequent condition of people is a promise that God's children will be completely restored. No more wandering. No more aching loneliness. No further disorientation or disillusionment.

One day we will finally be Home.

The Disappointment of Samson

When it comes to sin, few more tragic Bible stories can be found than the one recorded in Judges 16. That chapter relates how Samson the judge repeatedly stepped out of God's best plan for him. He finally arrived at the end of his life of disobedience. After four separate times of confiding in Delilah—one time too many—the supernatural powers of the world's strongest man evaporated in seconds. The tragedy was not that Samson's seven braids were shorn by Delilah. It was his presumption of God's faithful power in his life, in spite of his persistent infidelity. Judges 16:20b records the beginning of his life's end this way: "He awoke from his sleep and thought, 'I'll go out as before and shake myself free.' But he did not know that the LORD had left him." Although this uniquely powerful individual was specially called by God (both as Nazarite and judge), his stubborn rebellion caused his ruin.

Since the day of Pentecost in Acts 2, when the Holy Spirit permanently indwelt God's children, God will never leave us as he left Samson. However we can grieve or quench the indwelling Holy Spirit, so that the results are functionally the same as those in days of old. We Christians are like Samson when we presume God's presence in our lives. We are like him whenever we erringly expect divine power, while dismissing what God tells us to do.

At the center of this failure we show our ignorance of the Fall's severity. We forget how badly sin has marred us all. We tend to complicate this "Samson complex" by absentmindedly verbalizing commitment to God while our behavior fails to support our words. If the nonbelievers we meet rated our faith—and sometimes they do—many of us would be accurately described as "functional atheists." That's what happens when we presume God will always give us his best, even when we lead sinful lives of disobedience.

We are prone to another trait of the Samson complex as well. We quickly settle for a faith that is substandard. It, too, brings serious consequences. The question we must ask is this: "What if Samson had been fully dedicated to the Lord? What other great things could that Nazarite judge have accomplished for God's kingdom?" I guarantee that if you study Judges 13–16—read it again—not many paragraphs will go by before you catch yourself saying, "It seems that Jehovah used Samson not because he was a holy man. God used Samson *in spite* of the man he was." From his selfish attitudes, to his dishonoring behaviors toward his parents, and from his whining, belligerent reactions toward God to his immoral lifestyle, the world's strongest man was a huge disappointment.

Yet Samson had so much to offer.

And so do we. If we are serious about discipleship, we must constantly return to the perspective of sin that our Creator holds. To summarize the fourth principle of healthy Christian living:

Truth 4

God's model for discipleship requires a radical view of sin.
We saints should not settle for definitions of sin
that merely address legal issues (e.g., breaking the law).
Sin also unravels us, makes us less human.
Sin inauthenticates us, for sin distorts God's image.

I'm not saying we are imitators of every trait of this rebellious man, Samson. I am suggesting, however, that we often mimic his tendency to think we are "doing okay" as believers. Most of us—like Samson—haven't even come close to the full potential God has lovingly designed for us. C. S. Lewis diagnosed the root cause of our Samson-like mediocrity, when he wrote:

> Indeed, if we consider the unblushing promises of reward and the staggering nature of the rewards promised in the Gospels, it would seem that Our Lord finds our desires, not too strong, but too weak. We are half-hearted creatures, fooling about with drink and sex and ambition when infinite joy is offered us, like an ignorant child who wants to go on making mud pies in a slum because he cannot imagine what is meant by the offer of a holiday at the sea. We are far too easily pleased.[19]

We do not need to settle for less. That includes mediocrity, or "doing okay." Dare, with Christ, to dream of your greatest potential. Let Jesus start to reverse the distortions in your life.

Grab the gusto life he has planned for you.

1 From Millman's "Sachi" in *Chicken Soup for the Soul*, eds. Jack Canfield and Mark Victor Hansen (Deerfield Beach, Fla.: Health Communications, 1993), p. 290.

2 From Cornelius Plantinga Jr., *Not the Way It's Supposed to Be* (Grand Rapids, Mich.: Eerdmans, 1995), p. 2. My pastor, Glen Jones, in similar fashion refers to the believer's uncomfortable state of living in our finite bodies. He calls our physical makeup our "earth suits," based upon a message he heard at a Youth for Christ rally years ago, led by the Rev. Bill Gillham.

3 Plantinga, p. 13.

4 Ibid., p. 29. Later (p. 30) Plantinga describes the Flood as the ultimate *antithesis* of Creation; God's judgment of the exponential increase of sin in the early days of human *un*civilization.

5 George Macdonald penned these words in his preface to *Letters from Hell*, an anonymously published book by a Dutch author in 1866. Macdonald's preface contribution was made to the 1884 edition of that publication. The basic concepts from that original anonymous work would, one day—almost one hundred years later—influence C. S. Lewis to produce *The Screwtape Letters*. (See Rolland Hein's "A Great Good Is Coming: George Macdonald's *Phantastes and Lilith*" in *Journey to the Celestial City: Glimpses of Heaven from Great Literary Classics*, ed. Wayne Martindale [Chicago: Moody, 1995], pp. 123 and 127.)

6 The Reformers often employed the Latin term *curvatus*, meaning bent, for this post-Fall characterization of all human spirituality.

7 An excellent illustration of how sin causes people to "shrink" appears in C. S. Lewis's *The Great Divorce*. Near the end of his novel the author sets up a reunion between a very godly woman (who now dwells in heaven) and her former (still earthly) husband, characterized as a dwarf, who's holding a chain connected to a taller ghostly figure. As their conversation continues over several pages, the dialogue gradually lessens, because of the husband's fits of anger—bringing with them his gradual disintegration. At one point, she drops down on her knees to speak to this selfish man. The more he shrinks away, the less talking he does for himself; the taller figure—representing his ungodly attitudes and nature—takes over. Eventually, the taller ghost completes the conversation for the former husband, who is now smaller than a flea!

8 I have, elsewhere, listed these consequences of our sin as sevenfold refractions of our original, perfect reflection of the Creator (see *Teaching for Reconciliation*, revised edition, [Eugene, Ore.: Wipf and Stock, 2001], p. 32, table 2.1).

9 Several Scriptures refer to the unsaved mind—and even the potential of the believer's thoughts—as "darkness" (Eph. 4:17-18; 5:8-17).

10 Plantinga, p. 73. (See sidebar 4.3 in the *Supplemental Resource* regarding God's way and our waywardness.)

11 Lewis Smedes, *Shame and Grace: Healing the Shame We Don't Deserve* (San Francisco: HarperCollins, 1993), p. 116.

12 Kreeft (*Heaven: The Heart's Deepest Longing*, [San Francisco: Ignatius, 1989], p. 56). Peter Kreeft goes on to say "*No* one is really happy" (p. 57), then he offers "joy" as the believer's legitimate life purpose (pp. 56-57), along with this commentary:

> There is a very old wisdom, quite out of fashion today, that says we are not *supposed* to be happy here. In fact no one is really happy here, and the "pursuit of happiness," which the American Declaration of Independence declares one of our "inalienable rights," is in fact the silliest and surest way to unhappiness. This is not a wisdom we like to hear, and for that reason we had better give it extra hearing. It is wisdom not just from the past but also from within, from the soft spot in us that

we cover up with our hard surface, from the vulnerable little child in us that we mask with our invulnerable adult. Our adult pretends to want pleasure, power, wealth, health, or success, then gets it, then pretends to be happy.

To back his particular thought on our "inalienable rights," Kreeft cites this portion from Malcolm Muggeridge's "Happiness" in *Jesus Rediscovered* (New York: Doubleday, 1979), p. 179:

> The sister-in-law of a friend of Samuel Johnson was imprudent enough once to claim in his presence that she was happy. He pounced on her hard, remarking in a loud, emphatic voice that if she was indeed the contented being she professed herself to be then her life gave the lie to every research of humanity. . . . The pursuit of happiness, included along with life and liberty in the American Declaration of Independence as an inalienable right, is without any question the most fatuous that could possibly be undertaken. This lamentable phrase – the pursuit of happiness – is responsible for a good part of the ills and miseries of the modern world.

13 Our perpetual "longing for heaven's Home" has been noted by many influential thinkers. On the contemporary scene, three prominent contributors include Peter Kreeft, C. S. Lewis, and Malcolm Muggeridge. Kreeft (*Heaven: The Heart's Deepest Longing*, 1989, pp. 66-67) claimed: "We have a homing instinct, a 'home detector,' and it doesn't ring for earth. That's why nearly every society in history except our own instinctively believes in life after death. . . . Heaven is *home*. . . . We fit there; we are fully human there."

C. S. Lewis (in *The Problem of Pain*, pp. 147-48) said: "Your soul has a curious shape because it is . . . a key to unlock one of the doors in the house with many mansions. . . . Your place in heaven will seem to be made for you and you alone, because you were made for it—made for it stitch by stitch as a glove is made for a hand."

Finally, regarding our unsettled condition of the soul, Muggeridge (in *Jesus Rediscovered* [New York: Doubleday, 1979], pp. 47-48, italics mine) said:

> "For me there has always been—and I count it *the greatest of all blessings*—a window never finally blacked out, a light never finally extinguished. . . . I had a sense, sometimes enormously vivid, that I was a stranger in a strange land; a visitor, not a native . . . a displaced person. . . . The *only ultimate disaster* that can befall us . . . *is to feel ourselves to be at home here on earth. As long as we are aliens, we cannot forget our true homeland.*"

14 Leonard Verduin (*Somewhat Less than God* [Grand Rapids, Mich.: Eerdmans, 1970], p. 89) reminds readers that theologians have described "man's original condition as a condition of *posse peccare* (able to sin), his post-lapsarian condition as one of *non posse non peccare* (not able not to sin), his condition in the modality of savedness as one of *posse non peccare* (able not to sin), and his final condition, in glory, as one of *non posse peccare* (not able to sin)."

15 Peter Kreeft, *Everything You Ever Wanted to Know about Heaven* (San Francisco: Ignatius, 1990), p. 41.

16 Plantinga (1995) introduces the negative version of this term on page 2 and the positive side on page 10 of his book (*Not the Way It's Supposed to Be*; see note 2).

17 Plantinga (p. 5) cites, in the second half of this sentence, Geoffrey Bromiley's insights from Bromiley's article "Sin" in *The International Standard Bible Encyclopedia*, vol. 4, ed. Geoffrey W. Bromiley (Grand Rapids, Mich.: Eerdmans, 1988) p. 519.

18 Theologians have traditionally labeled this life objective as the "now and not yet" tension, but I believe our history is missing from that phrase. It might be more accurate to describe our predicament as our *"then* and *now* and *not yet"* three-fold life task.

19 From *The Weight of Glory* (New York: Macmillan, 1949), pp. 1-2.

CHAPTER FIVE

---✦---

PAVING THE WAY FROM SINAI TO THE CROSS

> *I want people to get past the idea that they*
> *understand Christianity because they went to*
> *Sunday School. You have to learn how to do it.*
> *You have to undergo an apprenticeship. Nobody*
> *really wants to love their neighbor as themselves.*
>
> — STANLEY HAUERWAS
>
> *I cannot, by direct moral effort, give myself new*
> *motives. After the first few steps in the Christian*
> *life we realize that everything which really needs*
> *to be done in our souls can be done only by God.*
>
> — C. S. LEWIS

March 17, 2000, marked the worst cult-related catastrophe in contemporary history. It was even worse than the 1978 mass suicide of 912 Jim Jones followers in Guyana. This Ugandan misfortune is all but forgotten. Even more regrettable, the lessons we should continue learning from such senseless human loss also verge on extinction.

Joseph Kibwetere, a leader in the Roman Catholic Church until his excommunication, invited hundreds of his cult members to gather that fateful day in March. His group was called the Movement for the Restoration of the Ten Commandments of God. They planned to dedicate their newly built chapel, located on the cult's sprawling farm in the rural southwestern corner of Uganda. Most individuals never exited the new 30-by-120-foot worship facility. A premeditated inferno extinguished their lives. The bodies of several children and adults were so badly charred that the remains of many were never identified. The fiery scene—along with multiple evidences of stabbings and stranglings—made it difficult to determine whether the case should be ruled a mass suicide or a mass murder.

A few years before that tragedy the cult's primary document, bound in a 163-page pamphlet, emerged. It was titled *A Timely Message from Heaven: The End of the Present Times*. Joseph Kibwetere claimed he could speak directly with God. His assertion brought the self-proclaimed revelation that the world would end at the close of 1999. He claimed the end would come specifically because the Ten Commandments were not being correctly observed. When the world didn't end, the disaster on March 17, 2000, resulted in its own self-fulfilling story of the apocalypse.[1]

This catastrophic event was heartbreaking. But what further compounded that misfortune was its presumptuous link with God and his truth. It particularly saddens me to see the erroneous tie this cult made with the Ten Commandments. They created yet one more twisted view of the Decalogue—as though the church and the world really need one more distortion. Former sect members who escaped this tragedy recalled that, springing from tangled interpretations of the Mosaic Law, the cult instituted several convoluted laws: Members had certain foods withheld from them as punishment; cult leaders explained "the Virgin Mary had told them" to do so. Sexual activity was discouraged even among married couples, and sign language replaced most verbal communication. This Ugandan cult reduced the Decalogue to a strict ascetic-communal life of contorted fasting, abstinence, and silence.

Worse yet, sect members were told that obeying these twisted ordinances served as "the only path to salvation."

A "Cult" of Another Kind

If a poll could somehow tell us how many Christians still consciously submit to the doctrine of the Cultural Mandate, statistics would be abysmal. I would guesstimate a single-digit percentage. Recall that I am broadly defining the Cultural Mandate as the disciple's challenge to journey to her heavenly Home through Eden. The Garden is not our destination, but our Mapmaker does plot it into the travel plans for his children. All disciples need to return to Eden first in order to discover their roots, their heritage. This widened view of the Cultural Mandate is upheld by Jesus' unflinching challenge for all to reclaim the Creator's "way from the beginning" (Matt. 19:8b). Our Lord's deliberate teaching here, which returned to Eden, is further reinforced by his broader instruction of who we are (image bearers), what we have (the Super Nine Gifts), and how we are to live (through our calling and our relationships). Besides these benefits of returning to the Garden, grounding ourselves in Eden also lessens the chances we will misunderstand the Ten Commandments (also known as the Decalogue or the Law). That's because the message of Creation, the Decalogue, and Jesus' teaching are far more complementary than we typically acknowledge.

Each of these three subjects connects with the truth of *imago Dei*.

Two Extreme Views of the Ten Commandments

The percentage of believers who value the Decalogue is significantly higher than the believers who value the Genesis Mandate. The erroneous roles those Commandments play in believers' lives, however, must not be underrated. On the one hand lies the distortion of legalism (or any faith-plus-works scheme; see sidebar 5.1 in the *Supplemental Resource*, for a detailed look at legalism.) On the other hand, the Ten Commandments are just as likely to convey complete irrelevance.[2] They are about as pertinent to today's believer as Charlton Heston's classic portrayal of Moses is to this year's Academy for the Oscar nominations.

I realize very few informed Christians ever come close to the excessive views of the Ugandan cult. Yet I'm afraid thousands and thousands of believers are regularly duped by one of these two extreme positions. Analogous to the African tragedy, either of these twisted mind-sets figuratively kills believers by fire—very, very slowly—throughout their lifetimes. (Both are comparable to the imperceptible process of oxidation, which gradually browns the corners of paperback books boxed in the attic for years.) The fire of legalism slowly destroys the core of Christian grace. It eventually chokes out any trace of joyful, liberated, and love-motivated behavior. The fire of irrelevance gags saints in a different manner. Another word to describe irrelevance is *antinomianism*, the extreme posture where virtually no rules exist for the Christian. No universal code of conduct pertains. Those who embrace irrelevance commonly hold to principles like love—the first fruit of the Spirit (in Gal. 5:22-23). Yet, oftentimes these same people forget about self-control (the last fruit). We usually coin phrases like "tough love" to balance these complementary obligations from the first and the ninth fruit. When the "no rules" version of Christianity is chosen, however, the inherent troubles of antinomianism arise. The toxic fumes of irrelevance eventually engulf the Christian, so that virtues like personal routines and corporate disciplines are strangled.

Faulty thinking at this point often starts with negative views about any rules or routines. That mind-set takes verses like John 8:32b ("the truth will set you free") and transforms them into half-truths like "the truth will set you free from every rule." Jesus never came close to this mind-set. Certainly he challenged the rules of his day (such as the

Sabbath), but he almost always clarified the intent of God's rules by offering stricter guidelines! There's absolutely no question that Christ not only advocated rules and disciplines but also personally complied with them. For instance, Jesus' routine of Sabbath worship could be best summarized by the potent Luke 4:16 phrase "as was his custom." Furthermore, the faithful testimony of Jesus' parents similarly honored such routines (see Luke 2:21-24, 27b, 39, 41-42). Jesus undoubtedly expected his followers, likewise, to discern the intent of God's rules and then to adhere to them. Later in this chapter I will describe Christ's support of the Law in more detail.

In sum, these two extreme versions of the Ten Commandments are not even remotely biblical.[3] Those who accept the redemption of Christ must not be swayed by either of these tempting options from what might be described as the Decalogue cult. The antidote for either disorder begins with a healthy dose of the Creation story as well as understanding who we are as image bearers. That includes the Creator's lifelong prescription for how to live, according to the Cultural Mandate.

Contributions of the Decalogue to Discipleship

The Cultural Mandate and the Ten Commandments fully supplement the Maker's image. Illustratively, each imperative contributes to the giant "jigsaw puzzle" of biblical discipleship, since both connect the puzzle's interlocking border of *imago Dei*. That's a simple way to state it. These two prominent Scriptures offer the twenty-first-century church a huge portion of the complete picture of discipleship. The Cultural Mandate, again, shows us *how to live*. It is one practical application of what it means to be shaped in God's image. The Ten Commandments' puzzle segment teaches us *how to love*. Christ's summative words in Matthew 22:36-40 endorse the Decalogue's focus on affection: love your God totally and love your neighbor as completely as you love yourself. This summary of love is as old as the Law itself (see Lev. 19:18; Deut. 6:5; Rom. 13:8-10).

Since the Commandments intrinsically relate to the Creation story, we disciples are to yield to these sacred directives specifically with his image in mind. We essentially obey all Ten Commandments because we still reflect the loving Creator who issued them. As we realign ourselves to its foundational truth about who we are, we tend to our lifelong objective: daily restoration of *imago Dei*.

Connecting the Puzzle of Complete Discipleship

For years, I used to wonder why Jesus made the provocative claim found in his apocalyptic instruction on the sheep and the goats: "Whatever you did [or did not do] for one the least of these brothers of mine, you did [or did not do] for me" (Matt. 25:40 and 45). That direct association really threw me. Our Lord consciously linked Himself with ministries to people who possessed a wide range of human needs: from those who needed food or drink to those who required hospitality, and from those who needed to be visited in prison to those who sought clothing. The outcome of Jesus' message was serious, too, for it held eternal consequences of "punishment" or "life" (v. 46).

I wavered between a salvation-by-works interpretation of this passage (which I knew wasn't true) and some mystical or symbolic view (which I knew couldn't stack up because of other literal features of Jesus' words). It didn't help, either, whenever I discovered additional passages that carried their own brand of new, troublesome message on the same topic.

One time I thought I had the problem licked. I took the view that the kindred association Christ referred to was needy fellow believers: Because disciples bear his name, what we do to other saints we essentially do to the Lord. I thought I had found the solution to Jesus' provocative claim. The first six verses in table 5.1 seemed to support this theory of Jesus' familial bond with his disciples.

TABLE 5.1

Key Verses for Complementary Image Obligations

Matthew 25:40: "The King will reply, 'I tell you the truth, whatever you did for one of the least of these brothers of mine, you did for me.'"

Matthew 25:45: "He will reply, 'I tell you the truth, whatever you did not do for one of the least of these, you did not do for me.'"

Matthew 10:40: "He who receives you receives me, and he who receives me receives the one who sent me."

Mark 9:40-41: "For whoever is not against us is for us. I tell you the truth, anyone who gives you a cup of water in my name because you belong to Christ will certainly not lose his reward."

Matthew 18:5: "And whoever welcomes a little child like this in my name welcomes me."

Hebrews 6:10: "God is not unjust; he will not forget your work and the love you have shown him as you have helped his people and continue to help them."

Proverbs 14:31: "He who oppresses the poor shows contempt for their Maker, but whoever is kind to the needy honors God."

Proverbs 17:5: "He who mocks the poor shows contempt for their Maker; whoever gloats over disaster will not go unpunished."

Proverbs 19:17: "He who is kind to the poor lends to the LORD, and he will reward him for what he has done."

James 3:9-10: "With the tongue we praise our Lord and Father, and with it we curse men, who have been made in God's likeness. Out of the same mouth come praise and cursing. My brothers, this should not be."

I found out I was only half right. There is nothing like finding "new" Scriptures that either totally negate or partially expand a working hypothesis. For me it was the latter. The four verses at the bottom of table 5.1 forced me to consider a larger solution. I labeled my broader outlook the "Creation Equation," which says: *The way we treat people is the way we treat their Maker.* That label's first word suggests that a proper anthropological view must return to the origin of human life. It affirms the Creator's image. Though sin severely distorted our once-perfect reflection, the Fall never canceled the Maker's presence inside everyone (e.g., in John 1:9 Jesus claimed there is a special light in "every man"). The label's second word implies there is a mutual and irreversible bond between God and all people (not just believers). Since this bond is reciprocal between Creator and creature, how we act toward either one of these two parties "equals" how we act toward the other.

The three Proverbs verses in table 5.1 (14:31; 17:5; 19:17) particularly stress this equation as it relates to the poor, while James 3:9-10 extends that principle to all people. Jesus' brother James concludes that saints must speak in a language that consistently honors Creator and creature alike. Anything less than this verbal standard is so inconsistent that James says there are no parallels found anywhere else in God's nature. In case his readers don't get his weighty point, James introduces his topic with a very concrete prohibition: "Out of the same mouth come praise and cursing. My brothers, this should not be."

The reason for introducing the Creation Equation in this fifth chapter is that it also unlocks a major secret to the Ten Commandments. The equation specifically enables us to see why the first four directives of the Decalogue (our vertical duties) link up with the six remaining imperatives (our horizontal obligations). The equation likewise helps us comprehend other Scriptures that refer to comparable reactions to other humans and to their corresponding rewards, such as:

- Why King Josiah's defense of "the poor and needy" led God to reward him, because that's "what it means to know" the LORD (Jer. 22:16).

- Why James can summarize commendable faith in God (our vertical duty) by only two (horizontal) attributes: "to look after orphans and widows in their distress"—as well as personal holiness (Jas. 1:27).

- Why Jesus refused to limit his answer to only one directive when he was asked what was the single greatest command. Certainly, loving God totally is the "first and greatest," Christ acknowledged. Yet, "the second is like it: 'Love your neighbor as yourself.'" His conclusion? "All the Law and the Prophets hang on these two commandments" (Matt. 22:36-40). The Master emphasized that the first and second commandments must stand together as "the single greatest."

The reason our vertical duties can never be fully separated from our horizontal duties is *imago Dei*. It's impossible to sever Creator from human creature. We share many attributes of our Maker, starting with his breath. To illustrate this inseparable quality, the following section describes the Ten Commandments through these integrated vertical-horizontal responsibilities. It portrays every one of these Laws within the framework of God's image.

How the Decalogue Honors God's Image

The Ten Commandments are, first and foremost, a statement about intimate relationships. This fact is striking from the start: Two powerful affiliations (the Passover and Israel's deliverance from Egypt) intertwine to form the historical events immediately prior to the Decalogue. These connected faith markers are so personal and powerful, it is not difficult to see how they (collectively) represent the Old Testament's prototype of the New Testament's cross. Both sets of stories in each Testament speak about God's love, demonstrated by his deliberate intervention for his people. Both stories have Creator-approved sacrifices. Both involve freedom of human choice to believe and to obey. Both reward their followers with deliverance from captivity. And each event is easily the most significant story of its respective testament.

With that relational context in mind, recall the introduction to the Decalogue: "I am the LORD your God, who brought you out of Egypt, out of the land of slavery" (Exod. 20:2). This verse leads to the initial Commandment: "You shall have no other gods before me" (v. 3). In Jewish tradition—because the prologue is so critical to each of these directives—verse 2 is actually classified as the first Commandment. Verses 3–6 comprise the second imperative, which prohibits idolatry. By recapturing the contribution this prologue makes for intimate Creator-creature relationships (like the Jews did), we see how the Decalogue's central message is sculpted by God's image.

This said, I've taken the liberty to paraphrase the Ten Commandments, using *imago Dei* as the interpretive key to unlock their meaning. I begin with the prologue, synthesizing all three Decalogue introductions (from Exod. 20:1-2; Deut. 5:1-6; Lev. 19:1-2). Then I proceed with the two halves of the Ten Commandments, the vertical and the horizontal duties of God's children.

The Prologue

"The Lord our God struck a special relationship with us at Mount Horeb. He created an intimate bond with us—not with someone else, not even our fathers. It was a personal meeting. And this relationship was not established aloofly from a distance. God is the very same one who demonstrated his deliberate love for us by magnificently delivering us out of our oppressive slavery in Egypt. Therefore, he calls us to be set apart as his unique people. We are unlike any other nation. We are to be holy as he is. Our holiness will be evident as we align ourselves with ten foundational imperatives."

The First Four Commandments

The Lord himself said: "If you really want to show your total love for Me, you will obey four particular commands that feature our special relationship. Here's how you can directly express your love to Me. . . ."

1. It is absolutely ridiculous for you to even look at other gods. They vainly try to compete with me! Every single one of them is totally inferior. Furthermore, you were created by me—in my image.

2. It is silly for you to create any human or animal picture to replace me! It's also contradictory for you, then, to worship that image. Ponder these truths in light of your creation, which mirrors me.

    Furthermore, I am trying to keep you from embarrassing yourselves. Don't you recall that one of my Creation principles is "you become what you worship"?[4]

3. If you really love me, you would never abuse my name. This means, for example, you won't make false promises or use my name in any shallow, irreverent way.[5]

4. To demonstrate your fullest love for me, you should imitate my own example of weekly rest. I personally inaugurated this schedule of priorities in the days of the Creation. I also set this time aside for you to worship me. This day should remind you of Eden's pleasures so much that you should "call the Sabbath a delight."[6]

The Last Six Commandments

"If you love Me completely, I have a half dozen more commands for you to show your love. They complement the first four, and they are equally important for you to obey because each draws upon a principle of My image."

5. You will express your fullest affection for me when you honor the parents I have given you.[7] You mirror me—but you also mirror their image.[8]

6. You will not murder—or even kill someone in your mind—since that ungodly behavior ultimately expresses your hatred of me, through my reflected image.[9]

7. You will not commit adultery, since that disgrace runs contrary to my Creation plan. The permanence and contentment I originally designed into marriage also represent extensions of my image.[10] (See sidebar 5.2, in the *Supplemental Resource*, for a phenomenal secular study that supports Christian principles of sexual behavior.)

8. You will not steal, because that means you disrespect other people (fellow image bearers) who own those possessions.[11] In the long run, stealing shows you are discontent—and your greediness is idolatry[12]—all of which dishonors me.

9. You will not lie or be deceptive in any way, since this trespass is similar to the dishonesty of the third command: It is the opposite of my command to be truthful.[13]

10. Finally, you will show your complete love to me, if you fully love your neighbor as you love yourself.[14] This means it is wrong to secretly desire what others have. As I said before, all people reflect me as image bearers. How you respond to them, therefore, is how you actually respond to me.[15]

In sum, the Ten Commandments uphold the foundational truths about our human origin. They remind us what it means to share our Maker's breath. The Decalogue sometimes sounds cold and aloof because we have journeyed so far away from Eden. These laws remind us of our sin (Rom. 3:20). But, as figure 5.1 illustrates, the Ten Commandments also remind us what we inherited in the Garden.

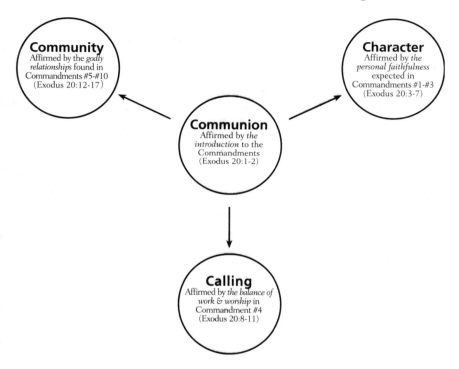

FIGURE 5.1

The Ten Commandments and the Garden Legacies

Community
Affirmed by the *godly relationships* found in Commandments #5-#10
(Exodus 20:12-17)

Character
Affirmed by *the personal faithfulness* expected in Commandments #1-#3
(Exodus 20:3-7)

Communion
Affirmed by *the introduction* to the Commandments
(Exodus 20:1-2)

Calling
Affirmed by *the balance of work & worship* in Commandment #4
(Exodus 20:8-11)

Why the Ten Commandments Are Still Relevant

So that we never disregard the pertinent place the Decalogue holds for today's disciple, contemplate two related topics: Christ's reverence for the Commandments and the believer's obligation to follow suit.

Jesus' Consistent Support of the Law

God's Son faithfully backed God's Law. He painstakingly reminded hearers of the Decalogue's original purpose, then he provided instructions for how followers are to comply. Probably the most controversial (and often confusing) two verses associated with Jesus and the Law are Matthew 5:17 and 18: "Do not think that I have come to abolish the Law or the

Prophets; I have not come to abolish them but to fulfill them. I tell you the truth, until heaven and earth disappear, not the smallest letter, not the least stroke of a pen, will by any means disappear from the Law until everything is accomplished." This testimonial from Jesus coincides with God's consistent message of hope throughout the Bible (see sidebar 5.3 in the *Supplemental Resource*).

The respected scholar Raymond E. Brown wrote that Jesus' teaching here indicated he was presenting "God's demand not by dispensing with the Law but by asking for a deeper observance that gets to the reason why its demands were formulated": to be holy like God is holy (see Matt. 5:48).[16] Brown further described contemporary believers who errantly think that Matthew 5:17 and 18 argue for Christ's death as the final historical event, as one which fulfilled this prediction of "everything is accomplished." Many falsely perceive (or behave in such a way) that the cross made the Law completely irrelevant to the church. Brown soberly renounced this misinterpretation by stating the Law's pertinent claim for today. He reminded his readers that this New Testament passage (Matt. 5) was "written in a post-resurrectional Gospel, and certainly some Christians were hearing this as an ongoing demand—probably Christians similar to 'the men from James' who opposed Paul at Antioch (Gal. 2:12)." Those who perpetrate this position of irrelevancy also miss the futuristic message found in its accompanying phrase: "until heaven and earth disappear" (Matt. 5:18).[17]

The primary conclusion of Matthew 5:17-18, then, shows that Jesus totally fulfilled—but did not cancel—the Mosaic Law. Contemporary disciples can benefit a great deal by discerning this fact (see sidebar 5.4 in the *Supplemental Resource*).

Finally, Christ proposes explicit support of Moses through his six amplified references to the Law (in Matt. 5). Each reference employs the phrase "You have heard that it was said . . . But I tell you. . . ." These half dozen sets (from Matt. 5:21-22, 27-28, 31-34, 38-39, 43-44) include the original intention of the Law regarding such practical topics as murder, adultery, divorce, oaths, duties to people, and obligations of affection toward our enemies. It is noteworthy that all six of these amplified references to the Law follow immediately after Christ's promise to "fulfill" (not "abolish") the Law, as well as his warning that believers must possess a "righteousness [which] surpasses that of the Pharisees" (in Matt. 5:17-20).[18]

The Saint's Need to Consciously Support the Law

Like their Lord, the Christian duty is to honor the Commandments without a "salvation by works" or legalistic mind-set. Such a commitment focuses on the consistency of God's plan throughout human history (review figure 5.1). The Law helps us become all we were created to become. The Law undergirded the same three legacies we received from Eden:

- Recovering holiness (character)
- Fulfilling livelihood (calling)
- Satisfying intimacy (community)

Table 5.2 summarizes both Christ's support of the Law and the present day disciple's obligation; its third column reviews each Commandment, noting (directly or indirectly) the Christian's lifelong purpose of image transformation (from Col. 3).[19]

The only exception to the exact and favorable repetition of all ten laws is the modification of the fourth Commandment about the Sabbath. Jesus' reassessment of that particular imperative (in Matt. 12:1-14) followed the formula he earlier used in Matthew 5: There, six times he says, "You have heard it was said . . . But I tell you. . . ." So, with regard to the Sabbath, the Master Teacher consistently expressed this same sentiment: "You were not taught God's truth correctly."

TABLE 5.2

The Ten Commandments: Then and Now

Moses' Historical Declaration of the Ten Commandments	Jesus' Support of the Ten Commandments	Christian Obligations to Ten Commandments (from Col. 3)
1 – "No other gods" (Exod. 20:3; also "Love God totally" [Deut. 6:1-5]).	Jesus clearly teaches that the "greatest commandment" was the first: to love God totally (Matt. 22:37-38).	Paul comprehensively teaches: "Whatever you do" give "thanks to God" (Col. 3:17)—to him alone.
2 – No idols (Exod. 20:4-6; see Jehovah's superior status over other idols/gods in Deut. 4:15-40).	The parable of the rich fool indirectly comments on idolatry in Luke 12:13-21, since greed is also called idolatry (Eph. 5:5; Col. 3:5).	"Greed, which is idolatry" (v. 5) is to be "put to death" (see Rom. 1:18-32 also refers to the perverse worship of creature over Creator).
3 – Don't misuse the Lord's name (Exod. 20:7; also Lev. 19:12: "don't swear falsely by my name").	Jesus declares: Don't swear at all; be sincere (Matt. 5:34; see Matt. 6:9 re: Father's hallowed name).	"Whatever you do . . . do it all in the name of the Lord Jesus" (v. 17; also re. Jesus' name: Matt. 28:19; John 14:13; Acts 2:21, and Phil. 2:10).
4 – Keep holy the Sabbath day (Exod. 20:8-11).	Jesus claims that he is Lord of the Sabbath (Matt. 12:1-14), recalling its Creation purpose.	(No Col. 3 reference) Church altered reverence for Sunday in Acts 20:7 and 1 Cor. 16:2, honoring risen Lord of the Sabbath. Also see Heb.10:25.
5 – Children should honor their parents (Exod. 20:12; Deut. 5:16).	Jesus condemns "Corban" tradition of children's disobedience to parents (Matt. 15:4; Mark 7:10).	The apostle repeats: "Children, obey your parents in everything, for this pleases the Lord" (Col. 3:20).
6 – Don't murder (Exod. 20:13).	Jesus adds the internal equivalent of "anger" to this command against murder (Matt. 5:21).	"Anger" and "rage" are condemned (Col. 3:8a; see Rom. 13:9).
7 – Don't commit adultery (Exod. 20:14).	Jesus adds the complement of lustful thoughts (Matt. 5:27-28, 31-32; also see Matt. 19:1-12).	"Sexual immorality, impurity, lust" are denounced (Col. 3:5).
8 – Don't steal (Exod. 20:15).	Christ: "For from within, out of men's hearts, come evil thoughts, . . . theft" (Mark 7:21).	Slaves are to serve faithfully, as serving the Lord, who rewards (Rom. 13:7-9; also Col. 3:22-25 and Titus 2:10).
9 – Don't give false testimony (Exod. 20:16).	Jesus similarly commands honesty; that our "yes" always be yes, and our "no" be no (Matt. 5:34).	Christians are not slander or lie, since old self has been "taken off" and new self has been "put on" (Col. 3:8-10).
10 – Don't covet a neighbor's belongings (Exod. 20:17; see Lev. 19:16b-18: "love your neighbor as yourself").	Jesus stresses "love your neighbor" in a few passages (Matt. 5:43-47; 19:16-30; 22:34-40).	"Holy" and "loving" fellowship is stressed in Col. 3:11-15; "love" is especially noted (v. 14).

Such an indictment did nothing to warm the frigid link between Jesus and the religious leaders. Yet he relentlessly pursued this same viewpoint throughout his ministry.[20] Jesus consistently condemned opponents for their stiff-necked stance on two pertinent facts: (1) The Sabbath was made for people (not the reverse, which was how they were interpreting it); and (2) Jesus is the Lord of the Sabbath. The Messiah drove home these two critical truths, which were based upon Creation. Conversely, his antagonists severely twisted those same truths. Jesus condemned his opposition's legalistic adherence to the Sabbath, because they never submitted to him—the Lord of the Sabbath. Christ judged enemies for diligently studying the Word but never loving its Author. A helpful cross-reference to this accusation comes from John 5:37-40, where Jesus concluded that Jewish leaders were fundamentally attempting the impossible: to achieve salvation from obeying Scripture, while ironically refusing to obey the Christ of Scripture.

True disciples were identified as those who began with Creation. They also valued Jesus' lordship. From those twin perspectives, they arrived at an end point that starkly contrasted with the Pharisees. The faithful members of the early church were, likewise, commended for their commitment to these twin principles. In fact, their endorsement of Creation and lordship was so significant that the church eventually shifted the day of weekly worship from the seventh to the first, because of their Lord's resurrection. The first Easter—Jesus' victory over the grave—so radically altered his disciples' lives that Sunday was deemed the new "holy day" to worship God. (See additional insights on holiness in the *Supplemental Resource*, sidebar 5.5.) Redeemed people in this century also follow the early church's lead. Every Sunday commemorates Jesus' victory over death (ours, as well). That's why we express gratitude to our risen Savior on the first day of the week. We consciously affirm that he is still our primary focus—he is still the "Lord of the Sabbath."[21]

The Only One Who Can Take Us Home

The Creator mercifully revealed his first signposts along the path of redemption, even before Adam and Eve were expelled from the Garden.[22] But, until the Christ himself arrived, those signposts were always limited in what they could do. God's covenants, laws, and prophecies could never fully satisfy our deepest human needs and longings.[23] Technically, they were never meant for that purpose, since every marker ultimately pointed to the Messiah.[24] So, in one sense, every marker along the Old Testament pathway made God's people long even more for Home. As Augustine reminded us, the sole (and soul) solution for our disquieted wanderings resides in our Maker: "You make us for yourself and our hearts find no peace until they rest in you."[25] Our creation in God's image forever links us with our Creator—even when we choose to rebel.

Jesus' salvation fully satisfies our longings. When individuals say yes to him, the image restoration process begins in their lives. They become holy for the first time since Eden. Their restless wanderings cease. (It is what one Christian mystic called "our again-making"[26]). I use the phrase "the image restoration process begins" because we believers are not *experientially* perfect (God helps us work on that task throughout our lives). But we are *positionally* perfect (God sees Jesus' perfect sacrifice through our lives and immediately "positions" us in heaven, as John 5:24 teaches). Table 5.3 indicates how Jesus' reconciling work at Calvary "buys back" all those Eden inheritances, so that God's image inside us begins to recover the full potential of Eden's gifts—and more.

After hundreds and hundreds of years of road paving and sign pointing, the Son of God fully embodied every Old Testament prophecy aimed at him. He brought with him all the "good news" from heaven's Home, which we desperately needed to hear. Christ's fulfillment of the predicted title Emmanuel ("God with us") indicated the Creator was

TABLE 5.3

Summary of Garden Doctrines and Legacies

GARDEN DOCTRINES

		Act 1 **What We Had** (Creation)	Act 2 **What We Lost** (Fall)	Act 3 **What We Regain in** **Christ** (Redemption)
G A R D E N L E G A C I E S	**Family Name** *Holy Living*	*The image of God presented each person with the original legacy of right-eousness. This truth is illustrated by the holy fellowship walks in Eden between the Creator and his once-perfect people. Paradise was never better.*	*The holy Family Name was rejected for greed and idolatry. Sin's con-sequences (especially from Cain's rebellion) left people "hidden" from God's presence. Humanity's unholy nature now described the essence of image in Paradise lost.*	*By Jesus' reconciling work, believers again receive their status of Holy Family Name. As individuals, we are new people, from our restored communion with God. Jesus' "Last Adam" role shows us Paradise's potential.*
	Family Business *Meaningful* *Livelihood*	*God's image also meant the legacy of human partnership with the Trinity to perform the important duties of dominion over and care for Creation. This fact is lovingly expressed by the Creator's assistance in Adam's first explicit chore to name the ani-mals. Paradise included the contentment of work done well.*	*The meaningful Family Business relationships turned chaotic, for God no longer partnered with his people. Sin's consequence is found in the phrase "restless wander." Its reality is symbolized by Cain's dissatisfaction—from his vocational shift to nomadic herding. Discontentment from livelihood now characterized image out-side of Paradise.*	*Following their salva-tion in Jesus, believers are to spread this Good News. We are given vocational insight into God's will, as he part-ners with us again in the Family Business. Jesus' roles of "Carpenter" and "Great Physician" show us how we should live, by our calling, in Paradise regained.*
	Family Ties *Satisfying* *Relationships*	*Image of God further meant intimate affinity between God and his people. This legacy is deliberately displayed by the Creator's institution of marriage in Eden. That intentional model of love was to typify all relationships in Paradise.*	*The once-perfect inter-personal bond between God and his people is broken first by defiance, then murder. Sin's con-sequence from this last image-despising act dis-torts every relationship thereafter, outside the Garden, the "hedging around delight."*	*Through Jesus' redemp-tion, a new found rela-tionship has been struck between all believers. Christians are fellow members of a new community, Christ's body. Our Family Ties must reflect the Trinity's cooperative ties and Jesus' "Faithful Brother" role in our renewed Paradise.*

now completing his superior and final redemption plan, which he introduced in the Garden (see sidebar 5.6 in the *Supplemental Resource*). God's gracious salvation plan in Christ simultaneously contained more promise along with more risk: The Maker of all life chose to literally live with his human creatures—and ultimately to die for them.

In sum, a biblical view of the Christian life reveals the fifth principle we need to apply to our comprehensive pilgrimage:

Truth 5

God's model for discipleship is far more connected than compartmentalized. Specifically, his Law faithfully extends his ongoing purpose, by reinforcing his image and by anticipating his Son.

Conclusion

We disciples are frequently tone-deaf to our Creator-Lover's complete song of redemption. Oh, we know the lyrics, all right. We even personally know the songwriter. But we don't always comprehend the harmony of the entire tune. This may seem odd, at first, for we uniquely breathe the Creator's breath. We mirror God through our inherited legacies. Still we typically don't concentrate on the song's connectedness throughout all its stanzas—how each stanza plays its part, how each relates to the other lines and how each contribution is necessary to the whole. Since we often overlook parts of this historical connectedness within the Creator's complete promise of salvation (from Gen. 3:15), we cannot always sing the full tune the way it was intended.

We particularly miss the role that the Ten Commandments' tough-love melody plays. It's a role that consistently extends from *imago Dei*. Because we don't always recognize that specific contribution, we don't always value those who faithfully sing their particular parts. So we don't always harmonize with fellow saints. Consequently, God's comprehensive heavenly score often goes unappreciated.

A biblical view of the Decalogue is neither one that gives us "more stuff to do" nor one that incarcerates us by legalistic chains. We are called to be set free. The promise of John 8:32 means just what it says: "Then you will know the truth, and the truth will set you free." God's rules for life certainly have boundaries, but—as a collective whole—they are liberating. They ideally provide deep-seated contentment, when we personally experience how they work for our good. Schaeffer and Koop drew those same implications from God's laws, when they summarized:

> This understanding of the chasm between what mankind and history are now and what they could have been—and should have been, from the way they were made—gives us a real moral framework for life, one which is compatible with our nature and aspirations. So there are "rules for life," like the signs on cliff tops, which read: DANGER—KEEP OUT. The signs are there to help not hinder us. God has put them there because to live in this way, according to his rules, is the way for both safety and fulfillment. The God who made us and knows what is for our best good is the same God who gives us his commands. When we break these, it is not only wrong, it is also not for our best good; it is not for our fulfillment as unique persons made in the image of God.[27]

Viewed through this complementary pair of lenses—the Cultural Mandate lens (after our Eden *creation*) and the Gospel lens (after our Calvary *re-creation*)—the Decalogue helps us achieve our fullest potential. We are reminded that:

• God knows us best.

- God wants our best.
- God shows us what's best.
- God provides us with the best.

Obeying God's Ten Commandments reminds us of his holy standards. Following God's directives still points us to Christ. They help us know, firsthand, how to love.

---

1 The details of this catastrophe are drawn from several Associated Press releases (following that Ugandan tragedy). The latest release was dated April 28, 2000.

2 Richard J. Foster comparably calls these two extremes the heresies of moralism and antinomianism. His illustration of this pair is helpful. Notice the conclusion of his analogy, pertaining to image restoration:

> Spiritual growth is the purpose of the Disciplines. It might be helpful to visualize what we have been discussing. Picture a long, narrow ridge with a sheer drop-off on either side. The chasm to the right is the way of moral bankruptcy through human strivings for righteousness. Historically this has been called the *heresy of moralism*. The chasm to the left is moral bankruptcy through the absence of human strivings. This has been called the *heresy of antinomianism*. On the ridge there is a path, the Disciplines of the spiritual life. This path leads to the inner transformation and healing for which we seek. We must never veer off to the right or the left, but stay on the path. The path is fraught with severe difficulties, but also with incredible joys. As we travel on this path, the blessing of God will come upon us *and reconstruct us into the image of Jesus Christ*. We must always remember that the path does not produce the change; it only places us where the change can occur. This is the path of disciplined grace.

From *Celebration of Discipline: The Path to Spiritual Growth* (revised edition; San Francisco: HarperSanFrancisco,1988), p. 8. Italics are mine.

3 For instance, the Apostle Paul painstakingly attends to the error of *legalism* in passages like Romans 4:1-12 and Galatians 3:1-14. Likewise, Paul addresses *antinomianism*— "grace only"—in passages such as Romans 3:27-31; 6:1-2; and 6:15.

4 See Psalm 115:1-8 (esp. v. 8); Psalm 135:13-18 (esp. v. 18); and Romans 1:21-25.

5 In ancient times, for all intents and purposes, *a person's name equaled the person*. The person essentially was his or her name. Sidebar 5.5 in the *Supplemental Resource* offers details as to why this commandment was so important, focusing on God's holiness.

Walter Brueggemann offers another angle to the subject of abusing the Creator's name. He claims that names are about who we put our allegiance in. So Brueggeman asks: "So who is really in charge? Answer carefully because we are expected to give an extraordinary answer. But if that answer is the right one, then every other answer is wrong. To suggest that any other is in charge, to name any other name, other than the Lord of disrupting, abiding freedom, is to answer wrongly. It is to embrace *idolatry*."

I especially like what this Old Testament scholar says next—how he assesses idolatry in terms of God's plan for holistic wellness: "Idolatry is at the heart of oppression and coercion. Idolatry is at the root both of our oppressing and our being oppressed. Idolatry—wrongly perceiving who is in charge—is the opposite of *shalom*. *Shalom*, as we are invited to perceive it, is premised on knowing who is in charge and making the life-reorienting pilgrimage to the mountain of freedom and obligation."

From Walter Brueggemann's *Living Toward a Vision: Biblical Reflections on Shalom* (New York: United Church Press, 1982), p. 59.

6 Notice how "delight" and "joy" relate to God's holy Sabbath in Isaiah 58:13-14.

7 Deuteronomy 5:16 and Ephesians 6:2-3 both state this Fifth Command is the "first command with a [two-part] promise": the dual blessings of a long life *and* a prosperous life.

8 The birth of Seth (in Gen. 5:1-3) is the first time this important biblical truth is identified. Seth reflects his father's image, humanly speaking. We use phrases such as "he looks like" or "acts like his father." The propagation of God's image (based upon the review of the opening verses in this chapter) is implied.

9 Genesis 9:6 leaves no doubt of this image connection when it comes to murder. Proverbs 14:31, 17:5; and James 3:9 also show the inseparable tie between Creator and creature, through this powerful reality of post-Fall image.

10 Matthew 19:1-9 mightily illustrates how Jesus—when pushed to conform to the permissive practices of divorce in his day—both *recalls* and *reinforces* God's *"way from the beginning."* Our Lord's apology-free apologetic is incredibly pertinent for saints, because it advances the crucial (and connected) truths of Creation with the place and purpose of marriage. By inference, Jesus also reaffirms *imago Dei*, for he perfectly quotes the *last half* of Genesis 1:27 (in Matt. 19:4)—and *twice* (in the *first half* of Gen. 1:27) the word "image" is found.

Sidebar 5.2 in the *Supplemental Resource* summarizes the most extensive research ever conducted on sexual behavior within American culture. Among several fascinating results, this nonreligious research repeatedly concludes, among other findings, that *conservative Christians are the most contented people in their sexual lives, when contrasted with all other competing peer groups.* That single discovery affirms the Garden legacies, especially Family Name and Family Ties.

11 Technically, nobody owns anything. Everything belongs to the Creator. Therefore, stealing from others essentially means stealing from God. At the "human level," see the apostle's guidelines (in Rom. 13:7-10) for owing respect to others, including material possessions and paying taxes.

12 Notice two connecting points in Colossians 3: (1) greed is idolatry (v. 5) and (2) Christ's disciples must particularly renew their minds and behaviors (regarding greed) "in the *image* of its Creator" (v. 10b).

13 Note the universal principle of truth-telling from Christ in Matthew 7:12. Also see Colossians 3:9-10.

14 See Leviticus 19:16b-18 and Matthew 22:34-40.

15 These remarkable concepts are played out in Matthew 25:31-46.

16 From Brown's *An Introduction to the New Testament*; New York: Doubleday, 1997, p. 179.

17 *Ibid.* Taken from Brown's comments in footnote 15 (on page 179) of his resource.

18 Merrill C. Tenney, in his revised *New Testament Survey* (copublished by Eerdmans and InterVarsity in 1985) also notes that, in Matthew alone, "at least sixty obvious examples"—between 1:23 and 27:48—connect Jesus with the Old Testament. Most references are found in Isaiah and the Psalms, Tenney adds, "yet the Old Testament as a whole is repre-

sented." More specifically, many of these sixty references include the phrase "the fulfill-ment" of prophecy, providing an even more direct link.

19 Note other lengthy portions of the New Testament (besides Col. 3) that verify the Ten Commandments and call for God's highest (and continuous) plan for holy living as well. Romans 13:6-14 is especially appropriate, as Paul refers to the ongoing growth phases of our holiness (in v. 11b): "because our salvation is *nearer now* than when we *first believed.*"

20 For example, see Christ's instruction on marriage and divorce in Matthew 19:1-9 (in which he called his audience back to God's original plan in the Garden) and Christ's proclamation of his seven woes in Matthew 23:1-39—especially verses 23-24 (in which he criticizes his opponent's lifestyle and leadership).

21 Note these significant post-Resurrection references to the early church's new day of worship on Sunday: Acts 20:7, 1 Corinthians 16:2, and Revelation 1:10.

22 The first promise of Messiah is made in Genesis 3:15. Notice how Romans 16:20 picks up on that prophecy for the church age.

23 Hebrews 9:8-10—especially verse 9—claim "the conscience of the worshiper" was never satisfied.

24 Notice Paul's brief historical review of God's multiple graces in Israel's past from Romans 9:3-5.

25 Saint Augustine, *Confessions*, book 1, paragraph 1, trans. R. S. Pine-Coffin; New York: Penguin, 1961, page 21, as cited in Charles Colson's *How Now Shall We Live?* Wheaton, Ill.: Tyndale, 1999, p. 140. To this truism Colson comments, "Only when we find God can we halt this restless search, because the very essence of our nature is the *imago Dei*—the image of God—implanted in us by the Creator."

26 Julian of Norwich combined the doctrines of Creation (image bearing) and re-creation in Christ:

> We know in our Faith, and believe by the teaching and preaching of Holy Church, that the blessed Trinity made mankind to his *image* and to his *likeness*. In the same manner-wise we know that when man fell so deep and so wretchedly by sin, there was none other help to restore man but through Him that made man. And he that made man for love, by the same love he would restore man to the same bliss, and over-passing; and like as we were *like-made* to the Trinity in our *first making*, our Maker would that we should be like Jesus Christ, Our Saviour, in heaven without end, by the virtue of our *again-making*.

In *Revelation of Divine Love* (p. 23), from Tinsley's *The Imitation of God in Christ* (p. 19); italics mine.

27 This citation was partially quoted earlier. This fuller quotation enables us to more broadly value the purposes of the law. It is taken from *Whatever Happened to the Human Race?* by Francis A. Schaeffer and C. Everett Koop (Old Tappan, N.J.: Fleming H. Revell, 1979), p. 155.

Section II

The Jesus We Wish We Knew

CHAPTER SIX

No Way in a Manger

> *God was given eyebrows, two kidneys, and a spleen.*
> *He stretched against the walls and floated in the*
> *amniotic fluids of his mother.*
>
> —MAX LUCADO

Several years ago I taught a summer studies course at a well-known seminary in the East. I visited the school library to place a dozen textbooks on the reserve shelves. One librarian (whom I'll call "Jill") never let me forget that experience: She grilled me on my intentions. She questioned my every move. In no uncertain terms, she managed to block all my efforts. I left, dumbfounded. I almost felt ashamed.

No books ever reached the reserve shelves.

Twenty-four hours later I had to return to the library on other business. It was the last thing I wanted to do. Entering the facility from a side door, I consciously avoided any additional contact with Jill. At least I thought I had. Before I was ten paces from the entry, Jill spotted me. She all but ran at me. Frozen in my shoes, I braced for more verbal blows. But—to my surprise—she welcomed me like a long-lost relative!

"I apologize," Jill began, not waiting for me to respond. "Yesterday, I acted quite rudely." By this time, I'm certain my mouth hung open in disbelief. "You see, yesterday I didn't realize you were a professor. I thought you were a student. I'll take care of your requests right away." As quickly as Jill arrived, she disappeared. Several minutes passed and I still felt shell-shocked. The numbness gradually subsided. To this day what troubles me was not the personal broadside I took but the double standard revealed by Jill's actions. Jill assumed that substantial differences exist between the categories of "teacher" and "student." Those differences were substantial enough in her mind to justify her rudeness. Jill's behavior reflected a disturbing inconsistency that is evident within Christian circles. Her actions collided with the "Creation Equation," which I introduced in chapter 5.

Let's review: The Creation Equation emerges from the powerful doctrine of the *imago Dei*—the fact that all people are created in the image of their Maker. I stress the word "are," for it is imperative we understand that the Fall did not cancel our image-bearing status. Sin severely distorted our once-perfect reflection, but the Fall did not totally cancel it. The Creation Equation says: "How you treat any person is the same as how you treat God." The inverse is also valid (with a small twist), because *imago Dei* is reciprocal: "How we treat God is how we should treat others."

Many Scriptures refer to this formula: Capital punishment is initiated because of this equation (Gen. 9:6); the Wisdom Literature supports this principle (Prov. 14:31, 17:5); the "Greatest Commandment" features not one, but two, directives because of its truth (see Matt. 22:34-40); and Jesus' lesson on the sheep and goats (Matt. 25:31-46) lends support when he connects our horizontal duties to our vertical duties. Finally, James 3:9-10 provides the most explicit link between this Creator-creature connection by noting unacceptable behavior for saints. What's great is that the rationale for the Creation Equation is clearly spelled out in those verses: "With the tongue we praise our Lord and Father, and with it we curse *men who have been made in God's likeness*. Out of the same mouth come praise and cursing. My brothers, this should not be."

So Jill violated God's principle of human dignity by substituting her own standard for the Creation Equation. Jill interfered with that Eden truth by exhibiting a bias for certain people, rather than treating all people equally—based upon image. Most of us do the same as Jill, if we are honest, though we may not be as public. Our unbalanced views of people frequently coincide with a couple of other kinds of imbalances. First, inappropriate views of people may lead to similar distortions in our perspectives about the Baby of Bethlehem. For example, if we erringly think that humanity inherently includes sin (even though our Eden parents were free from sin), we may have difficulty accepting Jesus' full humanity. Second, any warped view we hold of Jesus influences our perceptions about who he wants us to be now. We can't "follow Jesus" in any comprehensive way, for instance, if we believe his God side dominated his human side.[1] That perceived advantage we think he had over us makes him far too distant or aloof—and almost impossible to emulate.

Which Jesus?

Randomly ask people on the street which story they remember most about Jesus. Of those who are aware of any story at all, many will recall the time he walked on water. Many churchgoers would also select that story, for it is a picture of the Father's assistance in Jesus' life. That story was, ironically, one of the few times Jesus benefited from one of his own miracles. In other words, that story does not represent the rest of his life and ministry. It is an exception to his usual pattern of service to others.

The doctrine of the Incarnation has been correctly called a "mystery."[2] By definition, mysteries are never totally explained in this life. But our human nature can't handle that. We yearn for answers, even to life's toughest problems. We want fast, sound-bite solutions to sophisticated questions. That same mentality causes us to skip ahead and read the last chapter of a whodunit novel. Or we impatiently dial the 1-900 phone number to get the answers to this morning's newspaper crossword puzzle without having to wait for tomorrow's paper.

We should not be shocked, then, when many respond to major mysteries of our faith with convenient (yet abbreviated and lopsided) answers. We frequently settle for either/or viewpoints instead of holding mysteries within their proper tensions. When simplistic, black-or-white thinking is transferred to the Incarnation, Christ's humanity constantly takes second place to his divinity for most evangelicals. This dichotomized thought pattern produces an inferior Jesus. A diminished view of the Son's humanness also cheapens discipleship, because of the Creation Equation: When we minimize his humanity, we do the same to ours.

Understanding a Half Dozen Heresies

Six heretical views of Jesus are outlined in figure 6.1. The accompanying commentary helps us think through those falsehoods as well as Scripture's correctives. Awareness of church history may keep us from repeating past mistakes (Sidebar 6.1 in the *Supplemental Resource* describes more contemporary heresies).

These faulty views about Jesus are grouped into three major categories: (1) whether or not Christ was actually God or man or both (technically known as the subject of reality); (2) whether Christ was fully

FIGURE 6.1

Heresies About Jesus (Biblical Views in Parentheses)

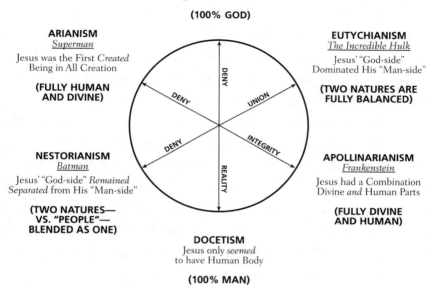

EBIONISM
Jesus was *only a special man*
through Whom God Worked

(100% GOD)

ARIANISM
Superman
Jesus was the First *Created*
Being in All Creation

**(FULLY HUMAN
AND DIVINE)**

EUTYCHIANISM
The Incredible Hulk
Jesus' "God-side"
Dominated His "Man-side"

**(TWO NATURES ARE
FULLY BALANCED)**

NESTORIANISM
Batman
Jesus' "God-side" *Remained*
Separated from His "Man-side"

**(TWO NATURES—
VS. "PEOPLE"—
BLENDED AS ONE)**

APOLLINARIANISM
Frankenstein
Jesus had a Combination
Divine *and* Human Parts

**(FULLY DIVINE
AND HUMAN)**

DOCETISM
Jesus only *seemed*
to have Human Body

(100% MAN)

divine and human (integrity); and (3) whether Christ remained God or man, after the Incarnation, when his two natures merged (union).[3] Figure 6.1 summarizes these heresies along with the evangelical response (parenthesized words in bold capital letters).

Heresies that Deny Reality

Ebionism proposed that Jesus was merely a man. Swayed by Jewish tradition at the end of the first century, this monotheistic mind-set denied that the son of Mary and Joseph could be God. For the Ebionite, Jesus displayed certain supernatural signs (for instance, at his baptism), but that's as far as his associations with divinity went. The Gospel of John and the book of Colossians raise specific arguments against this first heresy, asserting with certainty that Jesus was 100 percent God.[4]

Docetism was Ebionism in reverse, asserting that Jesus was not completely human. This movement was mainly influential between A.D. 70 and A.D. 170. Docetists held that any nonspiritual realities, like physical bodies, were automatically evil. Taken from the Greek word *dokeo* ("to seem"), Docetists said Jesus only "seemed" human but was actually more ghostlike, especially during times that required physical activity (e.g., eating, sleeping, and dying on the cross). Again, John's writings (both his Gospel and his Epistles) and Colossians reject this position, as does the book of Hebrews.[5] We can be sure that Jesus was 100 percent man.

For the most part, no one who claims to be a Christian today (especially evangelicals) still insists on either of these two misrepresentations of Jesus. That may not be true, however, when it comes to the remaining foursome.

Over the years, I've found that many adults say it is useful for me to explain abstract concepts through popular illustrations. Theological concepts are not exempt. So, without intending any irreverence, I have created analogies (from within contemporary fiction) to explain certain dimensions of the four remaining heresies.

Heresies that Deny Integrity

Arianism, for all intents and purposes, represented the historical roots of the modern-day Jehovah's Witnesses. Arianism equated Jesus with the first and highest of all created beings; therefore he was not totally God, since he did not possess an eternal past. The Church Council of Nicea in A.D. 325 condemned this heresy because it ignored the full divinity of Jesus found in verses like John 1:1 as well as Colossians 1:15-20. I occasionally meet people who say they are Christians, yet they're still sidetracked by this false doctrine. Many struggle with the functional implications of the Godhead as Trinity: Three-People-in-One. In those cases, Jesus' divinity is minimized, as is the Holy Spirit's. Others struggle with Jesus' earthly identity, for they can't believe that God could fully merge with humanity.

Because of Arianism's inappropriate picture of Jesus, it reminds me of the comic book hero Superman. The Man of Steel represents a mighty individual, yet one who's only a created being.[6] In this view, Jesus is one who is mighty, cloaked in a guise of humanity (like Clark Kent). Of course, Superman is virtually invincible, except for his susceptibility to kryptonite.

Apollinarianism also claimed Jesus was neither fully divine nor human. Its adherents proposed that he possessed parts of each category, such as a supernatural mind and spirit along with a human body and soul. The early church at the Council of Constantinople officially rejected this religious option in A.D. 381. Some Christians today struggle with this errant view. They find it very difficult (if not impossible) to resolve the tensions of the Incarnation. One troublesome area of Jesus' life, in their opinion, was his mental sphere. Apollinarians believed the Son of God didn't know the time of his Second Coming (Matt. 24:36); however they also believed he discerned peoples' thoughts (Matt. 9:4; 12:25; 22:18). Most evangelicals still believe those same two truths. Yet, rather than hold on to both ideas as a valid tension, this heresy resolved to "chop Jesus up into various body parts," which is theologically unacceptable.

My illustration of those still stuck on Apollinarianism is *Frankenstein*. This classic book featured an unsuccessful laboratory experiment that combined various human parts, like a body from one man and a brain from another. No single person was entirely represented by that macabre homo sapien "quiltwork." It is precisely this type of "monster" image of Jesus that we don't need roaming around the countryside, terrorizing the church or the world today.

Heresies that Deny Union

The final set of doctrinal fallacies about Jesus focus on something less than the full God-man, following the fusion of his two natures. *Nestorianism* claimed the Messiah never completely blended his divine and human natures. He retained two independent persons within Himself. Like Apollinarianism, this fourth heresy was condemned by the Patriarchate of Constantinople in A.D. 431. Several Scriptures also condemn this view, including Luke 2:40 and 52, which speak of Jesus' holistic and integrated growth, both as an infant and as a preteen entering adulthood.

Nestorianism, at best, offered a schizophrenic understanding of the Second Person of the Trinity—it asserted that the divine and human persons remained separate in the incarnate Christ. It operated in similar ways to the dual personalities of Batman's Caped Crusader and Bruce Wayne. In the movie *Batman Forever*, the hero critiques the two independent individuals within himself: "We are all two . . . one daylight; one evening shadows." Those who fall for Nestorianism today sound very much like the pastor I heard who taught that the frailties of Jesus' life (e.g., hunger, crying, and extreme anguish) exclusively represented his "human side"—nothing else.

Eutychianism completes our list of notorious falsehoods regarding Jesus' nature. Many well-intentioned people are still unwittingly duped by this heresy. I dare say (in some circles I know) this viewpoint is actually more popular than the biblical position! This distortion of Jesus claimed his divine nature always overpowered his human nature. That domination was so thorough that Jesus' humanity was all but silenced. Outcomes of this falsehood included the warped perceptions that Jesus really didn't feel pain or the full pull of human temptation, because his divinity protected him. Unfortunately this philosophy totally ignored passages like Hebrews 2:17-18; 4:14-16, and 5:7-9. Therefore our Lord's significant work as sympathetic High Priest was also marginalized. The Council of Chalcedon soundly condemned this view in A.D. 451.

"The Incredible Hulk" is similar to this misrepresentation of Jesus. In the 1970s TV series (inspired by the comic book character and updated in a recent movie), Bill Bixby played the human. Bixby's always-domineering counterpart was a green muscle-bulging monster (played by bodybuilder Lou Ferrigno) that generally wreaked havoc. I've known so-called brothers and sisters in Christ who have opted for this dangerous and unacceptable view of our Lord. Wherever Jesus' humanity is smothered for the sake of his deity, the disciple risks heresy.

Final Thoughts

These last four heretical beliefs about Christ threaten the contemporary church—whether they surface from the inside or invade from the outside. In every instance, these views leave us with one who's much less than the biblical God-man. They leave us one who is woefully ineffective in his early roles (beginning at the Incarnation) and in his later roles (at the Crucifixion), one who is schizophrenic, at best, and who thoroughly fails to live up to his current role as superior High Priest.

Thankfully, we don't need to be left with these inferior views. Thankfully, we have a better model toward whom we may turn. We have a far better example to emulate for our daily lives. He's the Jesus we need to know. He is the one who offers us much, much more for our daily life and faith.

Which Jesus Do You Know?

Some contemporary views of discipleship start off on the wrong foot by neglecting the essential features of Jesus' humanity. (I'm not suggesting active disbelief but passive neglect.) Authors like Max Lucado can help the church to understand part of that mystery of the God-man—especially his humanity. Resources like *God Came Near* blend certain helpful concepts about the Creator-become-creature.[7] Contemplate Lucado's earthy illustrations of the Incarnation below. (Especially notice his last line.)

For thirty-three years he would feel everything you and I have ever felt. He felt weak. He grew weary. . . . He got colds, burped, and had body odor. His feelings got hurt. His feet got tired. And his head ached.

To think of Jesus in such a light is—well, it seems almost irreverent, doesn't it? It's not something we like to do; it's uncomfortable. It is much easier to keep the humanity out of the incarnation. Clean the manure from around the manger. Wipe the sweat out of his eyes. Pretend he never snored or blew his nose or hit his thumb with a hammer. He's easier to stomach that way. There is something about keeping him divine that keeps him distant, packaged, and predictable.

But don't do it. For heaven's sake, don't. Let him be as human as he intended to be. Let him into the mire and muck of our world. For only if we let him in can he pull us out.

Take a moment to jot down your own mental pictures of Jesus. Without peeking at the two figures on pages 130 and 131, list at least a half dozen characteristics of his life that first come to your mind. What specific qualities or traits do you immediately associate with the Son of God? Drawn from the informal surveys I've made over several years in family camps, in college or seminary classrooms, and in adult Sunday school classes, figure 6.2 summarizes about 90 percent of what most people say about the man from Galilee.

Carefully examine each of the traits listed in figure 6.2. Do any of those characteristics surprise you? Can you think of a Scripture reference for each of the items listed? How many qualities did you find that match the entries on your own list? Which contributions, if any, did you note that were not found in this first figure?

Now study figure 6.3. This illustration also expresses biblical traits and experiences of Jesus—yet it refers to qualities that are infrequently noted by most people. In fact, reversing the statistics above, about 90 percent of the time these features are never cited in the surveys I've taken over the years.

Do any of the figure 6.3 entries appear on your personal list? Which ones don't? Do any items surprise you? Are there any traits for which you cannot think of a supporting Bible reference? Let me repeat an earlier point: Each of our perspectives of Jesus usually contains some level of distortion.

These exercises should help you get a better handle on your personal views of Jesus. Most disciples miss some feature of the Son's humanity. But here's the sad news to me: *Those very same human traits we ignore in Jesus' life tend to be the exact qualities we most struggle with in our own lives!*

Passages like Luke 2:40 and 52 remind us that Jesus matured in precisely the same spheres of humanity that you and I do. Mary's son grew in the same developmental patterns of growth that we experience. What was God's grand reason for designing Jesus' earthly life this way? So that disciples could purposefully follow the Son's example and become mature like him. To state it differently, Jesus showed us how to get the most out of life. Jesus demonstrated both how to celebrate life (as he did at Cana's first miracle) and how to mature from suffering; both how to look out for personal needs and how to selflessly serve others.[8] But this task of figuring out who Jesus really was is a tough assignment. It is so tough, in fact, that I have created this assessment about the church's 2,000-year-old struggle to identify the real Jesus: *Those who knew the man of Galilee best (from their day-to-day interactions) never, ever questioned his humanity. Yet all doubted his divinity. We who never knew the Lord in his earthly life have just the opposite problem!*

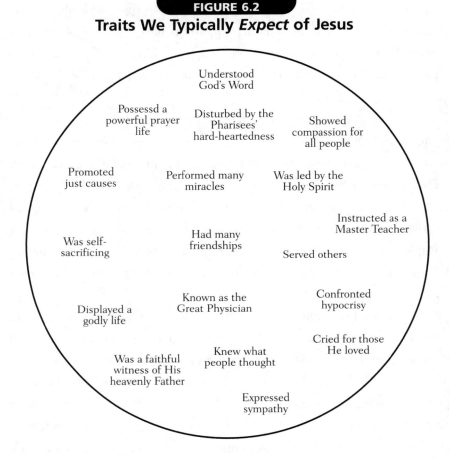

FIGURE 6.2

Traits We Typically *Expect* of Jesus

Understood God's Word

Possessd a powerful prayer life

Disturbed by the Pharisees' hard-heartedness

Showed compassion for all people

Promoted just causes

Performed many miracles

Was led by the Holy Spirit

Instructed as a Master Teacher

Was self-sacrificing

Had many friendships

Served others

Displayed a godly life

Known as the Great Physician

Confronted hypocrisy

Was a faithful witness of His heavenly Father

Knew what people thought

Cried for those He loved

Expressed sympathy

Rethinking Jesus' Humanity

When we analyze what we actually believe about our Lord's thirty-three years of flesh-and-blood existence on earth, most of us really don't believe some things we say. Our hearts and minds hold on to a different message. Again, I believe a large percentage of believers are functional *Eutychians*—believing Jesus' God side dominated his man side. Jesus, for them, was the original Incredible Hulk. Those who fall prey to this falsehood need to recall a couple of explicit Scriptures:

FIGURE 6.3
Traits We Typically *Don't Expect* of Jesus

Knew the Father's plan ("the hour") for His life

Was completely exhausted (and required rest)

Got angry

Became exasperated

Anticipated and experienced His Death

Became surprised

Often disturbed by His disciples

Was always learning

Doubted His Father's presence

Expressed sadness

Served people from many socially unacceptable groups

Needed the support of others

Experienced joy in the Holy Spirit

Sang Hymns

Got hungry

Deliberately wanted to be left alone

Publicly read the Scriptures

Experienced severe anguish (possibly fear)

Thoroughly enjoyed meals with His friends

Got severely stressed out

Claimed to not know everything

Didn't always get along with His family

- Jesus was "made like . . . [us] in every way" (Heb. 2:17a).
- Jesus was "not . . . unable to sympathize with our weaknesses, but . . . [he] has been tempted in every way, just as we are—yet was without sin" (Heb. 4:15).

When we examine Jesus' human nature and temptations—which he shared with us "in every way"—we sometimes conclude that his experiences were not as difficult as ours, since we may suspect his deity partially protected him. Many disciples I've met are convinced Jesus held an advantage over us. Some, if pushed, start backpedaling on earlier affirmations about his full humanity, sounding more contradictory than they realize (see sidebar 6.2 in the *Supplemental Resource* for more discussion).

A "Pop Quiz" Question

Let me test my assumptions with you by springing a pop quiz. (After all, that's what professors are supposed to do, isn't it?) Pretend I asked for your answer to this question: "Were Jesus' wilderness temptations really real—that is, was there any chance he *could* have actually sinned from those three encounters?" Which of the following two responses would you pick?

You might say yes, which implies that, unless the Son could have been able to sin, his temptations were less potent than ours today. "If each spiritual battle Christ faced was decided before it occurred (i.e., He could never sin)," you would argue, "then his temptations could not be equivalent 'in every way' with mine." With this first choice you also propose that, unless Jesus could have sinned, he did not demonstrate the fully human qualities that God's Word teaches.

If you chose to answer no, you might exclaim, "But Jesus was fully God, too! He was the only person to ever live a sinless life. If we say Jesus could have sinned, don't we question his deity?"[9] I have no problem whatsoever with the first two sentences of this second response. And I agree, in principle, with the third sentence. But I prefer to tweak that last phrase a bit, because this victory-is-guaranteed-even-before-the-first-skirmish position also seems to challenge Scripture—doesn't it? by questioning his full humanity.

How do we properly maintain the tension of Jesus' fully divine and fully human status when it comes to his temptations? (See sidebar 6.2 in the *Supplemental Resource* for more discussion.)

What If . . . ?

Review these two positions on Jesus and his temptations: (1) He was *able to not* sin (he could have sinned—because of his full humanity—but he always emerged victorious) and (2) He *was not able* to sin (he never could have sinned because of his full deity). What about a third option? What if Jesus *could not* have sinned (his deity) but—because he continued growing in every way (his humanity)[10]—he *never knew* he would be victorious every single time he faced temptation? Using the formula above, we could say: "He was not able to sin, but he was not able to know every outcome, in advance." If that combination is correct, *Jesus entered every spiritual battle virtually the same way we do:* He needed to trust the heavenly Father for deliverance.

Neither his divine nor his human nature is compromised by this third "what if" option. That position might be the best of both worlds, even though the Incarnation will always remain a mystery and a paradox.

Kenosis—A Self-Emptied Savior and a Model for All Disciples

These previous paragraphs have emphasized one aspect of the theological mystery known as *kenosis* (see sidebar 6.3 in the *Supplemental Resource* for other implications). This doctrinal term refers to the voluntary "self-emptying" of Jesus when he became a man, as described in Philippians 2:1-11. That concept not only helps us to understand our Lord more completely, but it enables us to comprehend our own discipleship better, for the apostle commands us in that passage, "Your attitude should be the same as that of Christ Jesus" (v. 5).

We all realize that the Incarnation necessarily limited certain divine traits of the Messiah. When he chose to become a human being, Jesus volitionally placed those divine qualities "on a shelf," so to speak. This thirty-three-year commitment did not, in any way, compromise the nature of his deity. It simply meant he freely chose not to exercise his powers independently. He was always God—before, during, and after the Incarnation. But he deliberately chose not to act separately from the Father's plan for him while he lived on earth (see John 10:17-18). For example, Jesus intentionally gave up the privilege to be omnipresent (simultaneously present in every geographical location). The Bible also records (as chapter 7 explains) that Jesus voluntarily laid aside his right to exercise omniscience so that he might grow in knowledge as every healthy person does. Jesus was so committed to this *kenosis* plan not to use his divine traits independently that—when he did do something superhuman—he relied upon the power supplied by either God the Father or God the Holy Spirit.[11]

One extraordinary application of how Jesus' *kenosis* directly affects the contemporary believer's life and responsibilities is this: Jesus consistently reminded us how he (in the very best sense) didn't have a life of his own. He fully submitted to everything his Father had for him to do,[12] and relied on his Father for provisions for every personal need. Each disciple is to emulate Jesus' reliance upon the Father.[13]

Kenosis—Jesus' Consistent Strategy

One of the most underrated passages on Jesus' *kenosis* is Matthew's version of Gethsemane (26:47-56). There, our Lord vividly demonstrated: (1) how he would not use his *own* powers independently (e.g., defeat enemies by himself) and (2) how he would *submit* to the Father's plan. After Judas betrayed Christ and Peter chopped off the servant's ear, our Lord called for the sword to be put away and healed the man. Then Jesus confronts his followers with the truth of his dependency upon the Father (which he displayed his entire life): "Do you think I cannot call on my Father, and he will at once put at my disposal more than twelve legions of angels? But how then would the Scriptures be fulfilled that say it must happen in this way?" (vv. 53-54).

Apart from the anguish of the cross, it didn't get any tougher in Jesus' life than the Garden of Gethsemane. Some might say Gethsemane was actually tougher because a battle of wills (between Son and Father) surfaced. All would agree that Gethsemane was pivotal for its revelation of *kenosis*. Throughout this fiery trial, the Son consistently adhered to the same protocol he followed his entire life: Jesus did not pull down his own divine powers "from the shelf," where he originally put them, even though he had every right to do so. He then reminded his disciples he could have called on his Father for deliverance (but he didn't do this, either). Jesus also expressed a desire for the Scriptures' fulfillment, a desire that led to his imminent arrest, trial, and death and exemplified Jesus' entire life of *kenosis*, his full submission to the Father. To rephrase it, when Jesus cited Scripture ("it must happen this way"), he was essentially saying, "I did what I was told. I did what was foretold" (1 Pet. 2:23 also affirms this testimony of the Son).

Furthermore (taking more liberties with my paraphrase), in Gethsemane Christ confessed: "I never used my powers apart from the game plan of the Father or the Holy Spirit. I voluntarily remained committed to my limited human nature throughout my life. Even here, at this betrayal in Gethsemane, I could have personally defeated my enemies. But I didn't."

In brief, Jesus could say, "I never took unfair advantage of my deity."

Jesus Was More "Like Us" than We Know

When I say we disciples must emulate Jesus our Lord, I am not saying we emulate everything he was and did. That's silly. Nobody believes that. We obviously are not called to be virgin-born or to die for the world's sin. That was the Messiah's unique life purpose. I hope no disciple would ever fall for such wild-eyed interpretations.

On the other hand, most of us look past his full humanity much too quickly. Jesus' contemporaries repeatedly acknowledged his humanness. That goes for friend and foe alike. John 10:33 expresses one of my favorite examples from the Gospels: Our Lord had been performing some miracles when his accusers took up stones to kill him. Their reasoning? Jesus had blasphemed, claiming to be God. They so much as said, "Everybody knows you are 'a mere man.'" Even when the Son of Man initially surveyed his own disciples for their opinion of who he was, they first came up with John the Baptist, Elijah, Jeremiah, "or one of the prophets" (Matt. 16:14). All these were human beings. Yes, they were godly men, but men nonetheless. To his disciples, Jesus exhibited every mark of full humanity. We have no record of anyone actually holding a Docetic view of Jesus while he lived on earth; nobody believed he was not a man but only "seemed" to have a body. That's because all who met Jesus knew he was truly human.

Here's another Bible truth that further shows Jesus' humanity. Apart from his messianic distinctiveness (e.g., dying for the world's sin), Jesus did not do anything inimitable. Jesus did not perform any unique miracles.[14] Similar miracles to those of our Lord's may be found elsewhere in Scripture. So Jesus' miracles alone do not prove his deity.[15]

Think about it. There were other righteous men and women in the Bible who, like Jesus, were led by God, spoke inspired words, produced several kinds of food miracles (though only Jesus turned water into wine), healed various illnesses, raised the dead, walked on water, were miraculously delivered from their enemies, knew people's thoughts, and performed miracles within nature.

Does this last paragraph surprise you? Disturb you? Reassure you?

So What?

What practical difference does this brief section on Jesus' humanity make in our lives? Let's review the implications of what a fully human Jesus means for us. We're reminded that Jesus really was "made like . . . [us] in every way" (Heb. 2:17a) and that he was "tempted in every way, just as we are" (Heb. 4:15). He really was fully human. Minimally, we must play down the "advantage" myth that Jesus was able to default to personal, divine help—which we can not replicate. Furthermore, the many passages that direct us to now "follow" or "imitate" Jesus mean exactly that. We don't need to invent some new mystical interpretation in order to spiritualize or rationalize such commands out of existence. First John 2:6 puts it as plainly as it can be stated: "Whoever claims to live in him must walk as Jesus did."

Consequently, since (1) Jesus was fully human, (2) Jesus never "unfairly" used his deity but always trusted the Father and the Spirit, and (3) Jesus' performing of miracles was not unique to him, then the Bible actually means what it says: *We can—we must—really follow Jesus!*

To assist believers in this straightforward view of discipleship, the next five chapters expand on the concepts introduced to this point: Chapter 7 features Jesus' model of character; his role as "Last Adam" captures what godly humanity looks like. Chapter 8 displays our Lord's model of calling; his titles of "Carpenter" and "Great Physician" show what comprehensive kingdom service looks like. Chapter 9 describes Jesus' model of community; his role as "Beloved Brother" informs us of what healthy relationships look like. Each chapter, again, is grounded upon *imago Dei*. Chapters 10 and 11 supply summary applications: what it means to "believe Christ" and to "follow Christ."

Fourth-century church father Athanasius correctly summarized Christian discipleship when he proposed a simple, yet revolutionary, idea about Jesus and us: "He became what we are that He might make us what He is."[16]

When we summarize this chapter, then, we lay yet another crucial foundation for our faith. This sixth principle not only provides the basis for a tested Christology; it likewise supplies the groundwork for biblical anthropology as a whole—helping us to understand ourselves and others with far more accuracy.

Truth 6

God's model for discipleship is intrinsically tied to the humanity of Jesus. Because our Lord was not only fully God but fully man, he also possessed the image of the Creator. So, the better we know him the better we know all people—a perfect application of the Creation Equation: "As we treat others, so we treat God."

Conclusion

Every Christmas season reminds us that the Creation Equation is as relevant as it's ever been. Since that Creator-creature bond is indestructible, disciples should annually recommit themselves to Christ at Yuletide. Cherished Christmas stories replay the historical valleys of human despair along with the mountaintops of hope. Thankfully, our "Desire of Nations" has come. God became flesh.

So we recommit ourselves to emulating our Master (enabled by the Holy Spirit within us). And we subsequently find a deeper, truer, healthier, and more satisfying life. By glorifying our Maker, the Creation Equation comes full circle.

That's the complete Christmas message—"The Greatest Story *Never* Told."

1 When I refer to Jesus' "God side" and "human side," I am emphasizing his two respective natures. Although it is permissible to analyze these natures independently, we must never treat Jesus as schizophrenic. Ultimately we must view the Son as one complete person.

2 See Romans 16:25; Ephesians 1:9; 3:4; Colossians 1:26-27; 2:2-3; and 4:3.

3 This organizational scheme was implied almost a hundred years ago in Augustus H. Strong's *Systematic Theology* (Volume II; Valley Forge, Penn.: Judson Press, 1907), p. 672.

4 For instance, see John 10:33 and Colossians 2:9-10.

5 See John 1:14; 10:33 (especially the phrase "a mere man"); and Hebrews 2:17.

6 If I had to come up with another illustration of how Christians often perceive the Holy Spirit, I would suggest "the Force" of *Star Wars'* fame. The Force was powerful and good, yet impersonal and somewhat unpredictable.

7 From *God Came Near* (Portland, Ore.: Multnomah, 1987), pp. 12-13.

8 Note this godly balance of self and others (in Phil. 2:4-5), which Jesus modeled: "Each of you should look *not only to your own interests*, but also to the *interests of others*. Your attitude should be the same as that of Christ Jesus."

9 Without getting into all the historical and theological details—including their respective Latin phrases—the next section will show that this first perspective says Jesus was "able to not sin," whereas the second view reasons that Jesus was "not able to sin." Although they play on the very same words, they are worlds apart in their presuppositions and outcomes.

10 See John 12:49-50; 14:31b; and 17:4, 8a.

11 Even as an adult, Jesus' limited mental abilities are displayed in two explicit ways: (1) Negatively put, Jesus confessed he didn't know when he was to return to earth (Matt. 24:36). (2) Positively stated, even in his final week of life, Jesus acknowledged he was still learning from the Father (John 15:15b). Also note the unusual twist on Jesus' learning from Hebrews 5:8.

12 A three-part "progression" of godly service includes the Father's work, then Jesus' ministry (John 5:17–9:4), and now it includes Christ's disciples (led by the Spirit). See this same progression in John 13:12-17, 34-35; 14:11-14, 23-24; 15:5-8, 9-12, 15-21; and 17:25-26.

13 Conversations with Dr. Michael Wilkens (from Talbot Theological Seminary) on this topic a few years ago prompted me to study this hypothesis further.

14 This statement, again, is not referring to Jesus' unique messianic experiences. Furthermore, this statement does not mean every precise detail of Jesus is reproducible elsewhere. For example, nobody healed ten lepers at once, but other people healed lepers.

15 It's the context of Jesus' doing miracles in the name of God and still claiming to be God himself that sets him apart from the other miracle workers of Scripture and gives us reason to believe (see John 20:30-31).

16 Several years earlier, Irenaeus put that same idea like this: "Jesus Christ, in his infinite love, has become what we are, in order that He may make us entirely what He is."

CHAPTER SEVEN

A HANDY WAY TO RECOGNIZE THE LAST ADAM

When Sir Thomas Malory wrote the tales of King Arthur, he included a list of 12 distinctive qualities that all true Christian knights shared. Among these characteristics were referre *(to obey all those that God had placed in authority),* frugalis *(marked by an evident thrifty stewardship),* abulere *(scrupulously clean in all personal habits and hygiene), and* sanctus *(piously reverent).*

—THE CHRISTIAN ALMANAC

I n these days of "nothing's sacred" swagger, one more irreverent item has made it to the shelves of children's literature. It's called *Jesus' Day Off.*[1] A handful of years ago, author/illustrator Nicholas Allan chronicled his fictitious account of the moment God's Son first realized he was "exhausted from saving the world." His miracles quickly turn defective. His teachings are found wanting.

After a thorough physical checkup, Allan's make-believe Jesus accepts his doctor's advice to take a day off. He chooses to cartwheel across the desert and play catch with his halo for pleasurable activities. However, at day's end, the man of Galilee wonders whether he's wasted opportunities to assist the needy. He seeks counsel from his heavenly "dad." Jesus is reminded that by helping himself he's also helped others. It is such a conveniently framed lesson for today's younger culture, already saturated with quasi-supernaturalism and self-centeredness.

The explicit falsehoods Allan teaches children are one thing. What's sad about *Jesus' Day Off*—though it's only one book—is that it symbolizes how we believers have failed to explain the whole Gospel. For starters, we neglect to paint a comprehensive picture of the Incarnation to fellow saints, a picture that extols Christ's humanity without compromising deity. We also neglect to exhibit that comprehensive portrait to the world at large. We particularly skip opportune moments to declare Jesus' fully mortal expressions of stress, humor, lifelong learning, suffering, questioning, intense agony, exhaustion, normal maturation, and pain.

It is fair to conclude we have disregarded Jesus' human need ever to take a day off! We have overlooked several Scriptures that tell us the Messiah carved out substantial time to be alone.[2] Bluntly stated, Nicholas Allan's views were partially right.

Because the church, as a whole, has violated the Scriptures—not "teaching [disciples] to obey *everything* [Jesus] commanded"—we have kept both saints and nonbelievers from recognizing Christ's full manhood. A second, possibly more damaging outcome emerges from our insubordination: By not teaching the total humanity of Jesus, we have unwittingly stiff-armed the very person many of us long to embrace. The Word-made-flesh wants to be our ultimate soul mate, our very best Friend. But our own defiance has forced us to go it alone.

Few disciples ever actualize Christ's offer of intimate companionship because we stumble over another related fact: The son of Mary was really like us. Specifically, as I showed in chapter 6, Jesus was like us in two critical ways: his human nature and his experiences.[3] The book of Hebrews takes great pains to establish these two facts, meticulously detailing how Christ was *"made* like [us] in every way" (2:17) and *"tempted* in every way, just as we are" (4:15). Jesus has "been there" and "done that," to use modern jargon. Our Lord is now poised as our heavenly High Priest to assist us with supernatural power when we daily cry: "What am I supposed to do?" and "How can I possibly go on?" That's the extraordinary potential he freely advertises. Yet, when we don't see his past earthly testimony as fully human, his present role as High Priest in heaven is severely hampered. He could do so much more for us if we would let him.

We inadvertently dismiss the exact Jesus we wish we knew.

What Jesus Taught Us About Ourselves (from His Own Example)

The Bible provides priceless insights into the nature of people, and a sizable portion of these truths is associated with Jesus' testimony. The Master Teacher, like a master painter, supplied at least two visual helps to illustrate Christian discipleship, drawing from his own personality. First, as a broad backdrop, our Lord embodied all the Garden legacies. This fact is especially seen in passages like his Upper Room instruction from John 13–16. Jesus identified the core of communion along with character, calling, and community. He deliberately and repeatedly blended these foundational components (see John 13:12-17; 14:10-14, 23-28; 15:1-17; 16:17-33). Figure 3.1 earlier noted how all three legacies are linked in partnership by our communion with the Creator.

On top of this broad backdrop, Jesus figuratively painted the second contribution of his portrait: the detailed brushstrokes from this first legacy of character. These finer features of Jesus' personal portfolio (as the Last Adam) are revealed, along with corollary traits of humanity as a whole. Table 7.1 embellishes this portrait, using the first three gifts. It arranges Jesus' personal names according to these first three Eden blessings, which represent character. In that table, those gifts are also matched with the Creation account and God's corresponding attributes. We better understand his humanity—and ours—through these comparisons. (Sidebar 7.1 in the *Supplemental Resource* shows the full complement of Jesus' names for the legacy of character.)

How Saints Must See Jesus—and Ourselves

Jesus was called "the Last Adam" only once in Scripture (1 Cor. 15:45b).[4] He was both similar to the first Adam and dissimilar. (Sidebar 7.2 in the *Supplemental Resource* discusses these two complementary Christian views of people.) He was similar to Adam (and to us) because he shared our complete humanity, minus sin. Sin was never an integral feature of original humanness. Sin was an aberration of our original parents. It was a deviation from the norm—and it still is. Chapter 4 taught that sin inauthenticates us, for it's not what the Author intended. In this sense Jesus was actually more human (more authentic) than Adam or Eve, when we see how they disobeyed, distorting *imago Dei*.

Several years ago my friend and mentor Ted Ward provided a simple perspective of people when he constructed the hand model of human development and spirituality.[5] Though Ward acknowledged the valuable truth that people are different, the brilliance of his creative model sprang from the universal traits found in every individual. His hand design accented what people have in common. Ward suggested that by symbolically using parts of the human hand, we better understand both Christ's humanness and our own, following this sequence: The thumb to the pinky finger portrays the physical, mental, emotional, social, and moral features of every individual. The palm represents the spiritual sphere,

TABLE 7.1

Summary of Our "Family Name" Legacy

	Complementary Descriptions of Super Nine Gifts	Super Nine References from Genesis	Attributes of God that People Mirror Through His Image	Comparable Super Nine Names or Traits for Jesus
Gift 1 God-like Physiques	We are **Physical** and **Spiritual** People.	• (2:7b) People were specially created (from God's breath) to become a "living being." • (2:9c) Trees "good for food" (implied need for nutrition and growth).	• The spirituality of God (John 4:24) refers to his immaterial nature; people partially reflect the Maker by their immaterial nature (Gen. 2:7; 1 Thess. 5:23). • Yet God is also something more than spirit—He "breathed" (Gen. 2:7) and walked in Eden (3:8) (see 2 Sam. 22:9, 10, 14, 16).	• A mere man (John 10:33) • A perfect man (Jas. 3:2) • Appeared in a body (1 Tim. 3:16) • God with us (Matt. 1:23) • Immanuel (Isa. 7:14; Matt. 1:23) • Made like his brothers in every way (Heb. 2:17) • The child Jesus (Luke 2:27) • The Last Adam (1 Cor. 15:45) • The Son of Man (John 1:51) • Who died and came to life again (Rev. 2:8)
Gift 2 Passionate Thinkers	We are an **Emotional** and **Rational** People.	• (2:18; 23-25) There was also potential to be lonely and loving. • (3:10) Fear resulted from sin.	• Intellectual abilities of God (knowledge and wisdom) are seen throughout Creation. • God's passion for Adam to have a "helper" (Gen. 2:18); also, God's grief arises from increasing wickedness (Gen. 6:6).	• The light of knowledge of the glory of God (2 Cor. 4:6) • The true light (John 1:9) • The truth (John 14:6) • The zeal for God's house (John 2:17) • The zeal of the LORD Almighty (Isa. 37:32) • Your light and your truth (Ps. 43:3)
Gift 3 Sensory Learners	We are **Sensory-Experience** People.	• Garden of Eden meant "hedging around delight." • (2:9b) Trees were created as "pleasing to the eye" (sight). • (2:9c) and "good for food" (taste). • (2:12b) There was "aromatic resin" (smell). • (3:3; 8) Post-sin references are made to touch and to hearing.	• Creator "saw" Creation was "good" (Gen. 1:4, 10, 12, 18, 25, and 31; also 2 Sam. 22:1-1, esp. vv. 7, 9a, 17; and Ps. 94:9); Creator God uses some forms of senses (cf. Eph. 5:2—Jesus was a "fragrant offering to God").	• A fragrant offering and sacrifice to God (Eph. 5:2) • Master teacher of experiential education (Luke 24:37-43) • The Bread of Life (John 6:35) • The spring of water welling up to eternal life (John 4:14) • Whose eyes are like blazing fire (Rev. 2:18) • Whose feet are like burnished bronze (Rev. 2:18) • You hear prayer (Ps. 65:2, 5)

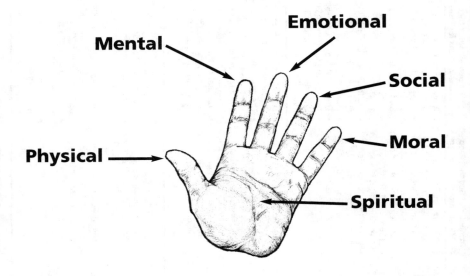

FIGURE 7.1

Hand Model of Human Development and Spirituality

Emotional

Mental

Social

Physical

Moral

Spiritual

which identifies the core of each person's existence—much as the church father Augustine reminded us.[6] Our spiritual life connects with each finger, yet it stands apart as a distinct entity (see figure 7.1).

The Apostle Paul referred to Adam as "a pattern of the one to come" (Rom. 5:14), namely Jesus. God's Son was patterned after Adam, but he was not exactly the same. First Corinthians 15:20-23 and 42-54 identify points of contrast, including phrases like heavenly versus earthly and imperishable versus perishable. So, where do we believers fit in? We share both the corrupt nature of the first man and the immortal nature of the last, as predicted, "And just as we have borne the likeness of the earthly man, so shall we bear the likeness of the man from heaven" (1 Cor. 15:49).

Consequently, there's a third perception about people that believers must acquire in order to fully understand their humanity: Besides viewing people as essentially different or the same, every saint must look in the mirror and see that the Last Adam (Jesus) is very similar to the one staring back at her. Apart from a few unique features (e.g., his deity and his messianic duties), the Last Adam gives us great hope, for we are told much about ourselves through his life. His thirty-three-year witness provides us with these immediate advantages:

- Jesus' earthly life enables us to see what our legacy of Name (character) ideally looked like (see sidebar 7.3 in the *Supplemental Resource*), since his name becomes ours.

- Jesus' life helps us see what a complete person looked like (Table 7.2 features the physical domain of Jesus; all remaining spheres are listed in sidebar 7.4 of the *Supplemental Resource*).

- Jesus' life shows us how we may access the power of the Father and Holy Spirit to live more "wholly holy" lives, as he did (see chapters 8 and 9).

Some Handy Applications for Discipleship

Ted Ward's model is biblically sound as well as practical. When we insert Jesus' example into Ward's design a couple of prominent concepts readily transfer to daily living. Our Lord's life, at an elementary level of discipleship, was intended for us to imitate. For instance, subsequent to studying the Son's display of emotions, we can be assured that "following Jesus" partially means we may experience those very same feelings—whether his anger, joy, or surprise.[7] We should understand our emotional life at a more substantial level as well: We possess the continuous need for image restoration. Unholy and unhealthy anger, as a case in point, must be rooted out of our lives—along with "rage, malice, slander, and filthy language"—as Colossians 3:8 instructs.

An oversimplified comparison of these two levels suggests that the

TABLE 7.2

Jesus' Holistic Model as "Last Adam"

- He had pain (Luke 2:21) from circumcision in the early days of His life.
- He had pain from the agony in the Garden (Luke 22:24), from being beaten at his arrest and trial (Matt. 26:67-68; John 19:1-3), and on the cross (Luke 23:32-34).
- He experienced hunger (Matt. 4:2; 21:19).
- He "ate" of "spiritual food" while never denying the value of physical food (John 4:32; Matt. 4:4; see also Matt. 11:18-19).
- Sometimes He was too busy to eat (Mark 3:20-21; 6:30-31) or to sleep (Luke 4:42; 6:12).
- He experienced exhaustion and need for sleep (Matt. 8:24).
- He refused drugs (Matt. 27:34), like narcotic gall to deaden pain.
- He required rest, quiet, and solitude (Mark 6:31-32).
- He ate . . . and will eat again in heaven (Luke 22:14-16).
- He was led by the Holy Spirit to a particular location (Matt. 4:1).
- He experienced thirst (John 4:7; 19:28).
- He experienced death (Luke 23:46).
- He used all five human senses (Luke 24:36-42).
- He ate healthy foods (figs, unleavened bread, lamb, wine, etc.).
- He exercised often (twenty years as a carpenter; walked regularly; climbed mountains—Matt. 5:1; 8:1; 14:23; 17:1; Luke 6:12; 9:28; John 6:15).
- He exhibited healthiness, fasting forty days (Matt. 4:1) and praying through the night (Luke 6:12).
- There were several indirect references to his health: (a) expressions of his emotions (humor, anger, bereavement); (b) close friendships; (c) intimate relationship with God and his Word; (d) his profession as a carpenter until age thirty (Mark 6:3); (e) his ability to potentially defend himself against wild animals (Mark 1:13).
- There were several indirect references to his own health via his teachings, such as: (a) the need for physical food, but not "bread alone" (Matt. 4:4); (b) the value of fasting (Matt. 9:15); (c) his orders to give Jarius's daughter "something to eat" (Mark 5:43) after he raised her from the dead; (d) his directions to His disciples to "retreat" because they didn't have a chance to eat (Mark 6:31); (e) his compassionate appreciation that, unless he fed the 4,000, they would "collapse on the way" home (Mark 8:3); (f) how he permitted his Twelve to pick grain and eat it on the Sabbath (Matt. 12:1-8); (g) how he used the "Great Physician" title (Luke 5:31); (h) his reference to being "Bread of Life" (John 6:35, 48); and (i) eternal water (John 4:13-14; 7:37, 39).

- He exhibited spiritual discipline "habits" (Luke 4:16; John 7:1-10; and Luke 9:62, re. perseverance; cf. his parents' similar habits and customs in Luke 2:21-24, 39, 41). Yet he also displayed some unconventional attitudes toward lawful routines, such as the observation of the Sabbath (Luke 6:1-11).
- He was not an ascetic like John (Matt. 11:18-19).
- There is controversy over what he may have "looked like." Some say "fairest of 10,000." Others refer to Isaiah 53:2 (before "Man of Sorrows" passage in v. 3); he possibly looked prematurely old—close to fifty (see John 8:57); the need for Judas to kiss him in the Garden, to distinguish him since he may have been "ordinary" looking (Matt. 26:48-49).
- He used his carpentry skills and money to provide for his family and friends (Mark 6:1-3; see also John 19:25-27).
- His body was the Temple of God (John 2:19-21; cf. 2 Cor. 6:16).
- God's power provided Jesus with the ability to heal the sick (Luke 5:17).
- He healed people—both spiritually (sins) and physically (Luke 5:18-26).
- He healed people with clay ointment (a possible reference to medicine; John 9:6-7).
- He had a need for angelic assistance from physical and spiritual trials (Matt. 4:11).

former category tends to be more *external* (we copy what we observe), while the latter centers on *internal* matters (we are transformed from the inside out). In other words, Jesus' example helps us disciples on an age-appropriate continuum of lesser to greater maturity (chapter 10 supplies a more detailed design of this model). Therefore, we may ideally progress:

- From Imitation—Disciples are called to "walk as Jesus did" (1 John 2:6)
- To Transformation—Disciples are called into the lifelong process of becoming like Jesus (Phil. 3:20-21; 1 Cor. 13:11-12; 2 Cor. 3:18)

Our restoration aim throughout life is neither private (independent) chores nor merely moral acts (i.e., Christians are not, first and foremost, just to be "good people"). These duties must be performed in conjunction with God the Holy Spirit. We work in partnership with him (following the lead of Jesus) and with each other in Christian community. We must also possess a greater objective beyond morality. Yes, Christians are to be "good," but that virtue (with scores of other virtues) is always—ALWAYS—a by-product, never the end in itself. "Goodness" is the sixth of nine "fruit of the Spirit." Fruit is always a by-product. Fruit is neither the root (cause) nor our ultimate aspiration.

Our greater objective is "being renewed . . . in the image of [our] Creator" (Col. 3:10b). When we are obedient to God, we are renewed in his image. And, as we are obedient and renewed, we simultaneously glorify our Maker.

The following section offers a practical analysis of Jesus' example through all five domains of his humanity. The spiritual sphere is wedded with each domain to maintain integration. Each pairing (of finger and palm) is also structured by realistic sets of tensions, which may (as in chapter 3) appear paradoxical. I hope these tensions will minimize simplistic either/or ways of thinking about humanity.

Table 7.3 was constructed as a reflective guide to personally assess and encourage growth. It may be used for one or all five of the subsequent studies on Christ's human domains.

Jesus' Physical/Spiritual Example: From Splinters to Sustenance

In chapter 4 I introduced the concept of *shalom* as one superb way to summarize the holistic health people once enjoyed. *Shalom* communicates holy and peaceful wholesomeness. Plantinga reminded believers that the authors of the Septuagint (the Greek translation of the Old Testament) chose the English equivalent of "hygiene" (meaning "holistic health") for the Hebrew *shalom*.[8] With that unusual English word, God's peace instantly takes on broader dimensions, both in terms of its comprehensive serenity and its physicality.

Just a quick reading of the Gospels supports Jesus' own spirituality

TABLE 7.3

A Reflection-Planning Tool to Follow Jesus' Example
(For one or all five human domains of Jesus' life)

1. Select one of the five integrated domains from Jesus' testimony in this section, then ask yourself the following questions, as they may pertain to you. What aspects from the human sphere you selected:
   a. Most excite you?
   b. Most convict you?
   c. Most surprise you?
   d. Most intrigue you (possibly for further study)?

2. What Bible passages (per human domain) would you like to analyze further? Why do these appeal to you?

3a. Recall the two application levels (imitation and transformation) and their meanings. In the next section, focus only on imitation.

   • First, select one subpoint within one domain of Jesus' integrated model, where you have noticed some signs of strength in your own life (e.g., building upon Jesus' joy within his emotional-spiritual sphere).

   • Second, on the following scale of 1–10 (10 is highest), place an "s" on the line at the point where you assess your present strength, in the category you chose. Be fair to yourself (not too critical or too lenient).

   1   2   3   4   5   6   7   8   9   10

   • Third, list a couple reasons why you made your evaluation the way you did.

   • Fourth, suggest one or two ways you may be able to further strengthen this area of maturity (your plan may include additional Bible study ideas, prayer, increased accountability, more intentional behavioral change, etc.)

3b. Within the category of Imitation, repeat these four steps, but think about—as opposed to a strength—an area of weakness. (Use the letter "w.")

4a & 4b. Finally, repeat the same steps you used in 3a and 3b, but focus on transformation instead. Keep in mind that transformation is much more substantial than imitation. Imitation is simple behavioral change; transformation is fuller personality change. Imitation is godly "doing"; transformation is godly "being" (it may be how someone else might describe you). Imitation is mostly external (from the individual who is growing); transformation is internal (inside the person). Imitation often focuses on alterations in your actions; transformation means character renewal to look like Christ.

as "hygiene" within this first domain. The Son of Man encountered growth, thirst, hunger, exhaustion, pain, and death to name only some of his physical needs and experiences.[9] As the first child of a carpenter—who worked in that trade for about twenty years—he was not immune to splinters, abrasions, and painful muscle pulls. It's a safe bet that Jesus smashed his thumb with a hammer more than once. And all that time he went without pain relief from ibuprofen or the benefit of a basic HMO.

Our Lord's normal physical frailties were, again, inseparably intertwined with his spirituality. Sometimes this first tensioned pair appeared to be in competition with itself. The most outstanding example of this potential for competition surfaced in the early wilderness temptations. The Devil's initial test (for Jesus to turn stones into bread) was intended to accent the internal rivalry between Jesus' physical and spiritual needs. But Jesus would have none of that dualistic thinking. He convincingly reminded the tempter that "man does not live on bread alone, but on every word that comes from the mouth of God" (Matt. 4:4).[10] He taught that every "man"—every person—requires this same blend of sustenance, both *literal* and *figurative* bread. The Son powerfully reinforced the daily physical/spiritual dependence that people should have upon their Maker.[11]

There are many additional references to Jesus' testimony from this first integrated domain. One interesting Scripture reveals that Mary's firstborn, as an adult, was sometimes so wrapped up in his ministries he neither ate nor slept.[12] Other Scriptures show how certain physiological routines had particular ties with Christ's faith. His parents taught him some of those integrated physical/spiritual habits (like the discipline of Sabbath-keeping).[13] And some of his holistic healings included a simultaneous combination of spiritual restoration and physical repair.[14]

Many other times Jesus attended to physical needs first, then spiritual. Often, our Lord focused only on the physical (healing) or the mental (teaching) domains. In fact, a careful study of Scripture reveals a shocking truth for those who are prone to narrowly define the spiritual domain (e.g., our duty to "save souls") as the only thing that Jesus was interested in. If we employ that restrictive definition, a thorough study of the four Gospels reveals that Jesus rarely did those types of "spiritual" things (chapter 8 discusses this subject further). Instead, Christ's teachings frequently coupled the physical and spiritual spheres of human need. One specific instance occurred when the Master Teacher chose his own body as a visual aid to explain the mysterious doctrine of the fleshly temple of God. The Apostle Paul later developed the significant lesson of our integrated human nature.[15]

In sum, Jesus repeatedly meshed the physical with the spiritual realities of people. He consistently spoke of our human needs as both earthly and heavenly. Then he purposefully modeled what it takes to feed the body as well as the soul. He proposed a consciously blended nutrition. Everything our Lord had to say about this first domain pairing comes down to one overarching hygienic, or healthy, principle: Take care of your body, for your God lives inside you.[16]

Jesus' Mental/Spiritual Example: From Surprises to Submission

Several instances from Christ's thought life tie us intimately to him as a fellow human being. One significant example of this is Jesus' testimony that he didn't know everything. There are two sides to this coin. The most familiar (and negative) example of his cognitive "deficiency" arises from our Lord's confession that only the Father knew when his Son would return to earth. On a more positive note, the Messiah similarly confessed limited human understanding when he admitted (during the last week of his life), "Everything I *learned* from my Father I have made known to you."[17]

This two-part testimony supplies an outstanding example of our Lord's *kenosis*—the voluntary self-emptying of his powers (earlier noted in chapter 6). Essentially Jesus learned the same way you and I do. He modeled a normal, lifelong learning pattern we may emulate, moving from lesser to greater knowledge. It should not alarm us, then, when we find that the man of Galilee was also trained in the school of hard knocks.[18] On a less grievous note, Jesus' ordinary mental capacity indicated he could be surprised, and he was.[19]

Another tensioned illustration of this discovery features our Lord's dependence upon both the human and the divine components of cognition. Multiple evidences of his "normal" mental growth are found in Scripture. Luke 2:40 and 52 remind us that Jesus grew up as most people do. So he was about as dependent upon the natural patterns of human development as any individual. The fundamental conclusions from this second domain steer us toward some exciting application points for today's saint. Much of Jesus' life paralleled what we encounter in our own mental/spiritual challenges. The Master Teacher intentionally provided us disciples with valuable ways to learn, including these lessons:

- Lesson 1: Learn truth wherever it is found—including "street knowledge" from any corner of the world.[20]
- Lesson 2: Value the exercise of serious, disciplined thought.[21]
- Lesson 3: Actively engage culture in the role of participant-learner, drawing understanding from careful observation.[22]

Learning may occur through these three categories, but that doesn't guarantee that insight will harmonize with God's revealed truth from his Word. On the other hand, there may be compatibility between these two sources. *This*-worldly truth—whenever it is truth—always complements *other*-worldly truth, since both originate with the same Creator.

The flip side of Jesus' "normal" learning patterns is that he also possessed divine insight.[23] We disciples are not explicitly told to replicate those aspects of his testimony. There are other features of his cognitive/spiritual domain, however, that are transferable. Jesus' study of God's *Word* (e.g., he intentionally memorized sayings from Moses[24]) and Jesus' study of God's *world* (e.g., he memorized cultural sayings about the weather[25]) are examples of Jesus' healthy thinking that never artificially divided itself between so-called sacred and secular knowledge. Whenever the Teacher highlighted the mental tasks of discipleship, he frequently linked—versus severed—heavenly and earthly duties. The Lord's Prayer taught disciples to consciously connect God's will "on earth as it is in heaven" (Matt. 6:10). In one less heralded passage (on the cost of following Jesus) our Lord essentially told the Twelve, "Use your heads!"[26] That's because logical thinking should not automatically be divorced from spirituality.

Jesus' imitable model for his disciples also included full submission to the Father and trust in the Holy Spirit. This balance is critical because, again, we tend to think in either/or categories, such as either Jesus' humanity was displayed or he exhibited supernatural abilities in a given situation. It's unusual for us to acknowledge the combination of his "normal" human growth stages, along with the times when he trusted God for divine outcomes. Yet that is precisely the combination Jesus teaches us to copy. For instance, the Son submitted to the power of the Holy Spirit to help him teach, then he told his followers to count on that same heavenly assistance.[27]

Jesus' Emotional/Spiritual Example: from Letting off Steam to Sympathy

The Man of Sorrows encountered every sin-free human emotion. Jesus' emotional display included astonishment, compassion, humor, exasperation, bereavement and tears, deep distress, empathy,[28] and extreme alertness (possibly even fear).[29] His example authorizes us to engage those same feelings. Jesus showed us what fully authentic humanness looks like. Only he could do that. And only he can give us power to transform our emotions to be more like his.

The setting for his first miracle—a festive wedding that probably lasted days—serves as an excellent case study to introduce this third domain. How we picture Jesus at that gala event says a lot about our perception of Jesus' humanity. It specifically tells us something about the repertoire of emotions we think he possessed. Our private imaginings also tend to reveal the emotions we deem acceptable for ourselves. So take a moment to contemplate the story of that initial miracle.

Since the Messiah never publicly accessed supernatural powers prior to Cana, we can assume that Jesus' personal invitation to that wedding signals the fact that he got along well with people. He knew how to have a good time. To restate it negatively (think of to some political figures during an election year), Jesus was not invited to the wedding because of celebrity status. And we can be certain he did not put in just a token appearance. I like to remind myself that our Lord stayed quite a while at Cana's wedding—long enough for the wine to run out.

We don't need to picture the Son of Man as "so serious he never enjoyed life," as one of my students once shared. He was clearly a man of passion. And that passion started with the fullest enjoyment of life and people. Christ's purposeful links between his emotional and his spiritual life (contrary to all other nonintegrated views) were revealed by his anger at the Pharisees' hard-heartedness, his zeal for the Father's work displayed during the temple cleansing, his personal joy in the Holy Spirit upon hearing the disciples' victorious missions report, and his struggling doubts about God's presence in the waning hours of his own life.[30] Because of the intense roller-coaster ride of passion that transported Jesus for thirty-three years—experiencing jubilant highs and turbulent lows—this third category of the emotional/spiritual domain may prove to be one of the most rewarding for future studies in discipleship (chart 7.1 in the *Supplemental Resource* gets us started in the right direction[31]).

Jesus' Social/Spiritual Example: From Solitary Moments to Subordination

The story is told of two brothers, six-year-old Javier and five-year-old Roberto, who are arguing over which TV channel to watch. After several minutes of scrapping, their mother steps in. Besides reestablishing order, she wants to offer some spiritual guidance. So she says, "Look, if you were Jesus, you would be willing to let your brother choose his channel selection first!" When she leaves, the boys sit in guilty silence—for about ten seconds. It takes Javier that long to craftily assess the situation. Turning to Roberto, he says, "Okay, you be Jesus first!"

As with the other three categories, "being Jesus" in this social/spiritual domain means we may embrace a refreshing array of human experiences. In Scripture we see our Lord's times of personal solitude (as well as times alone with his disciples) and his attendance at "black-tie" banquets thrown in his honor.[32] In addition to these events where the spotlight is focused on the Son, we notice that Christ also sought "offstage" settings to intentionally watch the behaviors of others. Jesus studied diverse people in many settings, ranging from interactions with adults to watching kids play in the marketplace.[33]

It doesn't take many of these Bible illustrations to conclude that Jesus needed people throughout his life. It's probably more accurate to say that Jesus was socially *dependent* on many people. That summary statement might initially sound strange to our ears. If we truly believe Jesus was 100 percent human, however, his dependence is a no-brainer. "Needing people" is so much a part of what it means to be made in God's image that it originally caused our Maker to essentially say (in Gen. 2:18), "Something's not quite right here, with Adam," before Eve came along. Remember, at that moment, Creation was still perfect. However, the image inside of Adam required companionship, much like the comradeship that the Trinity modeled. Adam was perfect—but not

complete—before Eve arrived. So the Creator judged it was "not good
. . . to be alone."

We find that Jesus' need for others literally came out of his own
mouth. That was true both at the start of his ministry—when Jesus
confessed his dependence upon John at his own baptism—and at the
very end—through Jesus' poignant cry for fellowship with his disciples,
as they convened for the Last Supper. Several other passages (between
this start and finish) likewise featured our Lord's interdependent nature.
One early reference recounts the Messiah's plan for the Twelve to be
"*with* him" as they began public service together.[34]

Another way we observe the Son's healthy dependency is to see him
when his social/spiritual needs were not met. We often forget that Jesus'
immediate family failed to support him.[35] At those precise moments,
Mary's son may have been more vulnerable than ever. Think about this:
his entire family deserted him. Jesus knew what it is like to grow up in
an unbelieving, nonsupportive family.

Where was he to turn? Back to his heavenly Home. Within the
setting of one of his family's rejections, Jesus redefined "family" as those
who perform the Father's will. Instantly, three things happened: He
galvanized everyone who has (or will have) a broken home (including
himself), by offering a larger, stronger, and superior familial support. He
also voluntarily associated himself with that very same group. He then
submitted himself to the caring hearts and loving hands of saints who
formed his newly designed family system.[36]

Jesus' Moral/Spiritual Example: From Scruples to Service

Morality and spirituality are similar, but they are not synonymous. Some
people miss this distinction, so this fifth domain of Ward's hand model
is not always associated with the Son of Man. Furthermore, two other
groups do their best to put Jesus' mature moral testimony on the endan-

gered species' list: Those who consciously choose to neglect Jesus' moral testimony because morality itself is too convicting (so it scares them off) and those who fear that an inordinate focus on morality could evolve into some "salvation by works" scheme. Lastly, many of us forget that morality is part of *imago Dei*. Gift 8 particularly addresses this Eden inheritance of ours.

For these and other reasons, Jesus' moral/spiritual example is often weakened, even though it is powerfully displayed in Scripture by:

- his preaching of the "Golden Rule"[37]
- his consistent evidence of personal character as a "man of integrity"[38]
- his famous plea for mercy in the story of the Good Samaritan[39]
- his noble instruction to especially help those who "cannot repay you"[40]
- his constant and faithful plan to help the poor[41]
- his motive to love, with pure intentions, even people of disrepute[42]
- his ethical call to be responsible stewards over Creation[43]

Because of the confusion that surrounds this final domain, it is necessary to first discern the major differences between morality and spirituality. Table 7.4 offers some crucial comparisons between morality and spirituality.

The Creator's highest purpose for all people begins with our core need for regeneration. This divine transformation reestablishes the converted individual as God's holy kin. Our Family Name is restored. But our life does not stop there. It only begins. Through the ongoing process of salvation (also known as sanctification), God does his daily work of refinement throughout our redeemed life. His intent is to bring all realms of our life into voluntary submission to his will, restoring us to be like the Son. That's why the phrase "born again" is so appropriate. We

---

TABLE 7.4

Morality and Spirituality

The two best biographies in Scripture that address this title subject are the comparable, yet contrasting, testimonies of the Rich Young Ruler and Cornelius. Both men exhibit splendid moral maturity while expressing their deep-seated spiritual need. Each man seeks God. Each desires more than what he has. Not "more" in terms of possessions, since both were quite well-to-do. Not "more" in terms of cultural status. One man was a Jew, one was a Gentile, yet both were well respected in their cultures. What each man sought was inner spiritual peace. Each longed for a lasting contentment the world couldn't provide. Each man desired salvation—God's *shalom*.

The Young Ruler and Cornelius inadvertently affirm a universal truth: *A mature moral life—as good as it is—is not good enough to satisfy people.* God's original image inside all people will *not* allow sensitive human beings to *not* ask the larger spiritual questions of life.

That is where these two cases diverge. Their lives end up at exact opposite points. The Ruler eventually says no to the Gospel, and the Roman centurion says yes. With that, this Gentile becomes the more complete person because he alone submits to the Father's restorative plan of redemption. He is rebirthed. Cornelius's strong moral self is reinvigorated by his new life in Christ. He is not perfect. But his divinely renewed spiritual "core"—for the first time since Eden—now provides the necessary growth potential for his moral domain to become all it was created to become.

In contrast, the Young Ruler does not repent (at least at this point in time). He leaves Jesus the way he came. The spiritual drive that prompted him to initially track down our Lord is still there. His hunger is still unresolved.

---

are reborn in every way, starting with the core of who we are. Changing metaphors, we then proceed as holy warriors, to fight for the King who has already won the war. We are called (among other tasks) to lay claim to the defeated territories within our own personalities formerly controlled by the old self.[44]

Hebrews 10:14 expresses this two-phase approach to God's holy work as well as any verse does, for it proclaims Jesus' "one sacrifice . . . has *made* perfect forever those who are *being made* holy." God's saving work is both an accomplished "done deal" (at Calvary, instantly giving new life to those who say yes to Jesus) and a continuous process (where daily restoration of every human domain is required). These grace-enabled daily accomplishments—reinforced by the saint's commitment—take us believers to the top of our game. They launch us into the highest levels of human potentiality found anywhere on planet Earth. A new understanding of and a new motive for moral maturity arise. Based upon image, for instance, justice is now viewed as nonnegotiable because God himself is just. When we seek justice for the poor, we intimately connect with our Maker.[45]

The hand model, then, allows us to see a significant wide-angle view of all people. When the hand model is interfaced with our three legacies from Eden, several parallels are drawn: Family Name, Family Business, and Family Ties each intersect with the five domains, grounded by the spiritual. And the moral domain offers connections to all three legacies (morality within character, vocation, and relationships). This comprehensive look at discipleship—returning to our heavenly Home, through the Garden, by valuing all we now have in Christ—yields the abundant life Jesus offered followers in John 10:10b. It is gusto living for his children. It is becoming fully human and fully Christian.

In sum, Jesus as the Last Adam enables us to understand the full potential for our individual lives, as indicated by Truth 7:

Truth 7

God's model for discipleship specifically focuses on what we received from our three Eden inheritances and how Jesus maximized each of those legacies by his own example— starting with his godly character, as the "Last Adam."

Conclusion

It has been said that no longer do people need to *seek* God, for we *see* him in Christ.[46] This is particularly true when we see Jesus as the personification of Family Name (character). Conversely, when we ignore even the smallest part of the Last Adam's testimony, we run the risk of missing the God-man. Creator-come-in-the-flesh did so for more than reasons of salvation. Jesus also wanted to demonstrate how to live a fully human life. It is here that comprehensive biblical designs, like the hand model, prove their usefulness. (To augment that model, the *Supplemental Resource* offers two helps: an overview of Elijah's holistic life in sidebar 7.5, and a listing of Jesus' holistic names in sidebar 7.6.)

Jesus wants to be our Redeemer. He also wants to be our life partner. He longs to be our best friend. He is more willing to be our soul mate than we will ever realize.

He makes these wonderfully intimate claims because he has always shared every breath we breathe.

---

1 Published by Doubleday (New York, 1998).

2 Sometimes these references to Jesus' solitary moments are linked with prayer: Mark 1:35, Mark 6:46, Luke 6:12, and Luke 9:18. The most useful passage on this theme is Luke 5:16, "But Jesus *often* withdrew to *lonely* places and *prayed*." But also consider Matthew 4:1-11, Matthew 14:13a, Luke 4:42a, John 6:15, and John 12:36. Especially study Jesus' intentional plan to get away for a while, when he purposefully traveled some distance to the non-Jewish seaport town of Tyre. His reason? Because he "did *not* want *anyone to know* . . . of *his presence* [there]" (Mark 7:24).

3 Because of his deity (including his unique calling), it is fair to say Jesus was *not* like us in (at least) two crucial ways: Jesus never possessed the negative features associated with sin and, conversely, he had a more pure and intimate tie with his Heavenly Father.

4 Contrary to many erring authors, preachers, and hymn writers, he is *not* "the Second Adam."

5 See Ted Ward's *Values Begin at Home*, 2nd ed. (Wheaton Ill.: Victor, 1989), p. 18.

6 Regarding God, Augustine concluded: "You make us for yourself, and our hearts find no peace until they rest in you" (Saint Augustine, *Confessions*, Book 1, paragraph 1, trans. R. S. Pine-Coffin [New York: Penguin, 1961], p. 21).

7 Certain domains overlap. "Surprise," for instance, can represent both emotional and mental domains. I like what Maria Harris says about the value of tensions in *Fashion Me a People*, published by Westminster/John Knox Press in 1989 (p. 27). First, Harris clarifies that

tension does not mean any mental or emotional strain. Rather, it's intended to convey "a tautness and a stretching, that positive condition created when important forces pull against each other." Harris prefers an artistic understanding of that term coupled with "the presence of intelligence." Harris concludes: "The lack of tension causes collapse. Tension is needed. Tension is good."

8 Plantinga plays out very practical implications of spiritual hygiene in today's believer, saying,

> Spiritual hygiene is the wholeness of resources, motive, purpose, and character typical of someone who fits snuggly into God's broad design for shalom. A spiritually hygienic person is one who combines strengths and flexibilities, disciplines and freedoms, all working together from a renewable source of vitality. . . . A spiritually whole person *longs* in certain classic ways. She longs for God and the beauty of God, for Christ and Christlikeness, for the dynamite of the Holy Spirit and spiritual maturity. She longs for spiritual hygiene itself—and not just as a consolation prize when she cannot be rich and envied instead. She longs for other human beings: She wants to love them and to be loved by them. She hungers for social justice. She longs for nature, for its beauties and graces, for the sheer particularity of the way of a squirrel with a nut. As we might expect, her longings dim from season to season. When they do, she longs to long again.

(From Cornelius Plantinga Jr., *Not the Way It's Supposed to Be* [Grand Rapids, Mich.: Eerdmans, 1995], p. 34.)

9 In subsequent paragraphs, to avoid too many endnote intrusions, I have put several Scripture references (cited in the preceding sentences) *into one endnote*. For example, for the six experiences of Jesus found in *this* sentence, see Luke 2:40 and 52; also John 4:7 and 19:28; also Matthew 4:2 and 21:19; also Matthew 8:24; also Matthew 26:67-68 and Luke 23:32-34; and also Luke 23:46.

10 This passage is special because Jesus quotes Moses' words from the Law. He purposefully recalls the comparable divine test that Israel was, likewise, given hundreds of years earlier in a parallel wilderness.

11 While wandering through their own desolate surroundings, Jehovah administers his final exam, so to speak, to his chosen people on the all-important subject of human anatomy. In a single sentence, through one quotable bumper sticker quote from Deuteronomy 8:3, Jesus standardized a crucial developmental fact about every man and woman: *All people require both literal bread and the symbolic Bread of Life.* Reminders like these instructions from the Master Teacher tell us who we really are. They endear us to the one "made like his brothers in every way" (Heb. 2:17a), to the one who knows us better than we'll ever know ourselves.

12 Mark 3:20-21 and 6:30-31; and Luke 6:12.

13 Luke 2:21-24, 39, and 41; Luke 4:16 and John 7:1-10.

14 Luke 5:18-26.

15 Jesus taught that he was both the Bread of Life (John 6:35, 48) and that he provided everlasting water (John 4:13-14; 7:37, 39). Also see John 2:19-21. In 2 Corinthians 6:16 Paul shows us—as Jesus taught—saints actually "house" God, in a certain sense, inside our bodies (see also John 14:17-18, 23).

16 Jesus promised the indwelling of the Trinity: first, from the Holy Spirit (John 14:16-17), then from the Son and the Father (John 14:23).

17 Matthew 24:36; also John 15:15b (along with Luke 2:52) acquaints us with Jesus' model of cognitive growth, both at the end of his life and at the start.

18 Hebrews 5:8 goes to great lengths to show that, even though he was God's Son, Jesus "*learned obedience* from what he *suffered*."

19 See Jesus' surprise reaction to the centurion's faith in Luke 7:9.

20 Luke 16:1-8.

21 Matthew 17:25 and 21:28.

22 Mark 12:41-44, Luke 13:1, and John 5:6.

23 For instance, Jesus knew what was going on inside the people he met (Matt. 9:1-8, esp. v. 4). See also Matthew 12:25, Luke 6:8, 9:47, and John 2:24-25.

24 Christ's first rebuttal of the Devil in the wilderness is found in Matthew 4:4, which quotes Deuteronomy 8:3b. Because of passages like Luke 2:40 and 52 (which refer to Jesus' intellectual growth), it's fair to assume that Jesus learned such truths the old-fashioned way: memorization. One thing's certain: Not having the conveniences of our day, Jesus didn't pull up Deuteronomy 8:3 on his personal laptop!

25 See Matthew 16:1-4.

26 Luke 14:25-33 demonstrate that clear and committed thinking must be employed to "count the cost" before following Jesus. It's a straightforward command, yet one that's rarely heard today.

27 Luke 4:14 and 18; also Matthew 10:20.

28 Matthew 8:10, Mark 6:1-6; Luke 2:49, John 3:10, and Matthew 15:28; also Matthew 9:36 and Mark 1:41. Humor includes Jesus' sarcasm (Matt. 12:3), puns (John 3:8), and wit (Luke 13:32); also Matthew 15:16, 17:17, and Mark 4:13; also Matthew 14:12-13 and John 11:35; also Mark 3:5; and also Luke 7:11-13.

29 This emotion of fear could have naturally resulted from Jesus' human responses to the various groups who opposed him (Matt. 12:14-15; Luke 4:28-30; John 8:59; 13:36) even toward those who wanted to make him king by force (John 6:12-15). Scripture is clear in distinguishing between an unhealthy, *ungodly fear* (which focuses on lies and emotionally paralyzes its victim) and a *godly fear* (which tells the truth and frees people to live with a wholesome respect for God). For example, five times in Luke 12:4-7 the word "afraid" or "fear" is used. There Jesus actually commands his followers to "fear him who . . . has power to throw you into hell." That's a healthy fear of God! Then (demonstrating the other type of destructive fear) Jesus commands, "Don't be afraid" (v. 7) of God in a paralyzing way, for he really does care for every person. All five uses of the word "fear" (or "afraid") come from the Greek root *phobos,* from which we get our English word "phobia."

Hebrews 5:7 refers to our Lord's "cries and tears," then concludes with his experiences of "*godly fear*" (RSV, see also KJV). The Greek root is *eulabeia,* which is also used in the Septuagint (the Greek translation of the Old Testament) within other contexts of healthy fear, as in Joshua 22:24 and Proverbs 28:14. To put it another way: *Not all fear is sinful.* Even apart from Jesus' fear (or godly respect) for the Father, it is quite possible that when the mobs charged him, Jesus experienced *sin-free fear, which precedes self-protection.*

30 Mark 3:5 expresses the only explicit anger of Jesus (in the NIV translation), although a few other passages imply it. Also see John 2:17; also Luke 10:21; and also Matthew 26:39 and 27:46-50.

31 Dick and Jane Mohline created this chart of thirty emotions that Jesus experienced. It represents extended insights from their earlier resource, *Emotional Wholeness: Connecting with the Emotions of Jesus* (Shippensburg, Penn.: Destiny Image Publishers, 1997).

32 Mark 1:45 and 7:24; also Mark 3:7a and 9:30; also Matthew 9:10, Luke 5:29, and Luke 19:1-10.

33 See Mark 12:41; Luke 13:1; and John 4:1-3, 5:1-6, 9:35. There are many other associations Jesus had with adults that can't be exhaustively listed here. Some of them are infrequently cited, like Luke 8:1-3, which implies "business ties" Jesus had with some women who financially backed his ministry. Also see Luke 7:31-32.

34 Matthew 3:13-15; also Luke 22:14-16; and also Mark 3:14.

35 John 7:1-5. Especially note the account detailed in Mark 3:21 ff.

36 See Mark 3:31-35, along with Luke 11:27-28. Also notice how (in Mark 5:18-20) *Jesus' ideal blend of family and faith is found:* Jesus commands the formerly demon-possessed man to "Go home to your family and tell them how much the Lord has done for you." Also see Mark 3:31-35; and John 14:18 and 19:25-27.

37 Matthew 7:12.

38 Matthew 22:16.

39 Luke 10:37.

40 Luke 14:12-14.

41 This biblical principle is, once again, totally grounded upon the *image of God*. See Old Testament connections between the Creator and the poor in Proverbs 14:31, 17:5, and 19:17; that tie is based upon image (note an extreme illustration of this principle in Gen. 9:6). See Jesus' model of this principle in Matthew 11:1-5; John 13:26-29 (esp. v. 29), and Acts 20:35.

42 John 8:1-11.

43 John 6:12.

44 Passages like Romans 6:1-14 and Colossians 3:1-17 speak about this battle-is-over-except-for-some-necessary-skirmishes metaphor within every believer's life.

45 See how Jeremiah 22:16 makes this connection: "'He defended the cause of the poor and needy, and so all went well. Is that not what it means to know me?' declares the Lord."

46 Leland Ryken, "Finding Heaven in Milton's *Paradise Lost*" in *Journey to the Celestial City*, Wayne Martindale, editor, Chicago: Moody, 1995, p. 75.

Chapter Eight

Honoring the Ways Jesus Worked for Restoration

> *Getting to know the God revealed in Jesus, I recognized I needed to change in many ways—yes, even to repent, for I had absorbed the hypocrisy, racism, and self-righteousness of my upbringing and contributed numerous sins of my own. I began to envision God less as a stern judge shaking his finger at my waywardness than as a doctor who prescribes behavior in my best interest in order to safeguard my health.*
>
> —PHILIP YANCEY

Disciples who lived at the time of our Lord asked a very normal question one day. It was logical and it was relevant to their faith. Every disciple since that day has raised the same query: "Once we trust Jesus as our Savior, what happens next—*what should we do with our lives?*"

I have referred to this topic as the believer's *calling*. It's what we were created to do. I have purposefully placed this subject between the corollary subjects of *character* (who we are, chapter 7) and *community* (how we are to relate, chapter 9). Each theme, of course, links to *communion* with our Creator.

Defining Terms and Reviewing History

When I define "calling," I am distinguishing that word from other synonyms like "job" or "career." A clever way to distinguish these terms comes from a story that was told about three workers who were interviewed at a construction site. Each was doing the same activity, yet each gave different responses when asked, "What are you doing?"

"Breaking stones," the first man replied.

"Making a living," the second one answered.

But the third person uniquely responded: "Building a cathedral."[1]

The first response conveys an attitude of work as merely a job—"punching the clock" of human employment. The second response has more of a sophistication attitude that is tied somewhat to a career. The third response comprehensively blends doing and being, calling and Character. There is also a supernatural mindset—a link with the Maker—for we are partners together in our Family Business.[2] The universal human quest for Calling is noted by Larry Crabb:[3] "*We all desire* to be adequate for a *meaningful task*, a desire to know that we are capable of taking hold of our world and *doing something valuable and well*." (See sidebar 8.1 in the *Supplemental Resource* for further insights on the Hebrew understanding of "work" as "worship.")

Church History

Church father Eusebius of Caesarea (A.D. 260–339) was one of the first prominent theologians to separate clergy from laity and sacred work from secular. As that myth gained popularity, so did the falsehood that "first-class Christians" were those who performed sacred work, uncontaminated by any manual labor. This bifurcation reached its apex by the Middle Ages.

The Reformers (emphasizing the priesthood of all believers) could no longer accept that misconception, which was now ingrained into more than a thousand years of tradition. They rejuvenated the word "vocation" (from the Latin *vocatio*, meaning "a calling" and its linguistic cousin *vocare*, meaning "to call"). They purposefully stressed that *every person* possesses a *calling* and that the *Creator* initiates that *calling* (as Caller). These supercharged ideas so radically influenced the Reformation that everybody was affected. For example, Martin Luther declared that the cobbler praised his Creator whenever he made a pair of shoes and "the plowboy and the milkmaid" also performed priestly work—he in his plowing, she in her milking.

All work became sacred once again. When we participate in our Business partnership, we do holy labor. That is why C. S. Lewis contended that "the work of a Beethoven, and the work of a charwoman, become spiritual on precisely the same condition, that of being offered to God, of being done humbly 'as to the Lord.'" He added, "A mole must dig to the glory of God and a cock must crow."[4] (Sidebar 8.2, in the *Supplemental Resource*, has additional insights on how calling was shaped by the Reformers.)

A Unique Prophet with a Pertinent Message

John the Baptist was a fascinating man of God. He was one of a kind, as these traits show:

- Both of John's parents were filled with the Holy Spirit (Luke 1:41, 67).
- Elizabeth (John's mother) was pregnant at the same time Mary (Jesus' mother) was, and they shared meaningful fellowship (Luke 1:39-45, 56).
- John was a close relative of Jesus.
- John's ministry spanned both the Old and the New Testaments.[5]
- John "prepared the way" for Jesus as Messiah (fulfilling Isa. 40:3-5).

- John's baptism[6] was unique, calling for Israel to repent of her sin, in anticipation of the Christ.[7] John had the awesome task of baptizing Jesus.[8]

We come to the undeniable conclusion that God's unique work in John's life yielded some very special blessings. Hold that thought, now, as you contemplate practical truths about calling from Luke 3:10-14. Three times in this short passage the crucial question that introduced this chapter is voiced: What should we do with our lives? And three times John the Baptist offers surprising, yet godly advice. Think about it this way: God's unique prophet—Jesus' kin, the one who alone prepared Israel for the Messiah, and the person who baptized the Son—now serves the vital role of *vocational guidance counselor* for believers. What does John say? As important as that question is, it is equally important to discover what John does *not* say.

I'll give you a clue as to what advice you can expect from John: It is based upon our creation, and it relates to our Maker's breath, which we inherited. Yes, *imago Dei* undergirds John's counsel regarding the Christian's vocation.

Vocational Advice That John Did *Not* Give

John the Baptist's initial answer to the crowd's natural question, "What should we do then?" (Luke 3:10), complements the definition of complete discipleship employed throughout this book. Quite frankly, anybody who does not opt for some type of wide-angle lens of Christian faith will have serious problems figuring out John's remarks in this passage—both what he *says* and what he does *not say*.

Consider those two categories in reverse, starting with what John did *not say*. John did *not* say to those who wanted to serve the Messiah: "Go to seminary" or "Sell your business and join Jesus' ministry." Those who take a conventional (more restricted) view of how Christian commitment should influence full-time professional vocation—whether back then or now—find John's advice an anomaly. They may exhibit confusion, as they attempt to discover "what's missing" from this prophet's comments.

Is this criticism fair? Could John have offered a "professional" option to his hearers? I believe he could. Recall that some form of professional ministry had long been a part of Israel's history, through its "school of prophets" (see 2 Kings 6:1-4). Also, although Jesus' ministry at this point had neither been made public nor had he come to John for baptism, those two events occurred shortly thereafter in Luke 3:21. The fourth Gospel tells us that Jesus made himself known "the next day" (see John 1:19-34, esp. v. 29). It's important to note that, although Jesus personally had no disciples at this time, John the Baptist did. The Gospel of John (starting in 1:35) tells us that Andrew was one of two disciples of John who, upon hearing his mentor proclaim, "Look, the Lamb of God!" left the baptizer and joined Jesus. Andrew represented (for want of a better phrase) the conventional "full-time ministry" position. He joined the ranks of the "professional disciples" who followed Jesus—one who left his business and was "schooled" for three years by the Master Teacher. But John the Baptist never indicates that Andrew's professional calling—which was perfect for him—was normative for the masses. (See table 8.1 for more reflections on so-called sacred and secular professions.)

Vocational Advice for All People

As table 8.2 indicates, John the Baptist's vocational counseling in Luke 3 consistently affirms Eden's three legacies, including its communion core. The reason John consistently takes the crowd's "vertical" question—"What do we now do for God?"—and answers it with "horizontal" advice based upon human character, vocation, and relationships is the image of God. Specifically, the prophet's advice to the crowd recaptures the Creation Equation, noted in chapters 3 and 5. John's instruction to

TABLE 8.1

Matthew and Zacchaeus as "Sacred" and "Secular" Workers

None of John's advice (in Luke 3) to tax-collectors and soldiers advocated "full-time, professional Christian service." John was not opposed to this vocational category, but this man of God realized that particular vocational category resembled the exception not the rule. Think of John's advice in terms of two other revenue collectors from the Gospels: Zacchaeus was the "rule"; Matthew (also called Levi) was the "exception" to the rule. The first man served Jesus by consciously remaining within the tax-collecting profession, as "salt" and "light" to a dark world. The second consciously withdrew from his tax-collection work, after Jesus' special invitation to follow Him. Both of these callings were part of the Father's broad plan for Christian vocations. Both were valid, since God blessed each man's choice. We can imagine these two complementary callings in Luke 3 (much like today) as dependent upon personal giftedness, leading of the Holy Spirit, differing personalities, varying opportunities, and other factors.

I am using the terms "rule" and "exception" merely to contrast group size, not to make a value-laden judgment. There have always been far fewer Matthews than Zacchaeuses. Furthermore, I am suggesting there is no vocational hierarchy. No single profession is "better" than another in God's eyes. There is no hierarchy within any particular profession. A committed Christian teacher, for example, should not automatically assume she is expected to instruct students at a Christian school.

God equally blessed Matthew and Zacchaeus, because each obeyed God's voice. Each was sold out to his particular calling. There was no competition between them, no rank ordering of one as "best" and another as "second best." Those guidelines are clear in Scripture. The problem comes when our cultures cloud that design. Rarely do our churches value "secular" vocations as equals when they stand alongside their "Christian" counterparts. Believers who have felt called to work in the health professions, in the arts, and in politics have especially encountered this two-tiered critique. It is the rare fellowship that shows a converted Zacchaeus how to return to his vocation (rather than withdraw from it) to vigorously serve Christ as salt and light. In sum, this is why John's simple advice on calling is so crucial for every disciple. Even what he doesn't say counts.

clothe and to feed the needy (Luke 3:11) sounds very much like Old Testament passages from Isaiah 58:6-7 and Jesus' later words in Matthew 25:31-46. John was essentially saying, "Don't forget that how you treat *people* is how you treat *God*."

TABLE 8.2

John the Baptist's Vocational Advice
(Based upon the Three Legacies)

Audience	John's Advice (from Luke 3)	How Each Legacy is Addressed
The Crowd	• "The man with two tunics should share with him who has none" (v. 11a). • "And the one who has food should do the same" (v. 11b).	• CHARACTER (Compassion) • CALLING (Use of material possessions) • COMMUNITY (Care for the less fortunate) . . . all linked with • COMMUNION[1]
The Tax Collectors	• "Don't collect any more than you are required to" (v. 13).	• CHARACTER (Integrity) • CALLING (Fair tax collection) • COMMUNITY (Justice) . . . all linked with • COMMUNION[2]
The Soldiers	• "Don't extort money" (v. 14b). • "And don't accuse people falsely" (v. 14c). • "—Be content with your pay" (v. 14d).	• CHARACTER (Honesty and contentment) • CALLING (Proper income and godly leadership) • COMMUNITY (The ninth commandment)[3] . . . all linked with • COMMUNION

1 John's advice affirms the Creation Equation (noted in chapters 3 and 5). Several other Old Testament portions connect these vertical and horizontal duties (e.g., Isa. 58:6-7 and Jer. 22:16), as do several New Testament portions (Matt. 22:34-40; 25:31-46 and Jas. 1:27).

2 In Luke 19:8-10, a parallel passage on the proper conduct of converted tax collectors, Jesus surprisingly links Zacchaeus's restorative plan of fourfold reimbursement (for those he has cheated) with "salvation." Here is an example of what a comprehensive picture of redemption looks like, through all the legacies.

3 The Ninth Commandment of the Decalogue is cited here, regarding false testimony (Exod. 20:16). Jesus reminds us how the last half of the Decalogue is summarized by "love your neighbor as yourself" (Matt. 19:18-19)—and how that summary is closely tied to loving God completely (Matt. 22:34-40).

True commitment to our Maker is always indicated by compassionate and practical service to human beings. It's impossible to divide godly devotion from moral behavior toward others.

Vocational Advice to Tax Collectors and to Enemy Soldiers

Aside from prostitution, there were no vocations more despicable than tax collectors and enemy soldiers. Consequently, John's advice becomes twice as potent (see table 8.2). If there were any professions that Christ's brand-new disciples should have been told to avoid, it had to be these two. But that's *not* what John tells these tax collectors and soldiers to do. He instructs members of both groups to do just the opposite: return to their jobs, then exhibit Christ's light in practical ways.[9]

The first group was virtually synonymous with "traitor" since, as Jews, they took as much tax money from their own people as they could get away with. The second group, the despised Romans, was Israel's oppressive enemy. Corruption within both vocations was normal and expected. Participants from both groups extorted money and abused people. Both vocations represented all the crookedness of Eden's legacies—specifically, the twisted consequences from Gift 4: *un*kind rulers.

John the Baptist's brief but notable words urged tax collectors and soldiers to obey the Cultural Mandate. Eden's directive to Adam and Eve was reinforced for John's audience.

What Jesus *Said* Disciples Are to Do

We now zoom in on the complementary categories our Lord personally created (in John 12:49–50; 14:31), which detail God's complete plan for restoration: (1) What *Jesus said* (and how he said it); and (2) What *Jesus did*. These two categories provide a basis for biblical calling, both his and ours. Sidebar 8.3 in the *Supplemental Resource* summarizes the overarching instruction of our Lord regarding vocation.

The best way to think about our calling—what we were all created to do—is to remember we are partners with our Maker. As partners, we are called to continue God the Creator's work from the Garden. We are called to listen to the Holy Spirit as he reminds us of Christ's complete message of redemption, and then we are to obey that voice. Such obedience brings God glory. It does not matter if we are paid for this work. What matters is that we are faithful partners.

That's the *first* message about calling that Jesus bequeathed to his disciples, and it is the foundational message. It is no less than the awesome task of continuing the Trinity's work. But that was not our Lord's only teaching about what we were created to do. Jesus also taught his followers some general principles about work (see sidebar 8.4 in the *Supplemental Resource*). Then he applauded praiseworthy qualities found within certain kinds of work.

Commendations for Specific Work-Partnerships

Since chapter 1 informed us that discipleship is a conspiracy, we followers should regularly attempt to "breathe together with Jesus" in our respective callings. We share his breath, as we likewise share his mission and passion. We represent junior partners with him in the Family Business.

A careful study of God's Word demonstrates that Jesus spoke positively about several professions, even though some of those references were not much more than illustrative. Undergirding each is *imago Dei*. Each derives value from our Eden inheritance. And each profession is uniquely applauded for its breathing-together-with-Jesus potential. Consequently, in the following sections, workers that Jesus specifically commended are labeled "conspirators." Each one serves within God's larger kingdom, cooperatively partnering with its King.

Conspirators Who Assist Needy People

Throughout Scripture we are told that those who advocate the cause of the oppressed share a special relationship with the Creator (e.g., Jer. 22:16). This group promotes a wide range of merciful human services that provide food, clothing, hospitality, and prison ministry. They perform their humane services secretly, not wanting to stand in the spotlight. Furthermore, these advocates act selflessly, not seeking any payback. They also offer godly counsel and they seek justice. These conspirators are particularly attracted to the underprivileged and to the powerless (including children, widows, the poor, and so forth).[10]

Conspirators Who Lead

Jesus made explicit references to leadership positions as well. He contrasted the Gentile "lord it over" model to his own servant-shepherd plan, whereby compassionate, godly leaders willingly die for those they serve. For Jesus, leaders must also be impartial, providing help for society's underdogs.[11]

Conspirators Who Work within Political Systems

When Jesus taught, "Give to Caesar what is Caesar's" (Matt. 22:21), he implied that government service is one more viable calling. His purposeful encounters with representatives from that group lends his support: The healing of the centurion's servant (Luke 7:1-10) brought an unexpected reward—Jesus' public declaration of the centurion's humility and faith. Also, Zacchaeus's noble plan of financial restoration to those he cheated brought Jesus' instant commendation. Jesus twice linked "salvation" to Zacchaeus's plan, again saying a lot about the Son's integrative view of complete redemption (see Luke 19:1-10).

Conspirators Who Serve Nurturing Roles

The fourth vocational group that Jesus affirms includes a potpourri of callings that heal and nurture. These individuals heal body, mind, and soul. And they incorporate a wide range of people—from those who care for children to nutritionists and from physicians to teachers and religious leaders.[12]

Conspirators Who Study and Research

Jesus said a lot about people who are thinkers, paralleling Gift 2 and Gift 6. This category included students in general (see Matt. 10:24-25), but it also included two kinds of scientists. Jesus' support for natural science was implied a few times by his use of these illustrations: the value of studying birds and plant life (Matt. 6:26-28); the importance of knowing "fruit" trees and their "root" system (Matt. 7:16-20); the significance of understanding the natural cycle of a seed's maturation (Mark 4:26-29); and the benefit of knowing about predictable weather patterns, from the study of atmospheric conditions (Matt. 16:1-4).

Support for social science is also implied by Jesus' instruction and through his own lifestyle. Usually we miss the point, for example, that when our Lord saw the widow drop her two small coins into the offering, the event was part of his consistent strategy of observation. Mark 12:41 introduces that story this way: "Jesus *sat down opposite the place* where the offerings were put and *watched the crowd. . . .*" His people watching was deliberate. In another example, Matthew 11:16-17 records Jesus' recitation of a children's poem-song he overheard in the marketplace. The fact that the Master Teacher intentionally took the time to memorize that piece, then to employ it in his instruction, tells us the value Jesus placed on the social science professions (e.g., anthropology), which study people and their cultures.

Conspirators Who Honed Skilled Trades

Multiple, positive references are likewise made to work that requires professional skills. I stress the word "positive," since it is one thing to allude to a profession in general; it's another matter to cite how a trade is done well. The One who handcrafted Creation also noted commendable vocational lessons for disciples from within particular trades (see table 8.3). Jesus consciously celebrated a half dozen professions. Each one portrays a vital link to our second legacy of calling. Each enables us to visualize how the Lord supported the Eden inheritance of what we were created to do. They also permit us to observe the Father's full, restorative design for his people since Creation; the Son's continuation of that original pattern and the church's duty to perpetuate that same

---

TABLE 8.3

How Jesus Affirmed Skilled Professionals

The Master Teacher identified a half dozen vocations that can assist today's disciple. Jesus' examples are more than illustrations, since he highlights commendable traits evident in superior workmanship. Specifically, Jesus tells us followers:

- How a respected baker purposefully takes yeast and mixes it into "a large amount of flour until it worked all through the dough." Jesus' positive analogy compares to the attention found in the unveiling of the kingdom of heaven (Matt. 13:33).
- How a wise engineer builds his house upon rock—not sand—which will stand the test of severe weather. This analogy relates to the importance of both hearing and applying Jesus' words as a blueprint for life (Matt. 7:24-27; also Luke 14:28-33).
- How an experienced farmer knows the value of planting seeds in "good soil" versus hardened paths, rocky places, or thorny ground. This analogy links the Gospel "seed" to soils of personal receptivity—how individuals similarly respond to the Good News (Matt. 13:1-9; 18-23).
- How a veteran fisherman separates "all kinds of fish" he catches in his net. He "collected the good fish in baskets, but threw the bad away." Again, this analogy compares to God's kingdom when, one day, the good and the evil will be separated (Matt. 13:47-50).
- How a smart financial investor makes sound decisions, minimally accruing basic interest from his banking deposits. This analogy has to do with making wise investments in eternal matters (Matt. 25:14-30).
- How a successful businessman makes shrewd purchases through a simple process: "looking for" valuable items (in this case, fine pearls); discovering an item of "great value"; making plans to go back home to sell everything; then returning to buy the valuable pearl. The kingdom of heaven, once again, is the featured point of this parable (Matt. 13:45-46)—how to exhibit a keen sense of "business" in this world and the next.

design by the Holy Spirit's power. These categories don't exhaust every single vocation that Jesus approved, but they represent a sizable portion of the complete restoration package he came to earth to offer. If these examples of work appear to look and sound like what the Garden might have been like, that's because they are. When we take our calling seriously, we receive both a larger picture and a greater power to do what we were put here to do. It's one more reason why "breathing together with Jesus" in our vocation just makes sense.

What Jesus *Did* to Show Us What to Do

So far I have reviewed what Jesus *said* about work. I have explained that his sayings were exactly what God wanted him to share (John 12:49-50). I have stated that the Son's work continued the Father's ministry since Creation. And I have challenged us disciples with our Lord's command to pick up where he left off. I have summarized this perpetual calling to be part of the complete restoration of God's people. I have also noted that *imago Dei* provides the foundation for our work, particularly expressed through our Eden legacies.

Now we turn to the second, complementary side of Jesus' witness: *What he did.*

Jesus the Carpenter

Eighteen to three, or six to one.[13] Those ratios contrast the length of Jesus' professional carpenter years to his last three years of life. What's even more stunning is that almost nobody pays attention to that lopsided contrast, including the four Gospel writers.

But we can't afford to neglect those ratios if we want to know what complete discipleship means.[14]

I didn't say Jesus' eighteen years of carpentry totally escaped the notice of Matthew, Mark, Luke, and John. They *do* say something about this topic, to which we now turn our attention. Josh McDowell's excellent book on apologetics reminds the church that Christ was *More Than a Carpenter*. To arrive at the conclusion that he was "more," however, we must initially realize that *Jesus was a carpenter*. Yes, he was called the "son of Joseph" and "the carpenter's son." But Jesus was called "the carpenter" as well.[15] This blue-collar tradesman made a handful of references to his former profession when he later referred to items like "sawdust" and "planks" of wood, "the measure" people use, "narrow" and "wide" gates, and wise and foolish "builders." His parables included the building of barns. He predicted his role as the Cornerstone who would be rejected by builders. And he foretold his own death and resurrection in terms of the temple demolition and reconstruction.[16]

Carpentry and Discipleship

One might ask: "What does this review of Jesus' first profession have to do with discipleship?" If a conventional perspective of the Christian life is chosen—one that's narrower and disintegrated—the answer is "Nothing." However, if we remain committed to a comprehensive and connected view of discipleship, the proper answer is, "Quite a bit." Jesus' eighteen years of carpentry *were* part of the Father's best plan for him. Those years *were* an integral component of God's calling. Jesus was *not* just biding his time—"Punching a time card" in the carpenter's shop, so to speak—anxiously awaiting God's "real" calling at the end of his earthly life.

Jesus' eighteen years as a carpenter were not wasted.

Whenever we settle for the conventional pattern of Christian vocations, we reach a radically different end: Jesus' role as carpenter implicitly gets pitted against his role as Savior. When that occurs, Jesus' blue-collar years quickly vaporize. For all intents and purposes, those eighteen years don't exist. We must be very careful not to fall for "the-more-a-truth-is-mentioned-the-more-truthful-it-must-be" myth. Just because the Scriptures rarely mention Jesus' carpentry years does not mean they are unimportant.

Carpentry and the Cultural Mandate

Faithful disciples must consciously alter our "this-versus-that" thinking in favor of a "this-*and*-that" mindset. We must pledge our allegiance to this inclusive principle, when it comes to Christ's vocational example, for *Jesus' eighteen years of carpentry uphold the Cultural Mandate.*

A couple of years ago I was privileged to speak to an internationally recognized author-pastor (I'll call him David) about this subject of vocation. Because David was a man of God who deliberately thought through the *why* of our faith, I purposefully sought him out. I asked something like: "How do you preach to individuals in your congregation to help them fulfill their personal calling?" Without waiting for his reply, I moved to a follow-up question, which really got at the heart of what I was after: "How do you help those 95 percent who *won't* sense God leading them into full-time Christian work?"

I grew excited by David's opening response: "Well, I know what I would tell them *not* to settle for—to just 'witness on the job' or just 'do their job well.'" David's answers hooked me. "We're on the same page," I excitedly told him. But I wanted more. "Okay, so what do you actually tell them *to do?*," I pressed. His brief pause made me hold my breath. After a few seconds of reflection David confessed: "I don't know." My shoulders sagged at the letdown.

The Cultural Mandate—along with image restoration—now satisfies my query of David. I wish I had known the implication of that Bible doctrine years ago. Today I'm certain our Lord's eighteen-year example in Nazareth strengthens our Eden Mandate, since all three legacies were displayed by his carpentry trade:

- *Family Name* (character)—Jesus' physical prowess (gift 1) was undoubtedly affirmed. Furthermore, his mental skills and passion for excellence (gift 2), along with his sensory abilities to learn and to grow (gift 3) were accentuated.

- *Family Business* (calling)—Jesus' personal maturation "in favor with God and man" (Luke 2:52) correlated with the dual dimensions of gift 5 (worshipful worker). More than likely, both parts of gift 6 (creative and logical problem solving) figured into the daily challenges of his trade.

- *Family Ties* (community)—The fact that this carpenter was the primary breadwinner for his earthly family (gift 7)[17] can't go unnoticed. Likewise, Jesus' work skills and reputation met the needs of Nazareth (gift 8) and its vicinity (gift 9).[18]

The English Reformer Hugh Latimer put his finger on the core contribution that Jesus' carpentry made to *all* vocations, when he said: "Our Savior Christ . . . was a carpenter, and got his living with great labor. Therefore let no man disdain . . . to follow him in a common calling and occupation. For as he blessed our nature with taking upon him the shape of man, so in his doing he blessed all occupations and arts."[19]

Returning to this chapter's focus on calling, table 8.4 supplies an overview of Jesus' names that are pertinent. Scriptures record several of his titles—based upon gifts 4, 5, and 6—each of which connects with this second legacy of Family Business.

A couple of final thoughts about how Jesus' carpentry relates to discipleship are found in sidebar 8.5 in the *Supplemental Resource*. The first contribution is quantitative and the second is qualitative.

To oversimplify at the risk of disintegration: Jesus' carpentry years largely represented the Cultural Mandate, whereas his three post-baptismal years primarily represented the Gospel Mandate. Combined, Jesus' personal "job description" within his Father's business included *both*

TABLE 8.4
Image, the Legacy of Family Business, and Jesus' Names

	Complementary Descriptions of Super Nine Gifts	Super Nine References from Genesis	Attributes of God that People Mirror Through His Image	Comparable Super Nine Names or Traits for Jesus
Gift 4 Kind Rulers	We are **Regal** and **Ecological** People	• (1:28b) People were commanded to "*subdue*" and to "*rule* over" the Garden. • (2:15b) People were also commanded to "*take care*" of the Garden.	• *El-Shaddai* values God's power and *faithfulness* to his people, through his consistent blessings and comfort (see Gen. 17:1; 28:3; Exod. 6:2-3).	• Gentle (Matt. 11:29) • Judge of the Living and the Dead (Acts 10:42) • King of Kings (Rev. 19:16) • That Great Shepherd of the Sheep (Heb. 13:20) • The Lord of All the Earth (Josh. 3:13) • The Lord of Peace (2 Thess. 3:16) • The Ruler of God's Creation (Rev. 3:14)
Gift 5 Worshipful Workers	We are **Restful** and **Worshipful** People	• (2:2-3) There was an implied command to rest as the Creator did (compare Exod. 20:8-11). • (2:15a) People were commanded to "*work*" the Garden.	• Creator modeled his commendable work pattern through his Creation (Gen. 1:1-31). • Creator rested on the seventh day, making it holy (Gen. 2:2).	• Lord of the Sabbath (Mark 2:27-28) • Master-Builder of Firm Foundation (1 Cor. 3:11; Matt. 7:24-25) • One Who faithfully Worshiped (Luke 4:16) • One Who Took Purposeful Time Off (Mark 7:24; 6:30-32)
Gift 6 Artists & Scientists	We are **Creative** and **Orderly** People	• (2:19-20) *Multiple capacities for curiosity, adventure, and organization for creative problem solving were first given to people.* • (3:1-6) *This same potential within people was found in the very first sin.*	• (Gen. 2:19b) *The Creator shows personal "curiosity": He personally "brought [the animals] to the man to see what he would name them" then "God made woman (vv. 19-22). In Ps. 147:4 God similarly names the stars* • *The orderliness of God is displayed in Creation (Gen. 1:1-31; a parallel order is found in the church 1 Cor. 14:33, 40).*	• A Precious Cornerstone (Isa. 28:16) • A Teacher Who Has Come from God (John 3:2) • He Who Created (Rev. 106) • One Who Creatively Escaped Entrapment (Matt. 22:22) • One Who Carefully Observed Life (Matt. 6:26-30; Mark 12:41) • One Who Sang Hymns (Matt. 26:30) • Physician (Luke 4:23) • Teacher (Matt. 10:25) • The Carpenter (Mark 6:3) • The Potter (Jer. 18:6)

duties. Both ultimately intertwined. We never need to settle for a mindset that figuratively portrays the Gospel Mandate as Sunday and the Cultural Mandate as Monday. *Both* require calling, and *both* play a significant role in "whole person" restoration. Illustratively, the outcome of the Gospel Mandate *births* an individual through new life in Christ, while the Gospel *and* the Cultural Mandate *grow* that individual. Table 8.5 provides several comparisons and contrasts of these complementary directives.

Jesus, the Great—and Holistic—Physician

Before we focus on what Jesus did for the last three years of earthly life, we should reacquaint ourselves with his view of people. What Jesus believed about humans affects every significant area in his life: his Incarnation, his ministries as Carpenter and Great Physician, his death and resurrection, his Great Commission to every disciple, and his present service as our Great High Priest. *Whenever we cut corners on Christ's understanding of people, we are always left with an inferior form of discipleship.* (Sidebar 8.6 in the *Supplemental Resource* provides an overview of Jesus' beliefs about people.) Jesus concisely summarizes his own restorative ministry as *"healing the whole man"* (John 7:23b). That pivotal phrase aids us in our own calling, if we obediently imitate our Lord's efforts on earth. To join him as junior partners in God's Family Business, we start by respecting our "clients" the way he did.

A Trio of Tasks

After we remind ourselves of who people are, we review the job description of our partnership, which Jesus modeled. All four Gospels show us that Jesus' last three years included three consistent activities: *teaching*, *preaching*, and *healing*. This is particularly true in Matthew's Gospel,[20] but it is also true for Luke and for John.[21] Once we acknowledge these three tasks, we face two questions. The first relates to cohesiveness: "In

TABLE 8.5
The Disciple's Calling from Two Prominent Mandates

	Jesus' Personal Example	Original Primary Audience	Primary Purpose	Explanation in Terms of God's Image	Mandate Status	Complementary Points of Emphasis (within the Hand Model)
The Cultural Mandate (Gen. 1:28; 2:5b, 15, 19-20)	*The Carpenter*	God's First Two People: *Son Adam and Daughter Eve* (who were created)	To show us *how to live* (Stewardship focus)	*Perfect* image bearers knew precisely *how to live* the way God intended them to live.	*Unique* to Every Disciple (Resulting in an Individual Partnership)	*Outward/Inward* — Begin by expressing one's calling through five *domains* (fingers); "palm" is seen as source of divine empowerment (see Luke 3:7-14)
The Gospel Mandate (Matt. 28:18-20)	*The Great Physician* (preaching, teaching, and healing)	God's Kingdom People: *Sons and Daughters* (who were ransomed and recreated)	To show us *how to live again* (Redemption-focus)	*Redeemed* image bearers were recreated to live as God originally intended.	*Common* to Every Disciple (Resulting in a Collective Proclamation)	*Inward/Outward* — Start with "palm" as source for new life in Christ (Col. 2:6), then focus on implications for the five *domains* (Col. 3:1-17)

what way, if any, do these three activities relate to each other?" The next question (discussed in this chapter's conclusion) is one of transference: "To what extent is Jesus' three-part model also ours?" The answers we provide help unlock the challenges of calling.

Our options for the first question about cohesiveness include:

- Randomness: Essentially no relationship exists between Jesus' teaching, preaching, and healing ministries.

- Eliteness: Some relationship between the tasks may exist, but preaching is so predominant that it tends to exclude the contribution of the other two.[22]

- Complementariness: Each of these three tasks serves its own purpose. Each task is necessary, and each works in harmony with the other two, promoting the total well-being of *shalom*.

I prefer the third option since that corresponds with Jesus' view of people as "whole man." Complementariness also coincides with the thoroughness found in Jesus' Great Commission[23] and the testimony (at the end of his ministry) where our Lord confesses he said and did "exactly" what the Father planned for him.[24] Jesus' vocational tasks were balanced this way: *Teaching* emphasized the healing of the mind. It stressed the *proximate* health of *shalom*, insights that may promote godly well-being.[25] If godly teaching is well received, it may literally cause participants to "come near" fuller health and restoration. One example is obeying the teaching of the fifth Commandment (to honor parents), for it holds the potential of "long life" (Exod. 20:12; Matt. 15:3-6; Eph. 6:1-3).

Healing was aimed at restoring the body. In Christ's ministry this second category included a range of miracles that brought sick persons back to health. But it likewise included food miracles—maintaining a well person's health.[26] Furthermore, this activity broadly incorporated Jesus' call for justice, in which social and moral needs are met (see Luke 4:14-21). One could even claim that Jesus' restorative healing extended beyond the individual to her environments with implications that included care for animals and ecological goals (based upon the Cultural Mandate).[27] In short, healing primarily focused on the holistic health of the body. It represented the *immediate* health of *shalom*, yet that health was tempered by temporal life. Lazarus, though blessed by Jesus' touch of new life, eventually died a second time.

Preaching was the core of Jesus' design for godly well-being.[28] It held the potential for *ultimate* health within the Creator's *shalom*. Preaching focused on the healing of the human soul and spirit, reuniting believing individuals with their Maker. Though central (see Luke 4:43), as we have seen, preaching was not the exclusive activity of Jesus' daily agenda. An inseparable relationship between all three ministry tasks and Jesus' Great Physician role was regularly featured in all four gospels.[29] Each task supplied an important contribution to the Creator's promise of *shalom*. Table 8.6, along with sidebar 8.7 (in the *Supplemental Resource*), supply more comparisons and contrasts of these three tasks.

Conclusion

When we ponder the numerous passages where Jesus' holistic healings occurred, key principles about biblical calling surface:

- We must value *the complete story of human origin*, especially our creation in God's image.
- We must value *the complete picture of human beings*, especially our holistic nature (versus a souls-only perspective).
- We must value *the complete message we bring to every human*, both the Cultural Mandate (which customizes the individual's conspiracy with Christ) and the Gospel Mandate (which describes the common directive for all disciples).
- We must value *the complete methods we use to communicate the message* of our calling. This is particularly true when it comes to

TABLE 8.6

Jesus' Trio of Complementary Tasks

	Primary Focus of Restoration	Explanation of "Holy Wholeness" (*Shalom*)	Types of Well-Being or *Shalom* (with Sample Passages)	How Each Task Promotes Full Humanness	Scriptures Where All Three Tasks Occur Simultaneously
Jesus' Task of **Teaching**	Healing of the *Mind*	Wholeness That Is *Pedagogically Envisioned* (via kingdom-consciousness, such as in Matt. 5–7)	*Proximate Health:* Truth that *may* lead to health (e.g., "Don't worry" about life, food, clothes, or tomorrow, but seek first God's kingdom [Matt. 6:25–34])	"A student [literally 'disciple'] ... who is fully trained will be like his teacher" (Luke 6:40). Jesus consistently taught *maximum* and *integrated* wholeness in every human sphere: • Physical-spiritual health (John 4:13-14) • Mental-spiritual health (Luke 14:25-33) • Emotional-spiritual health (John 15:11) • Social-spiritual health (Mark 3:31-35) • Moral-spiritual health (Matt. 25:31-46)	1. Jesus' ministry throughout *Galilee* (Matt. 4:23-25) 2. Jesus' work "through *all* towns and villages" (Matt. 9:35) ... 3. ... with his ensuing command for his *"workers" to do the same* (v. 38; also Matt. 10:24-25) 4. Jesus' response to John's doubt involves all three tasks (Matt. 11:1-6; Luke 7:20-23) 5. Jesus' first sermon in hometown of Nazareth addresses these same three tasks, as predicted by Isaiah 61:1-2 (see Luke 4:14-21, esp. v. 18-19)
Jesus' Task of **Healing**	Healing of the *Body*	Wholeness That Is *Partially Encountered* (via miracles of healing, nutrition, and healthy relationships)	*Immediate* (yet temporal) *Health:* by healing (Matt. 8:14-17) and food (Matt. 14:15-21) and justice (Luke 4:18)	Jesus consistently expressed his concern for holistic health through miracles that integrated the physical domain with the other five domains: • Physical-spiritual (John 5 re: blind man) • Physical-mental-spiritual (Luke 5:17-26 re: healing of body, truth, and sins [see v. 24]) • Physical-emotional (Mark 5—two cases of healing and emotional well-being, featuring peace [v. 34] and fear [v. 36]) • Physical-social (Luke 7:11-17—Widow of Nain's son raised from the dead, "and Jesus gave him back to his mother" [v. 15b]) • Physical-moral (Matt. 12:15-21— Jesus' healing is linked to fulfillment of Isaiah's prophecy, involving the proclamation of justice)	
Jesus' Task of **Preaching**	Healing of the *Soul and Spirit*	Wholeness That Is *Permanently Experienced* (via salvation)	*Ultimate* (and eternal) *Health:* both abundant (temporal) life (John 10:10) and eternal life (John 3:16)	Jesus constantly *preached* a fuller eternal and abundant (temporal) health (especially see John 10:10b *"life* ... to *the full"*) • With blind man (John 9:35-39) • At Lazarus's funeral (John 11:25-26) • To unbelieving Jews (John 12:37-50) • To disciples: He *"has eternal life* [now] ... *has crossed over from death to life"* (John 5:24); see also "Gospel" ties in Rom. 8:28-30; 1 Cor. 10:31–11:1; 2 Cor. 3:12–4:6 (esp. 3:18; 4:3-4); Gal. 4:13-19; Phil. 3:15-21	

the noncoercive options we supply our hearers, as we offer them God's *shalom* (see sidebar 8.8 in the *Supplemental Resource*).

When we take a serious and a comprehensive view of Christian vocation, we intersect with another popular concept: our life purpose to glorify our Creator. Many believers consider "glorifying God" their primary life objective. Yet—since that objective involves theological jargon—I suspect fewer than 20 percent who claim that purpose could explain what that phrase actually means, using both accurate theology *and* everyday (jargon-free) language.

As I noted earlier, one useful synonym for "glory" is "reflection." We glorify God whenever we obey him, which positively reflects his Name. We also glorify God when we mature, growing through our image-reflecting lives (see 2 Cor. 3:18–4:6). Again, a parallel from family life is worth repeating: Whenever a child accomplishes a praiseworthy feat, it reflects both on her and on her parents. That principle applies, in reverse, when a child is associated with a degrading activity. Calling provides one more avenue through which we disciples may glorify our Maker. And Jesus modeled the pattern we must emulate. Our Lord testifies to his Father at the end of his life: "I have *brought you glory* on earth *by completing the work* you gave me to do" (John 17:4, italics mine; see John 15:7-8). When we finish our own godly calling—just as Jesus did—we similarly shower our Creator-Savior with glory.[30] Jesus' model is still pertinent today. We follow Christ's lead, as junior partners in the Family Business, by attending to both the Cultural Mandate and the Gospel Mandate.

Furthermore, as the Carpenter-Great Physician modeled for us—and the rest of the New Testament taught—when we obey these two mandates, we embrace the "Image Mandate," as well. This collective focus (see figure 8.1) allows us to become the complete disciples we were created to be.

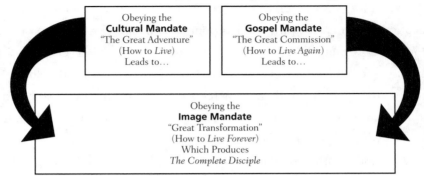

FIGURE 8.1

Mandates for the Complete Disciple

Obeying the
Cultural Mandate
"The Great Adventure"
(How to *Live*)
Leads to…

Obeying the
Gospel Mandate
"The Great Commission"
(How to *Live Again*)
Leads to…

Obeying the
Image Mandate
"Great Transformation"
(How to *Live Forever*)
Which Produces
The Complete Disciple

In sum, this chapter has enabled us to understand how to pursue our vocation, the lifelong plan that God has for us. Putting it another way, we could say:

Truth 8

God's model for discipleship emphasizes the second legacy of godly calling—through Jesus' complementary roles as "Carpenter" and "Great Physician"—promoting both the Cultural Mandate and the Gospel Mandate.

Years ago, someone used the analogy that evangelism is like one beggar telling another where he could find bread. That phrase was very helpful, especially because of its jargon-free charm. When I think about a comparable analogy for biblical vocation—for evangelism *and* discipleship—the analogy I suggest is this: "Discipleship is one needy person telling another *how to be wholly holy again*."

1 This story is attributed to Peter Schultz in the *Hope Health Letter* (Vol. XV, No. 1), January 1995. Published by the Hope Heart Institute in Seattle, Wash.

2 James W. Fowler says, "Vocation is the response a person makes with his or her total self to the address of God and to the calling to partnership," in his *Becoming Adult, Becoming Christian* (San Francisco: Harper & Row, 1984), p. 95.

3 From Crabb's *Understanding People: Deep Longings for Relationship* (Grand Rapids, Mich.: Zondervan, 1987), p. 114. Italics are mine.

4 From Lewis's *The Weight of Glory and Other Addresses* (New York: Macmillan, 1949), pp 48-49.

5 Technically speaking, John was an Old Testament prophet, since his ministry was before the church age, which started on the Day of Pentecost in Acts 2.

6 One of the best phrases for understanding what baptism means is "public identification with . . ."—such as identification with Jesus. See how that phrase helps unlock the meaning of Paul's instruction in Romans 6:1-7 See endnote 8 below.

7 See Luke 3:3 and John 1:19-34.

8 Since John was preaching repentance, he seemed somewhat confused when Jesus also asked to be baptized (Matt. 3:13-14). But Jesus' baptism was different—it uniquely displayed the Son's *public identification with* the Father's righteous plan for him (Matt. 3:15-17).

9 It's useful to see how Cornelius (in Acts 10:1-7, 23-48) represents the vocational exemplar for soldiering, just as Zacchaeus does for tax collecting. Both remain within their professional discipline, and both exhibit a similar lifestyle of pragmatic godliness in a fallen world.

10 See Matthew 6:2-4; 10:40-42; 25:31-46; Luke 6:36; 10:25-37; 14:13-14; and John 19:25-27.

11 See Matthew 9:36, Luke 2:24-30, and John 10:11. Also note Jesus' personal fulfillment of Isaiah's prophecy on justice (in Matt. 12:15-21), along with his indictment of Jewish leaders (from John 10:34-36), who ignored their primary *image* duty of dominion (based upon Ps. 84).

12 See Matthew 18:1-11 and Luke 11:11-13; Mark 5:36-43 and Matthew 15:32; Matthew 9:10-13; Matthew 7:28-29 and Luke 11:52; Mark 12:38-40 and Luke 18:9-14.

13 Within Jewish culture, a boy became a man at age twelve. Consequently eighteen years of carpentry work includes Jesus' years of twelve to thirty (even though his early years were served as an apprentice).

14 Remember that John 21:25 tells us, "Jesus *did many other things* as well"—but it would be impossible to exhaustively record everything he accomplished.

15 See John 6:41-42, Matthew 13:55, and Mark 6:3.

16 See Matthew 7:3-5 and Luke 6:41-42; Matthew 7:1-2 and Luke 6:38b; Matthew 7:13-14, Luke 13:22-27 and John 10:6-11; Matthew 7:24-27 and Luke 6:46-49; Luke 12:18; Matthew 21:42; and John 2:19-22.

17 Tradition has it that Jesus' earthly father, Joseph, died sometime during Jesus' early teen years, so Jesus, being the oldest, probably provided for his mother and siblings.

18 I believe that *part* of the reason that his hometown "*All* spoke *well* of him" in Luke 4:22a is because of his respected reputation as a carpenter in their village for so many years (notice the connection with "Joseph's son" in verse 22b).

19 Cited in Alister E. McGrath, *Spirituality in an Age of Change* (Zondervan, 1994), pages 146-147.

20 See *Encountering the New Testament: A Historical and Theological Survey* by Walter A. Elwell and Robert W. Yarbrough (Grand Rapids, Mich.: Baker, 1998), p, 83.

21 See Luke 4:14-21, especially vv. 18-19. The fourth Gospel repeatedly notes the *integration* of this trio of tasks in John 3 (with Nicodemus); John 4 (woman at the well); John 5 (man at Bethesda's pool); John 6 (the Bread of Life message); John 9 (the blind man); and John 11 (raising Lazarus).

22 This view has historically represented the conventional position of most conservative believers. Verses like Luke 4:43 are cited by its members.

23 Matthew 28:20 commands Christ's followers to be "*teaching* [future disciples] to obey *everything* I have commanded you." Teaching is the only one of the three tasks explicitly commanded—preaching and healing are not publicly featured.

24 See John 12:49-50 and 14:31. The sheer time commitment that Jesus made to "teaching" and "healing" tells me option 1 is not feasible and option 2 is too lopsided.

25 "Proximate" comes from the Latin *proximare,* meaning "to come near."

26 Luke 9:11b-13 combines these two categories. Notice how Jesus, possessing an excellent knowledge of human nature, tells his disciples that sending the crowd of four thousand away—without feeding them—may cause them to "collapse on the way" (Matt. 15:32b).

27 The latter category includes Jesus' stilling of the storm (Luke 8:22-25), his attention to nature's wildlife (Matt. 6:25-33), and his concern for the "leftovers" from his miracle feeding (John 6:12). The former category extends from verses like Proverbs 12:10: "A righteous man cares for the needs of his animal." Consequently, in certain pockets of revivals throughout church history—like those influenced by John and Charles Wesley—converts were recognized by how they subsequently cared for domestic animals.

28 Some people struggle with the question "How is teaching different from preaching?" For me, they are more alike than dissimilar. Preaching represents a certain kind of teaching— specifically, how to be "born again" and related topics. In contrast to the many *divergent* topics of Jesus' teaching, his preaching was *convergent,* centering on the Good News of salvation. Elwell and Yarbrough [in their book *Encountering the New Testament* (Grand Rapids, Michigan: Baker, 1998), p. 83] describe the latter topic, from Matthew, like this: "As a preacher, Jesus had the prophetic ministry of expounding the Word of God, calling the people to repentance, warning of the coming judgment of God on sin, announcing the arrival of the kingdom of God (4:17), and proclaiming the end of the age with his glorious second coming (24-25)."

29 All four Gospels emphasize some aspect of the Great Physician role: Matthew 9:10-13 refers to the crowd's perceived healthiness and sickness, then cites Hosea 6:6; Mark 2:17 brings up this same truth, minus Hosea; Luke 5:31 (without Hosea) adds a holistic dimension of spiritual health with Jesus' mission: "I . . . call . . . sinners to repentance"; and John 9:35-41 note the literal and symbolic uses of blindness, along with its personified cure.

30 We tend to forget how *human "work"* and *God's plan* are frequently connected in Scripture to honor the Creator. Consider these well-known passages: Matthew 5:16, 1 Corinthians 15:58, Ephesians 2:10, Colossians 1:9-10, 2 Timothy 3:16-17, and Hebrews 13:20-21.

Chapter Nine

Following Our Beloved Brother's Maturing Ways

> *Everywhere a greater joy is preceded by a greater suffering.*
>
> —AUGUSTINE
>
> *Pleasure and Pain are represented as twins, as though they were joined together, for there is never the one without the other. . . . They are made . . . out of the same trunk because they have one and the same foundation.*
>
> —LEONARDO DA VINCI

Have you ever thought: "I wonder what it would have been like to be Jesus' parents"? I have.

Which would have been harder, as his parent—to know Jesus was God's Son or to realize you had a perfect human living under your roof? Years ago, that subject wasn't even an issue for me. I was always awestruck whenever I contemplated the first category. Now I'm not so sure which would have been more difficult. If anything, I revere Jesus' deity more than ever. My respect for his humanity, however, has grown by tremendous leaps and bounds.

Consider that topic of parenting Jesus from this angle: Jesus' sinless life was lived in the context of his experience that illustrated his humanity: pain and hunger; curiosity, coupled with the ceaseless question "Why?"; the craving for hugs, along with other needs to be loved; the desire for belonging within supportive relationships; and the drive to do right.[1] My sense is that—along with his perfect character—came perfect expectations, for Himself and others.

So I say this in the very best sense: Jesus was a demanding child. If you believe that's too harsh, picture in your mind's eye a perfect boy encountering a very imperfect world. And before you are tempted to think that encounter would have ended in a draw—an irresistible force meeting the immovable object—remember that Jesus never compromised. He never backed down. He never lost.

Mary's Reactions to Her Perfect Child

One of my all-time favorite questions I ask my students is this: "Where are the two Scriptures that say Jesus' mother 'pondered' and 'treasured' personal memories 'in her heart'—and what was it that Mary was personally experiencing both of these times?" Listeners often mention the second event more quickly than the first, even though both passages are found in the same Bible book—and the very same chapter. (Though only several verses apart, it is helpful to know these verses are separated by twelve silent years of Mary's life.) The first time that Mary ponders comes right after the shepherds' encounter, on the night of Messiah's birth (Luke 2:19). The second time, the more familiar story, occurs subsequent to Mary and Joseph's discovery of Jesus in the temple, after a panic-filled search for three stressful days (Luke 2:51b).

Mary cherished both experiences, though her emotions ran the gamut of highest highs and lowest lows. Each event was so poignant and so personal that she could not even confide in her own faithful husband.

At a Crossroads

But why these two particular times? What was their common denominator? I propose each was a "crossroads moment"—a special time when our Maker deliberately enters into our lives to mature us. Ironically (as this chapter illustrates), a crossroads moment involves two traits we believe are mutually exclusive: the trait of pleasure and the trait of pain. Don't twist that proposal into saying God is sadistic. He does not delight in cruelty. Our Father is sovereign and redemptive. He graciously intervenes in our sinful lives, takes the painful consequences of our transgressions, then transforms them into his godliness.

Return to Luke 2:19 and 51. The first crossroad followed Mary's divine encounter with the shepherds. Sounds like all "pleasure," right? Don't forget that meeting occurred within hours of Mary's delivery—without any anesthetic, midwife, or medical help. The second crossroad put the ultimate spin on the phrase "lost and found," evoking feelings of extreme anxiety and urgency in Jesus' parents. I say the next sentence tongue-in-cheek—but full of reverence—imagining the dialogue between these parents on that third day of searching in Jerusalem. What if Mary and Joseph, at the peak of exasperation, said to each other: "Just think what the history books will say about us! 'They lost the Son of God!'"

And these two episodes were probably not the only "pondering" moments for Mary. It is likely she made many other similar entries into her spiritual journal. (There's an excellent chance, in fact, that one more entry occurred after another experience in that same chapter when Mary received her "blessing" from Simeon in the temple.[2])

These were not Kodak® moments.

In both cases from Luke 2, it appears the mother of the Son of God deliberately stopped and asked herself: "What just happened here? How am I supposed to interpret these experiences in my life? Am I doing all that I'm supposed to do?" And possibly a more stressful inquiry, "Have I unwittingly become an obstacle in God's master plan?" If you empathize with any one of Mary's questions, it's because you have probably raised those same issues. Those are the kinds of questions most disciples ask, each in their own way.

What This Chapter Offers

Chapter 9 analyzes how Jesus related to others—and how those relationships brought about his own maturity as a human being. This chapter covers the third (and last) legacy of community. It is a crucial topic for discipleship, because it helps explain a very complex subject: how Jesus grew and how we can mature, as well—how we become complete disciples.

You may have trouble with that last sentence. You may have never considered the idea that Jesus matured, because he was God and sin-free. But Jesus was also a person—and since he modeled healthy humanity, Jesus matured. Think of Jesus' maturity like this: Nobody ever dismisses the notion that Jesus grew up physically. Not even his critics. We all can imagine him being a normal human—growing up and wearing out his clothes, becoming stronger, his voice deepening, starting a beard, and taking longer strides as he walked beside his dad.

However, millions of Christians have a very difficult time with every other human domain in our Lord's life—even with convincing Bible facts in full view. Just days ago, for instance, I was talking to a respected Christian leader (within the field of mental health) about the Son's testimony of cognitive growth (from John 15:15b). This professional exclaimed: "I've never thought about Jesus in those terms at all!" I became as surprised as he did, but for a completely different reason. My surprise was one of disappointment, saddened by the prospect that his response represented the vast majority of believers. The implications of such widespread ignorance within the church are even more disheartening.

We disciples must recover the provocative truth that Jesus matured, from infancy to adulthood, in every single sphere of his manhood. Furthermore—and this fact signals one essential application for discipleship—the Bible never portrays Jesus' holistic development in some isolated or unique way. Our Lord grew, for the most part, like any other person. He matured in conventional human patterns.[3] He modeled what it means to mature in the precise ways God wants all his people to grow. If we believers apply just this single truth to our lives, discipleship would radically transform first us, then our culture. Whenever this fuller message of Scripture is told (i.e., the facts about Jesus' total human life and the believers' greater potential), broader implications of the Good News emerge as well.[4]

Consider a relatively unknown passage, in 1 John 2:5b-6: "This is how we know we are in him: Whoever claims to live in him *must walk as Jesus did.*" Based upon this straightforward instruction, one would be hard-pressed to defend the view that the Apostle John was settling for only the spiritual features of his Savior's life (such as how he prayed or preached). Certainly spiritual issues lie at the heart of John's message, but these two verses stress our Lord's complete testimony—and our emulation of it—consistently lived seven days a week and twenty-four hours a day.[5]

One More Glance at Mary's Heart "Treasures"

Take Mary's ponderings one step further. I already noted how those two explicit references (Luke 2:19, 51) portray crossroad moments of maturity in her life—times of blended pain and pleasure. But these same two events were times when Jesus also matured: first, when he was an infant and then, second, as he entered adulthood (according to Jewish custom). Both passages succinctly explain Jesus' holistic growth. Just one verse following Mary's second treasured moment, Luke described the Son, at age twelve, in these refreshingly human terms of development: "Jesus *grew* in wisdom and stature and in favor with God and men" (Luke 2:52). Likewise, with Mary's first "pondering"—exactly one week after meeting the shepherds—Luke similarly records: "And the child *grew* and became strong; he was filled with wisdom, and the grace of God was upon him" (Luke 2:40).

The point I am making is that Jesus' mother experienced her own memorable moments, in part, because she was an eyewitness to the holistic growth of the God-man! How many questions have you ever had about the God-became-flesh mystery? They may have been as simple as "Why did the God-man get tired and hungry?" or more complex inquiries like "How could the God-man cry as well as learn?" Ask yourself how many of those same questions—and so many more—Mary must have processed in her daily thoughts. She watched the Creator grow up! Mary's ponderings, then, partially occurred because she watched this unique phenomenon.

If we want to comprehend how Jesus related to others and matured, we must review who Jesus was and how he grew. His age-appropriate growth provides the backdrop for our own growth.

Where Chapter 9 Fits into Complete Discipleship

I have made it a point to stress the biblical fact that Jesus was far more than our Savior. That's neither disrespectful nor compromising. The Son's purpose was to redeem us *and* to show us how to live. Anything less than this two-part objective cheapens "life to the full," which Jesus offered believers in John 10:10b. His human example—as one who mirrored God as we do—revealed who we are. His Last Adam title (chapter 7) showed us what to do, first by his carpenter role and then by his Great Physician role (chapter 8). Correspondingly, chapter 9 reminds disciples that our Lord went before us to demonstrate how to relate to others, as our Beloved Brother. The book of Hebrews describes how Jesus is our brother:

- Hebrews 2:11: "Both the one who makes men holy and those who are made holy are of the same family. So Jesus is not ashamed to call them brothers" (also see Matt. 28:10).
- Hebrews 2:12: "He says, 'I will declare your name to my brothers; in the presence of the congregation I will sing your praises.'"
- Hebrews 2:14: "Since the children have flesh and blood, he too shared their humanity so that by his death he might destroy him who holds the power of death—that is, the devil."
- Hebrews 2:17: "For this reason he had to be made like his brothers in every way, in order that he might become a merciful and faithful high priest in service to God, and that he might make atonement for the sins of the people."

This familial tie between Jesus and his disciples was consciously established by Christ early in his ministry, just after his own family publicly opposed him (Mark 3:20-35). We become members of Jesus' newfound family when our Savior rebreathes new life into us through the Holy Spirit. We express evidence of that new birth by obeying our Father's will—exhibiting our legitimacy as sons and daughters. Table 9.1 reminds us of the last three gifts from the legacy of community—especially as they connect with Jesus' names and traits. Table 9.2 proposes some pivotal points for this chapter. The rest of this chapter analyzes particular features of Jesus' pattern for human maturity, as they pertain to the legacy of community.

TABLE 9.1

Image, the Legacy of Community, and Jesus' Names

	Complementary Descriptions of Super Nine Gifts	Super Nine References from Genesis	Attributes of God that People Mirror Through His Image	Comparable Super Nine Names or Traits for Jesus
Gift 7 Intimate Families	We are *Individual* and *Relational* People	• (1:27) God created people as "male and female." • (2:18) It was "not good for the man to be alone." • (2:20-25) The woman was created for man.	• Yahweh features the covenant faithfulness of God (Gen. 28:3; Ex. 3:12-16; 6:2-3) • Relational references to God (plural pronouns "us" and "we") refer to the communitarian (or fellowship) attribute of the Trinity (Gen. 1:26 and 3:22)	• Brother of Every Believer (Mark 3:35) • Family Advocate (Matt. 19:1-9) • Not Ashamed to Call Us Brothers (Heb. 2:11-12) • The Bridegroom of the Bride (John 3:29) • The Brother of James, Joseph, Judas, and Simon (Mark 6:3) • The Son of Abraham (Matt. 1:1) • The Son of David (Matt. 1:1) • The Son of Joseph (John 1:45) • The Son of Mary (Mark 6:3) • Who Loves Us (Rev. 1:5)
Gift 8 Good Neighbors	We are *Morally Helpful* People	• (2:9, 17) The "tree of the knowledge of good and evil" implied moral potential. • (2:20-24) Eve was Adam's "suitable helper." • (3:7-8) Moral shame resulted from the first human choice to sin.	• The holiness of God is witnessed in Creation, related to the Sabbath (Gen. 2:2-3) and that trait continues to the end of the Scriptures (Rev. 4:8; 21:2, 27; 22:19) • God's holiness causes him to evict unholy Adam and Eve from the Garden (Gen. 3:22-24)	• A Friend of Tax Collectors and Sinners (Matt. 9:11; Luke 7:34) • A Refuge for the Needy in Distress (Isa. 25:4) • A Refuge for the Poor (Isa. 25:4) • Defender of the Widows (Ps. 68:5) • My Helper (Heb. 13:6) • The Father to the Fatherless (Ps. 68:5) • Who Heals All Your Diseases (Ps. 103:3) • Who Satisfies Your Desires with Good Things (Ps. 103:5) • Wonderful Counselor (Isa. 9:6)
Gift 9 Responsible Citizens	We are *Broadly Cultural* People	• (1:28a) God commanded people to "be fruitful and increase . . . and subdue" (Cultural Mandate). • (3:1-6) The human capacity to communicate and work together was demonstrated, even for evil.	• The positive cultural traits of God—modeled by his own attributes of communication and cooperation—are constantly evident within the Trinity (Gen. 1:1-2 and 3:22)	• Carpenter (Mark 6:3) • Cross-cultural skills (Mark 7:24ff; Luke. 10:25ff) • Faithful Citizen of Earth and heaven (Matt. 22:21) • Humble (Matt. 11:29) • Master Communicator (Matt. 7:28-29) • Multilingual (Mark 7:26; John 7:35, 12:20-22, 20:16) • Pure (1 John 3:3) • Servant (Acts 4:27) • Supporter of Music/Art as "Song" (Isa. 12:2) • Taxpayer (Matt. 17:24-27) • The Lily of the Valleys (Song of Solomon 2:1)

TABLE 9.2

Some Hypotheses for Chapter 9

Here are the sequential themes that lay the foundation for community—how Jesus related to others and matured and how we can, too:

- The disciple's lifelong objective is to glorify her Maker by constantly maturing toward Christlikeness;

- That maturation process involves all healthy relationships—with oneself, with others, and with God;

- Undergirding every healthy relationship is the basic need to trust God;

- A significant illustration of this trust is dependence upon God for personal, daily needs ("Give us today our daily bread");

- A common test related to those daily needs is also requesting God's help for personal sufferings;

- Jesus set a deliberate pattern for maturity by his own testimony:
  - He lovingly engaged his needy culture;
  - He regularly encountered suffering;
  - He trusted the Father and the Holy Spirit;
  - He experienced God's blessings; and
  - He matured ("perfected") as a whole person

- Thus, Jesus is our example for every relational challenge in life. His model was grounded upon *imago Dei*. We are enabled to mature as his disciples whenever we emulate his design for interpersonal growth (blending pain and pleasure), established on hope in God.

How Jesus Lovingly Engaged the World, Suffered, and Matured

As I noted in the introduction, I don't want to consciously repeat something about discipleship that has been said elsewhere. So when I speak of Jesus' capacity for love, I will emphasize his progressively maturing stages of human affection—from childhood to youth to adulthood. If we wholeheartedly believe the truth of Luke 2:40 and 52, we will come to terms with our Beloved Brother's age-appropriate emotional growth. We will also value how every stage within that domain reflects and glorifies the Creator.

The Apostle Paul provided a superb starting point for age-appropriate maturity when he testified: "When I was a child, I talked like a child, I thought like a child, I reasoned like a child. When I became a man, I put childish ways behind me" (1 Cor. 13:11). Paul was not criticizing childhood. The apostle was implicitly validating childhood as a normal time of age-appropriate communication, thought, and reason. What Paul *was* criticizing were adults who still acted like children. So, *childlikeness* (for kids) was esteemed while *childishness* (for adults) was not.

The Greatest Commandment—in Reverse

We all know Jesus' answer to the query about "the greatest commandment": Love God completely. And we know that every time our Lord mentioned this first command, a complementary directive was always added—"the second is like it"— "Love your neighbor as yourself" (Matt. 22:34-40; Mark 12:28-33; Luke 10:27). Those references are the only times this two-part command is featured in the New Testament. That is, the greatest commandment *never* appears by itself. Not many know, however, that that's *not* the last we read of the second commandment. Five additional New Testament references highlight our horizontal duty to love others as ourselves.[6] That's a ratio of three to eight passages, a ration that favors the *second* directive.

If the first command to love God completely is superior, why is the second mentioned more often?

I believe the most reasonable explanation is a developmental one. These two commands—to ("first") love God completely and then to ("second") love our neighbor as ourselves—take the reader from the most complex to the least, moving from the top down in its hierarchy. It answers the "adult" question, "Which is the greatest commandment?"

Yet all people (based upon the design of image) mature in the opposite direction: from simple to complex stages. That's true, regardless of whether we are studying the physical, mental, emotional, social, moral, or spiritual spheres of humanity. Therefore, we Christian leaders, educators, and parents must ask, "Which is the 'first' commandment a young child must face?" The answer honors the Creator's plan for sequential growth, starting at birth. We begin from the child's perspective.

Consequently, it's logical to see that far more people (children, youth, and even adults) can relate to the love-neighbor-as-self category than the love-God-completely category. Everybody must enter the former phase before the latter, so the eight-to-three ration of total verses matches this progression. This pattern of Christian maturity is substantiated in the Bible (see sidebar 9.1 in the *Supplemental Resource*), based upon the notion of mature love (specifically *agape* love).[7] This sequential pattern also carries some helpful implications.[8]

Complete discipleship is distinct from either a worthless self-image or a false humility that merely accommodates others. That is why the popular acronym JOY—Jesus first, Others second, You last—does more harm than good, in my opinion. It is far too simplistic, as it unrealistically creates competing compartments of affection. It blatantly ignores God's design for a healthy self-understanding, and Jesus' own example is misunderstood. The JOY acronym fails to present the significant implications of image, such as the Creation Equation.[9]

To illustrate, when we contemplate the developmental pattern of how Jesus loved, we need to think of the analogy of a musical arrangement, not a mathematical sequence. Though there is obvious progression in a musical score, certain themes repeat and intertwine. Much more than a "1-then-2-then-3" view of maturation, disciples must value the ebb-and-flow patterns of maturation, based upon passages like those featured in this section. Healthy emotional growth progresses from mature love *for* self to mature love *for* others to mature love *for* God—all of which is based upon the love *of* God (1 John 4:7, 10, 19). Elementary stages are never

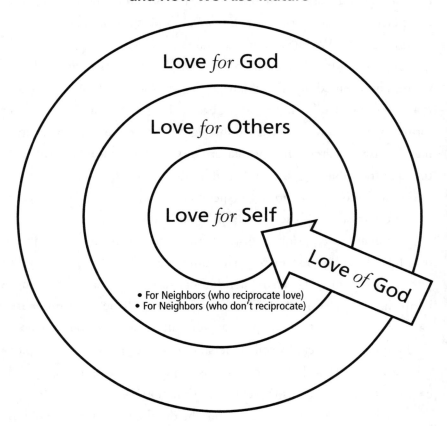

FIGURE 9.1

**How Jesus Matured in His Love Relationships—
and How We Also Mature**

Love *for* God

Love *for* Others

Love *for* Self

Love *of* God

• For Neighbors (who reciprocate love)
• For Neighbors (who don't reciprocate)

abandoned as maturity progresses. Love for self is incorporated in more sophisticated phases of love for God. (See figure 9.1 above.) Sidebar 9.2 in the *Supplemental Resource* illustrates how this progression might look.

How Jesus Suffered as a Person

Every time I ask one of my standard questions on human maturity to the adult audiences I teach—regardless of who or where they are—the answers are predictable. I have asked hundreds of adults: "When you think of the times you matured in your life, how many of those times came during 'mountaintop' periods versus 'valley' experiences?" Very rarely do adults mention personal growth during "mountaintop" periods—when things are going exceptionally well. Probably 5 to 10 percent vote for that category. As a rule of thumb, about 85 percent or more identify with their "valley" moments—when things were really tough. Valleys cause people to reflect, to prioritize, to lean strongly upon someone—sometimes God. Last week I asked that question again. Same results, but even more extreme. Nobody raised a hand for the first choice. Twenty-seven out of thirty (90 percent) chose the second option. (Three didn't vote.)

That's precisely how Jesus matured as well. Hebrews 5:8-9 are the most provocative verses on this topic. My paraphrase of these verses spells out an invaluable (yet simple) pattern for maturation:

"Even though Jesus was the Son of God, he matured just like every other disciple. He learned how to obey the Father's plan for him, through suffering—as he trusted God. When Jesus came to the end of that plan—that is, he had completed or perfected it—he personally became mature. Once that happened, the Father made Jesus the source of eternal salvation for everybody who, in turn, now obeys Christ."

Also, Jesus testified that by maturing this way—which contributed to the larger, completed "work" that the Father assigned him—he glorified God (John 17:1-5).

Pleasure and Pain

The Father's pattern of human maturity for his Son included a blend of pleasure and pain. It's fair to say that, through his perfect humanity, Jesus experienced both the highest highs a person could ever have, as well as the lowest lows. Several verses address this pleasure-pain combo in Jesus' life. No Old Testament chapter is more convincing of that truth than the Suffering Servant prophecy of Isaiah 53. Even though Christ was an innocent person (see v. 9b), "it was the LORD'S will to crush him and cause him to suffer" as "a guilt offering" for God's children (v. 10). After that sacrifice, Jesus would then "see the light of life and be satisfied" (v. 11a).

Hebrews 12:2-3 provides more helpful details, for there Jesus has two complementary roles: (1) "Author"—literally one leading off and (2) "Perfecter" or Pioneer—one who blazes a trail. That's because Jesus didn't come to Earth only to save us from death; he demonstrated how to live life. Notice the pleasure-pain pattern in Jesus' mission in the opening verses of Hebrews 12: ". . . who for the joy set before him endured the cross, scorning its shame, and sat down at the right hand of the throne of God" (v. 2b). The immediate application for disciples follows: "Consider him who endured such opposition . . . so that you will not grow weary and lose heart" (v. 3).

I like how Brent Curtis and John Eldredge approach this paradox of blended pain and pleasure. They speak about our heart's capacity to mature—to actually expand to include more pleasures and greater pains. In one section, Curtis and Eldredge make the connection between new converts to Christ and a newfound pleasure. They refer to a missionary friend of theirs who serves Muslims in Senegal. After observing post-conversion behaviors, this missionary reported that many Muslims "will often notice flowers for the first time." That's because, in their somber, rules-filled culture, Muslims tend to prize doing, not being. They value a tree, for example, only if it yields fruit, not merely for its inherent beauty. Curtis and Eldredge paralleled that view of life with other modern fundamentalists, even those within our churches: "Their hatred of pleasure is not a sign of their godliness; quite the opposite. The redeemed heart hungers for beauty."[10]

Curtis and Eldredge also refer to the maturing disciple's growing capacity to know pain—an increasing threshold that accommodates more suffering. "You can keep *that* 'gift,' thank you," we might react, sarcastically. But we miss our Maker's best plan with that attitude. If our wish were granted, we would become emotional and spiritual dwarfs. We forget, for example, that the Latin root for *passion* means "to suffer." Pain is inextricably linked with pleasure.[11] Think about it like this: Being blessed with a close and loving family is a kindness from God that's hard to beat. Yet, within those same relationships, we also run the risk of more severe pain from hurt, disappointment, or loss.

Most of us know the shortest Bible verse, John 11:35: "Jesus wept." But how many of us recall the next verse: "Then the Jews said, 'See how he loved him!'"? Our Lord's deep bereavement mirrored his deep love for one of his closest friends. Saints who choose an alternate route, who "play it safe" when it comes to affective expressions, hedge on their emotional commitments and their potential for growth.[12] Certainly the potential pain of a love relationship is enough to make anybody shrink back into a self-preservation mode. But C. S. Lewis reminds us: "God whispers to us in our pleasures . . . but shouts in our pains."[13] (Sidebar 9.3 in the *Supplemental Resource* offers a refreshing view of our future as it pertains to healthy relationships in this life.)

The Many Ways Jesus Suffered

Numerous biblical examples feature the pain and suffering of Christ. Here are some of the more outstanding incidents:

- Foremost was his suffering from his payment for the sins of us all, which included the horrible prospect of being made sin for us;[14]
- the suffering from various types of pain in his early childhood years;[15]
- the suffering from his temptations with the Devil;[16]
- the suffering from various threats to his life;[17]
- the suffering from rude attacks on his personal background and heritage;[18]

- the suffering from the hard-heartedness of his enemies;[19]
- the suffering from the rejection of his beloved Israel;[20]
- the suffering from his own followers' "slowness of heart";[21]
- the suffering from the religious leaders' entrapments and tests;[22]
- the suffering from his own thirst, hunger, and exhaustion;[23]
- the suffering from his family's rejection of him and his ministry;[24]
- the suffering from his sharing of others' pain, even that of strangers;[25]
- the suffering from shared pain of close friends, including personal loss;[26]
- the suffering from insults, taunts, and scoffing thrown at him;[27]
- the suffering from physical pain "in his body";[28] and finally,
- the suffering from personally sensing God's forsaking Him[29]

Besides these numerous references to Jesus' sufferings, there are an astonishing number of additional references to his sufferings.[30]

How Jesus Trusted God While He Was Suffering

Just as Hebrews 5:8 provides a pivotal verse on our Lord's suffering, 1 Peter 2:23 highlights his trust in God during times of need or persecution: "When they hurled insults at him, he did not retaliate; when he suffered, he made no threats. Instead, he entrusted himself to him who judges justly." What's so crucial about 1 Peter 2:23 is its context. Just two verses earlier, we are commanded "follow in [Jesus'] steps." In recent years this phrase became extremely popular through the "WWJD?" fad. What was not so popular was the fact that "in his steps" is based upon Jesus "example" of suffering—spelled out in the first part of verse 21. Verse 23 goes beyond our calling to suffer, by reminding us how we should suffer: Like Jesus, we are to trust God for every need we have.

Figure 9.2 illustrates Jesus' elementary, yet effective, pattern of nonretaliation. It also shows how Jesus committed himself to the Father

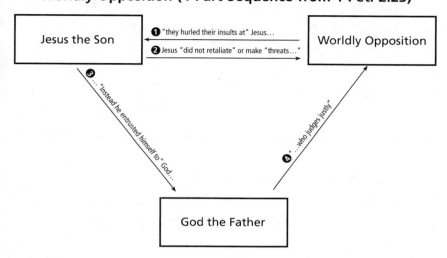

FIGURE 9.2

How Jesus Trusted God Whenever He Faced Worldly Opposition (4-Part Sequence from 1 Pet. 2:23)

and Holy Spirit in times of personal struggle or need. To avoid over-reaction, Leslie B. Flynn pointed out what Jesus' model of nonretaliatory love was not:[31]

- Nonretaliation did not rule out Jesus' responses.[32]
- Nonretaliation did not rule out Jesus' rebukes.[33]
- Nonretaliation did not rule out Jesus' righteous wrath.[34]

In chapter 6, I introduced the all-important doctrine of *kenosis*, Jesus' voluntary self-emptying of his divine powers (not his divine nature). Among other implications, I concluded that Jesus, when tempted, could not sin (since he was God), yet he did not always know that he would come out victorious (since he was human). Consequently, Jesus felt the full pull of evil. As Hebrews 4:15 claims, Jesus really was "tempted in every way, just as we are. . . . ." I also said that since Jesus put his powers "on the shelf," he never held an unfair advantage over us. Each of the miracles Christ performed (apart from his unique calling) is essentially reproduced elsewhere in Scripture. Therefore, when our Lord directs us disciples to now pick up the work of the Father where he left off (through the Holy Spirit living inside us), he really means just that. We, too, can trust in the Father, the Spirit, and God's Word, just as Jesus did.[35] We can follow—emulate—the man of Galilee.

Table 9.3 (pp. 212-213) extends these *kenosis* implications to every disciple: first, how Jesus trusted God; second, how other people in the Bible also committed themselves to God; and third, how that same trust, in both cases, resulted in personal maturity. Seventeen practical areas are identified in this table, along with accompanying examples of growth.

How Jesus Matured as a Human Being

Recall that Jesus' ultimate purpose for his Incarnation consisted of two key roles: once-for-all Savior and ongoing Great High Priest. The first occurred at a specific point in time, the second is still taking place, based upon all thirty-three years of his life, as he slowly matured. That's why he is both the Author and the Pioneer of our faith (Heb. 12:2). Greek scholar A. T. Robertson concluded in his comments on Hebrews 2:10, "If one recoils at the idea of God making Christ perfect, he should bear in mind that it is the humanity of Jesus that is under discussion. . . . One cannot know human life without living it. . . . Jesus . . . lived his human life in order to be able to be a sympathizing and effective leader in the work of salvation."[36]

The late Ray Stedman effectively argued for this same tie between Jesus' completely matured human life and his finished work on the cross when he emphasized his complementary roles of Savior and sympathetic High Priest. Stedman also chose the provocative Hebrews 2:10 phrase that says God made Christ "the author of their salvation perfect through suffering," then Stedman claimed Christ's full life of suffering (which shaped his maturation) was absolutely necessary for him to fully identify with our present-day struggles. Stedman speculated: *What would have happened if God's Son had come to earth as a fully grown adult rather than as an infant?* Then he wondered what if, as a grown adult, Jesus lived only his last week of life before dying on the cross? Could he have still been our perfect Savior? "Certainly he would have been perfect as far as bearing our guilt is concerned," Stedman concluded, because "that only required a sinless Savior. But he would not have been perfect as far as bearing our infirmities, our weaknesses, is concerned."[37]

What a fascinating distinction! Salvation for our mortal sins, yes. Empathy for our daily struggles, no. Drawing one more implication about his own hypothetical picture of Christ, Stedman claimed: "He would have been able to fit us for heaven someday, but never able to make us ready for earth right now."[38] Both aspects of Christ's life, then, are absolutely necessary for the complete Christian life: his salvation, which grants our eternal life, and his empowerment for our temporal life. Only that combination allows us to comprehend the importance of Jesus' historical and current ministries to believers; his past atonement as well as his present merciful service.[39] A. T. Robertson, extending his earlier comments (now based on Heb. 2:18, which says Jesus is "able to help those who are being tempted"), noted, "This word strikes at the heart of it all. Christ's power to help is due not merely to his deity as God's Son, but also to his humanity without which he could not sympathize with us (Heb. 4:15)."[40]

Peter Kreeft concisely summarized why the Creator chose to transform all his human children—including Christ, our Beloved Brother—using this suffering-trusting-maturing pattern. In brief, Kreeft stated that sequence is how people, firsthand, come to know what they personally believe.[41] This process is often called "personal ownership" in educational philosophy and human development literature.

TABLE 9.3

How Jesus—and Others—Trusted God for Maturity

Key Verse: "Jesus . . . went around doing good and healing . . . *because God was with him*" (Acts 10:38).

Categories of Human Trust	How Jesus Purposefully Trusted God the Father	How Others in Scripture Similarly Trusted God	How Trusting God Promoted Human Maturity (in Jesus and in Others)
For the Creator's Provisions	Jesus praised the Father for his assistance (Matt. 11:25) and he thanked him for his answered prayers (Matt. 14:19).	• Jesus told his disciples to seek God for "our daily bread" (Matt. 6:11). • The church thanked God for his sovereignty (Acts 4:23-31 [esp. v. 31, where all the people were filled with the Holy Spirit])	God's children matured when they trusted the Creator for daily needs.
For Revelation of Thoughts	Jesus sometimes knew what people were thinking (Matt. 12:25-28 [esp. see the Spirit's power in v. 28]; also Matt. 9:4 and John 2:24-25).	• Daniel was enabled to know dreams and their interpretation (Dan. 2) • Peter supernaturally knew the private thoughts and plans of Ananias and Sapphira (Acts 5:1-4)	God's children matured because their Maker gave them special knowledge, as they needed
For Revelation of Words	Jesus testified that what he said and how he said it was from God (John 12:49-50; see John 14:10).	• Peter gave his godly confession of Jesus according to God's power (Matt. 16:13-16) • Disciples were promised God's words by the Holy Spirit (Luke 12:11-12; John 14:26)	God's children matured when they could count on the Creator to give them just the right words at the right time.
For Divine Leading (to specific locations)	Jesus was "led by the Spirit" into the wilderness (to be tempted), then the Spirit empowered Jesus to return to Galilee (Luke 4:1, 14).	• Peter was led by Spirit to Cornelius (Acts 11:12) • Paul and Barnabas were led by the Spirit to go serve as first missionaries (Acts 13:1-4) • Paul was led by the Holy Spirit (and the "Spirit of Jesus") to Macedonia (Acts 16:6-10)	God's children matured because they trusted the Spirit to go to places they were supposed to go.
For Heavenly Visions	Jesus was occasionally enabled to see visions (Luke 10:17-21 [esp. notice God's power in v. 21]).	• Stephen had a heavenly encounter (Acts 7:55-56) • Peter was given a series of visions (Acts 10:9-23)	God's children matured when they had the confidence their Father would provide special insight, as necessary.
For Godly Wisdom	Jesus particularly sought God's guidance regarding the selection of his twelve disciples (Luke 6:12-15; Mark 3:13-19).	• Stephen so powerfully possessed the Spirit's wisdom that nobody could stand up and argue against him (Acts 6:10)	God's children matured as they relied on the Spirit's wisdom to help make decisions and defend the faith.
For the Spirit's Joy	Jesus was "full of the joy through the Holy Spirit" (Luke 10:21).	• The disciples also experienced joy in the Lord (see Luke 10:17) • Jesus promised more joy (John 15:11; 17:13)	God's children matured, because they experienced godly joy.
For Spirit-led Prayers to the Father	On the cross, Jesus prayed that the Father would receive his spirit at death (Luke 23:46).	• Being stoned, Stephen prayed the same prayer as Jesus: for God to receive his spirit (Acts 7:59)	God's children matured by knowing God would answer their final prayer of hope.
For Divine Comfort	Jesus sought God in solitude and prayer during times of bereavement (Matt. 14:13).	• The Ephesian elders prayed, wept, and grieved when they heard Paul's prediction that they would not see him again (Acts 20:36-38)	God's children matured as they sought the Father in times of loss and mourning.
For God's Deliverance	Jesus was protected and delivered from his enemies because...	• Peter was miraculously delivered from prison by an angel, as "the church was earnestly praying...	God's children matured when they trusted him for intervention and...

TABLE 9.3
Continued

For God's Deliverance *(continued)*	of God's timing, will, and power (John 8:20; Luke 4:28-30 [esp. note the Spirit's role in v. 14, 18, and 21]).	to God for him" (Acts 12:1-17 [esp. v. 5])	deliverance, according to his will.
For Miracles over Nature	Jesus was enabled to walk on water (Matt. 14:25-27) and to calm the storm (Mark 4:35-41).	• Moses performed several miracles over nature (the Nile River turned to blood; frogs; gnats; etc., in Ex. 7:14–10:29) • Elisha made an axhead float (2 Kings 6:1-7) • Peter also walked on water (Matt. 14:28-29)	God's children matured as they participated in the Creator's power over Creation.
For Food Miracles	Jesus was empowered to feed the crowds by God's answer to his prayer (Matt. 14:17-21 [esp. v. 19]; John 2:1-11).	• Elisha supernaturally resolved the dilemma of poisonous stew, then provided enough food for one hundred men (2 Kings 4:38-44 [esp. v. 43b-44])	God's children matured after they observed that the Lord could miraculously provide food, if necessary.
For Exorcism	Jesus regularly exorcised demons—and he did so by "the finger of God" (Luke 11:20; also Luke 4:31-37; 8:26-39; 9:37-45).	• The disciples, likewise, followed their Lord's example of exorcism, both the Twelve (Luke 9:1) and by the seventy-two disciples (Luke 10:17-20)	God's children matured when they experienced God's consistent power over Satan.
For Divine Healings	Jesus performed a broad range of healings because "the power of the Lord was present for him to heal the sick" (Luke 5:17b); some were healed by just touching Jesus (Mark 5:22-43; 6:56).	• Several disciples participated in miracles of healing, like Moses (Num. 12:1-16) and Elisha (2 Kings 5:1-19) • Peter was enabled to heal by having his shadow fall on the sick (Acts 5:12-16)	God's children matured as they realized the Father's care and power as the Great Physician.
For Resurrection of the Dead	Jesus raised the dead: Jairus' daughter (Luke 8:49-56), the widow's son (Luke 7:11ff), and Lazarus (John 11).	• Elisha predicted the birth of a son to a well-to-do Shunammite woman (without children), then raised the boy from the dead when he died (2 Kings 4:8-37) • Paul raised Eutychus from the dead (Acts 20:7-12)	God's children matured following eyewitness involvements of the Maker's power over death.
For the Power to Do "Good"	Jesus was "anointed" by the Father and given "power" by the Holy Spirit to serve by "doing good"—"because God was with him" (Acts 10:37-38).	• The church perpetuated that model to "do good," whether it was Tabitha's personal and practical displays of kindness (Acts 9:36) or the leadership's mercy, extended to Gentile believers (Acts 15:28)	God's children matured as they utilized God's power to "do good."
For Divine Judgment	Jesus refused to retaliate when his enemies mocked and insulted him (Mark 15:31-32); Rather, Jesus prayed for their forgiveness (Luke 23:34) and Jesus "entrusted himself to him who judges justly" (1 Pet. 2:23). Through these sufferings, Jesus "learned obedience . . . and . . . [was] made perfect" (Heb. 5:8-9).	• This model of maturity ("perfect") was exactly the design that Jesus' disciples were to emulate, as we "follow in his steps" (1 Pet. 2:21) • Stephen also sought forgiveness of his enemies (Acts 7:60) • Paul modeled Jesus' "slander-for-kindness" example, then told believers to "imitate" him (1 Cor. 4:11-16)	God's children mature when they followed the pattern of nonretaliation and trusted in God as Judge.

How We Disciples Mature "in His Steps"

Our Father's plan to nurture us children should never be perceived as a cloning method. Metaphorically, his maturing pattern is much more like a garden than an assembly line. That's because complex variables within human growth include dynamic elements like age, gender, circumstances, spiritual warfare, giftedness, calling, willingness, and the overall maturity level of the disciple.

One of my favorite literary examples of the disciple's individual growth journey is found in C. S. Lewis's *The Lion, the Witch, and the Wardrobe*. When Lewis first introduced Christ as Aslan in the *Chronicles of Narnia* series, he pointed out the varying reactions that the four heroes and heroines display. Mr. Beaver, hosting these four children, does the honor of this introduction, announcing that Narnia has a new Guest:

> "They say Aslan is on the move—perhaps already landed."
>
> And now a very curious thing happened. None of the children knew who Aslan was any more than you do; but the moment the Beaver had spoken these words everyone felt quite different. . . . It was like that now. At the name of Aslan each one of the children felt something jump in his inside. Edmund felt a sensation of mysterious horror. Peter felt suddenly brave and adventurous. Susan felt as if some delicious smell or some delightful strain of music had just floated by her. And Lucy got the feeling you have when you wake up in the morning and realize that it is the beginning of the holidays or the beginning of summer.[42]

Following Christ as a Maturing Person

Having noted human differences, it is also important to reemphasize the common elements of Jesus' own maturation, since Christ presents a basic pattern of maturity for every person. We are called to follow our Faithful Brother, who pioneered the path of holiness we must also take.

We, like him, lovingly engage our world. To be "in" the world, but not "of" it, perpetuates the passion we find throughout the Son's testimony (to repeat, "passion" means "suffering").

When we realize the remarkable number of references to our Lord's suffering, it should never surprise us that we are also supposed to suffer. Recall the Apostle Peter's version of this pain-pleasure design, which Christians should expect: "Dear friends, do not be surprised at the painful trial you are suffering, as though something strange were happening to you. But rejoice that you participate in the sufferings of Christ, so that you may be overjoyed when his glory is revealed." (1 Pet. 4:12-13).[43] The Apostle Paul corroborates this attitude in 2 Timothy 3:12: "In fact, everyone who wants to live a godly life in Christ Jesus will be persecuted." (See sidebar 9.4 in the *Supplemental Resource* for a thorough listing of citations that connect obedient disciples with suffering, persecution, and pain.)

We, like the Son, are called to mature by trusting our Father. There's "good news and bad news" for every disciple at this juncture. The "bad news," so to speak, is that many times God does not supernaturally intervene to stop his children from suffering. That may sound odd (and even a bit "unspiritual") to some people. Yes, God may decide to intervene and to prevent suffering at the outset. And, yes, subsequent to suffering, God still performs miracles today. I have witnessed the Great Physician's healing power in a very serious medical case where James 5:14-16 was appropriated. But our Father does not always deliver us from suffering. I am not saying God does not answer our prayers. Those two sentences express two different concepts.

Throughout the entire history of humankind there are only a handful of times when we see miracles clustered together: during Moses' life, the period of the Judges, the days of Elijah and Elisha, Daniel's lifetime, Jesus' ministry, and the early years of the church. That proposal neither says God was not present throughout all of history nor that he did not intervene at certain points (e.g., in the Flood). I am saying that "clusters of miracles" are found only within those half dozen periods, discounting the Creation and the end times.[44]

In light of the many occasions when miracles don't occur, it isn't surprising that the Apostle Paul was not delivered from his own "thorn in [the] flesh"—even though he prayed for healing three times and he healed many others. Again, I'm not saying his prayers weren't answered. They were—just not the way he initially wanted them answered. Second Corinthians 12:7-10 details the wise principle behind God's decision not to heal this apostle. God replied: "My grace is sufficient for you, for my power is made *perfect* in weakness" (v. 9a).

If that word "perfect" sounds familiar, it should. Based on the Greek root *telos*, God was essentially saying to Paul: "Trust in my grace—that's all you need. For, as you trust me, you'll experience my strength in your weakness. Over time, that trust relationship will make you complete, or mature." In other words, God's answer to Paul's three prayers for healing was the precise pattern Jesus modeled for his own human maturation.[45] When that ultimate trust in God is displayed, we—like Christ—can have confidence (even in suffering) that we are untouchable, until God's plan for us changes.[46] (Sidebar 9.5 in the *Supplemental Resource* further explains human maturing by the biblical concept of "disciple." Sidebar 9.6 in the *Supplemental Resource* offers an overview of this discipline process, utilizing verses that raise the subject of "perfection," or maturity.)

The ninth of twelve truths about complete discipleship, then, may be summarized in this fashion:

> **Truth 9**
>
> God's model for discipleship features the third legacy of godly community, demonstrating both how to relate to others and how to personally mature. Jesus' role of Beloved Brother intentionally helps us disciples to grow and, thus, to honor God.

Conclusion

Four feet, three inches. Four feet, eight inches. Four-eleven. Five feet even. Five feet, three inches. These increments scale the doorjamb that leads into our laundry room. Each mark signals growth—healthy growth, expected growth. Slow growth. And yet, those penciled lines provide only one dimension of growth for my three daughters over the years. Human growth is slow. The dates of each entry prove that—even though observing the entire vertical pattern at a glance seems to say the opposite.

When Israel was about to enter Canaan, God promised he would help them drive out the heathen nations "little by little" (Deut. 7:22). That's because Israel had to gradually and patiently attain her own "maturity," as it were.

Christian maturity is a lot like these two examples. It is incremental and it is ongoing. It is almost imperceptible at times, yet it is expected and necessary.

That's why it helps to have the earthly example of Jesus Christ. He is one who has already finished the race. He has pioneered our course. He has shown us how to run the race and how to finish strongly.

1 I have deliberately reviewed the hand model from chapter 7, respectively moving from the physical to the mental to the emotional to the social and to the moral domains.

2 Simeon's prophetic words about Jesus in the temple—exactly *one week* after the shepherds' encounter—may have prompted another "crossroads moment," as "the child's father and *mother marveled at what was said* about [Jesus]." Then Simeon blessed them and said to his mother: "And *a sword* will pierce your own soul too" (Luke 2:33-35—notice both "pleasure and pain").

3 Four obvious exceptions to this fact are that Jesus was also God, he didn't sin, he had a special and intimate tie with his Father, and he had a unique calling as Savior.

4 I'm not saying that the Gospel message would change in its substance. First Corinthians 15:1-5 provides the Gospel's *unchanging core* of the death, burial, and resurrection of Jesus. What I am referring to are the "implications." So, rather than referring to "saving souls," we would refer to the redemption of the "whole person," just as the complete biblical message in the Old Testament (e.g., see Prov. 4:18-22) and the New Testament (e.g., see John 7:23) have always taught.

5 Notice how James describes the "perfect man" in these holistic ways (from Jas. 3:2), as one who keeps "his *whole body* in check."

6 Matthew 19:19 and Luke 10:27 answer the Rich Young Ruler; Romans 13:9 says the whole law is "summed up in this *one rule*" to love neighbor as self (also see Lev. 19:18); Galatians 5:14 likewise summarizes the entire law "*in a single command*"; James 2:8 calls that same imperative the "royal law found in Scripture"; and Matthew 7:12 essentially expresses that same truth via the so-called Golden Rule.

7 In 1 John 4:16b-21 and Ephesians 5:28-33 (two of the key passages cited in sidebar 9.1 in the *Supplemental Resource*), the Greek word *agape* is consistently employed, whenever the word "love" is used. That fact is critical, since *agape* is always used in the Bible whenever people are commanded to love God. (*Agape* is the highest, purest form of love in the Bible.) The only exception to this rule, to my knowledge, is in John 21:15-17, where Jesus asks Peter three times, "Do you love me?" The Lord's word (for the first two usages) is *agape,* but he chooses *phileo* the last time. (*Phileo* represents a lesser love, more commonly associated with "brotherly love.") There are a few different theories as to why Jesus would switch words on his third question—but I believe a strong theory comes from the text itself: Peter, in his first two replies (prior to Jesus' third inquiry), answers Jesus' two *agape* questions with two *phileo* answers. I believe that Jesus is simply doing the developmentally prudent thing: modifying his request to the level that his student is willing to make an affective commitment. Thus, with this sensitive alteration, Peter repeats—for the third time—his willingness to love Jesus in (only) a *phileo* way.

The very best contrast to these Scriptures that command proper, godly self-love (based on *agape,* as sidebar 9.1 shows) is found in 2 Timothy 3:1-5. Five references are made to *ungodly* love in those five verses (the phrase "without love," in verse 3, uses a word other than *agape* or *phileo*). Here is a key point: *Every single time* the word *phileo* is chosen to portray the *ungodly* love, the apostle is warning his readers to avoid it.

8 Barry J. Wadsworth, an expert in Piaget's theories, has made an extremely sobering statement that *one-half of the adults in the United States never develop beyond the concrete operations* stage of thinking. This means that about 50 percent of adults will never function at the next cognitive level of abstract thought. Practically speaking, they can't consistently process, for instance, symbolic doctrines like the Trinity. (From Wadsworth's *Piaget's Theory*

of Cognitive and Affective Development, 4th ed. [New York: Longmans, 1989], p. 115).

Virtually every human development theory claims that people can *neither* "jump over" the subsequent stage they are entering (i.e., they must "go through it") *nor* prematurely accelerate their way through a stage. One useful implication is that parents, teachers, and other community leaders are similarly discouraged from challenging a person two (or more) stages beyond where he currently is. In this light, the eight-to-three ratio of these two commands is both a sound theory and a gracious strategy.

9 A helpful Bible study would analyze Jesus' healthy self-love—the various ways he took care of himself and was mindful of his own needs. Consider how Jesus spent time alone (Mark 7:24-30), how he sought out the Father during his own grief (Matt. 14:6-13), and how he overtly expressed his gratitude for his disciples' presence at the Last Supper (Luke 22:15). Another potent example is found in Philippians 2:3-5. Verse 4 clarifies that a healthy focus on "own interests" and on "the interests of others" does not need to be mutually exclusive. They may be concurrent. Verses 5-11 indicate that Jesus displayed harmony.

   The Creation Equation says "how we treat others is how we treat God." To say "others" is to include ourselves.

10 From their book *The Sacred Romance* (Thomas Nelson, 1997), pp. 200-01.

11 Simone Weil (*Waiting for God* [New York: Harper & Row, 1973], p. 180) draws the following understandings about God from human encounters with nature and pain and pleasure:

> Through joy the beauty of the world penetrates our soul. Through suffering it penetrates our body. We could no more become friends of God through joy alone than one becomes a ship's captain by studying books on navigation. The body plays a part in all apprenticeships.

Cited in Diogenes Allen's *Spiritual Theology* (Cambridge, Mass.: Crowley, 1997), p. 122.

12 Curtis and Eldredge (*The Sacred Romance*, p. 201) caution disciples about such a strategy, saying: "This is why many Christians are reluctant to listen to their hearts: They know that their dullness is keeping them from feeling the pain of life. Many of us have chosen simply not to want so much; it's safer that way. It's also godless. That's stoicism, not Christianity. Sanctification is an awakening, the rousing of our souls from the dead sleep of sin into the fullness of their capacity for life."

13 *The Problem of Pain* by C. S. Lewis (New York: Macmillan, 1978, p. 93).

14 See Isaiah 54:3-6, 10-11; Romans 4:25; 1 Corinthians 15:3; 2 Corinthians 5:21; and Hebrews 9:28.

15 Jesus lived through a range of painful issues like infanticide, a refugee flight into Egypt, and his family's return to Nazareth out of fear. Certainly, Jesus later heard about and retained these tragic stories of his childhood.

16 Review the wilderness temptations from Luke's account (4:1-13), especially the last verse which implies more than this one, solitary encounter: "When the devil had finished all this tempting, he left him until an opportune time." Regarding Jesus' personal torment in these situations, analyze the concise and insightful truth of Hebrews 2:18a: "[Christ] himself suffered when he was tempted."

17 Matthew 12:14; John 5:18; 6:15; 7:1, 19; 8:59; 10:31; 11:8; 11:53; and 12:9-10. Especially see John 10:39 re: Jesus' full "experiential" escape from his enemies, at the very last second. Contrast John 8:20b: "No one seized him, because his time had not yet come."

18 In John 8, the Pharisees began a methodical argument with Jesus about religious heritage. They first asked, "Where is your father?" (v. 19). Then they crudely said, "*We are not ille-*

gitimate children," inferring that Christ *was* (v. 41b). Finally, they speculated that Jesus was a demon-possessed "Samaritan" (v. 48).

19 Mark 3:5 records the only explicit reference to Jesus' anger, based upon the fact that he was "deeply distressed" at the "stubborn hearts" of the religious leaders.

20 Luke 13:34-35.

21 See Mark 7:18 and 8:21 along with Luke 24:25-27 and 45-47.

22 Mark 12:15 and Matthew 22:34-36.

23 All three of these physical needs are noted in John 4:6-8.

24 See Mark 3:20-35 and John 7:1-5.

25 See Jesus' immediate response of total empathy to the widow of Nain, who appears in this text as a virtual stranger (Luke 7:11-17).

26 Within minutes after writing this section on suffering I was informed by my wife that a mature, godly fifteen-year-old member of our church's youth had just accidentally drowned during a family outing. Believers, like nonbelievers, experience the same grief from loss and also cry out "Why?" By God's grace, however, we also have hope and peace, though the pain of lost fellowship remains. Jesus experienced these very same feelings in Matthew 14:12-13a and John 11:33-37.

27 Matthew 27:39 and 44. Also see Psalm 22:7 and 42:10, which tie physical decay with taunting.

28 Matthew 26:67-68; 27:27-31; and 1 Peter 4:1.

29 Matthew 27:46; see Psalm 22:1.

30 Notice the consistent reminders of our Savior's suffering: Mark 8:31; 9:12; Luke 9:22; 17:25; 22:15; 24:26; 24:46; Acts 3:18; 17:3; 26:23; Romans 8:17; 2 Corinthians 1:5; Hebrews 2:9-10; 2:18; 5:8; 13:12; 1 Peter 1:11; 2:21, 23; 4:1, and 4:13.

31 In *Jesus in the Image of God* (San Jose, Calif.: Magnus, 1997), pp. 15-25, Leslie B. Flynn notes these key points of Jesus' trusting strategy.

32 Flynn (pp. 21-22) gives this prudent advice: "Nonreviling doesn't necessarily mean a person should not answer back. Before the Sanhedrin Jesus was asked if he were the Christ. At this point he did not keep silent, but affirmed unequivocally that he was the Messiah. When an answer was needed to vindicate the truth, Jesus answered. When an answer was pointless, no reply was given. When reviling was in progress, an answer was not forthcoming because it would only have added fuel to the fire."

Flynn adds other examples of Jesus' justifiable self-defense, such as why he continued healing on the Sabbath, why he associated with the tax collectors and sinners, why Mary's use of the expensive perfume was not only acceptable—but why it would become a memorial. In short, Flynn concluded: "Nonretaliation doesn't rule out defense. Response doesn't mean retaliation."

33 Flynn (p. 22) also proposes that a nonreviling attitude does not forbid rebuking: "Jesus rebuked his disciples for their little faith. He reproved Martha for excess agitation on mundane matters. He scolded Peter for denying the announcement of his coming sufferings and death. To their faces he called the Pharisees 'a wicked and adulterous generation' (Matt. 12:39)."

34 Finally, Flynn (p. 22) notes: "He even became angry at times, in righteous indignation pronouncing woes on the hypocrisy of the scribes, and castigating the cheating money

changers in the temple. Jesus' scathing scorn was never the result of personal vindictiveness, but stemmed from a love of righteousness."

35 Jesus' high view of Scripture (John 10:34-35; 17:17) as God's unbreakable truth led him to logically conclude that, by accurately knowing Scripture, one could experience the power of God (Matt. 22:29).

36 From Archibald Thomas Robertson's *Word Pictures in the New Testament*, Vol. V, (Nashville: Broadman, 1932), p. 347. Italics are mine.

37 From Ray Stedman's sermon "The True Man," based upon Hebrews 2:5-18, preached March 14, 1965 (see Hebrews Series 1, Message No. 2, Catalog No. 85). Discovery Publishing, a ministry of Peninsula Bible Church, Palo Alto, California, ©1995.

38 Ibid.

39 See Hebrews 2:17b.

40 Robertson, p. 351.

41 Peter Kreeft, *Three Philosophies of Life* (San Francisco: Ignatius, 1989), p. 86.

42 Lewis, *The Lion, the Witch, and the Wardrobe*, [New York: HarperCollins, 1994], pp. 74-75.

43 Other biblical examples of this pain-pleasure pattern—*from just 1 Peter alone*—include 1 Peter 1:3-6; 1:7; 2:11-12; 2:19-23; 3:9; 3:14; 3:17; 4:1-2; 4:14-16; 4:19; and 5:1, 10.

44 In Luke 4:22-30 Jesus infuriated his hometown by alluding to this historical point—even though that was not his main reason for reflecting upon the lives of Elijah and Elisha. These two prophets clearly portray a special time when the Creator regularly intervened with miracles. Yet, Jesus matter-of-factly pointed out the *enormous needs* for healing and assistance that *were not met* during the same time frame. Christ was partially communicating that God normally does *not break* into history—because he wants needy people to trust him, in order to be "made perfect in weakness," as Paul experienced in 2 Corinthians 12:9.

45 The ultimate trust that Daniel's three friends exhibited in the fiery furnace (Dan. 3:17-18) represents exemplary trust. Essentially they confessed that they trusted God for *who he is* (faithful, wise, just, etc.) *not* for *what he does* (whether or not he would deliver them).

46 John 7:30 states that "*no one* laid a hand on him, because *his time had not yet come.*" Also see John 8:20.

Section III

The Jesus We Want Others to Know

CHAPTER TEN

THE COMPLETE WAY TO BELIEVE IN JESUS

> *God cannot give us . . . peace apart from Himself,*
> *because it is not there. There is no such thing.*
>
> —C. S. LEWIS
>
> *Evil's greatest triumph may be its success in portraying*
> *religion as an enemy of pleasure when, in fact, religion*
> *accounts for its source: every good and enjoyable thing is*
> *the invention of a Creator who lavished gifts on the world.*
>
> —PHILIP YANCEY

This is a true story: About ten years ago, during a special service on the first Sunday of April, young Michael was dedicated by his parents to the Lord. Michael's parents were good friends of my wife, Mary, and me. Dan, Michael's father, recounted this momentous event, which was completed in only six minutes: "Michael was noticeably anxious that morning," Dan began his reflection. "We just figured he was nervous because his grandparents were visiting, and he had to stand in front of a large congregation and answer a couple questions. But, later that night, we discovered there was more to his anxiety."

With those opening words, Dan secured my attention.

"Actually," the father of the five year old continued, "knowing what I know now, I am amazed Michael let us perform the dedication at all." My curiosity was piqued.

"Michael thought that, by being dedicated to the Lord, he would be expected to serve God the rest of his life. He didn't have a problem there. But Michael also thought that public service meant he could no longer live at home! He would be immediately taken from his family!"

I recalled an Old Testament story that paralleled what Dan was summarizing, but I was careful not to jump to any conclusions. "So, where did Michael think he was supposed to live?" I quizzed, selecting my most neutral voice.

"In the church building itself!" Dan answered. "I guess we didn't realize how literally our son was taking our home instruction. We read about young Samuel's similar dedication by his mom, in preparation for Michael's commitment. After Samuel's dedication, the temple became his new residence."

My suspicion was confirmed. Little Michael's limited knowledge of the Bible was playing tricks on him. And nobody detected it for weeks preceding his dedication.

I must add that Dan and Linda were extraordinary Christian parents. Both were bright, sensible, well-educated, sensitive, and caring. In many ways they represented ideal caregivers. But it was those precise facts that caused me to wonder (almost out loud): "If this is how well-nurtured Christian homes can mis-educate their kids, what does this say about homes that don't have any of these advantages? What other Bible truths are being misunderstood in our homes, how do we discover those trouble spots, and how do we reverse such negative instruction and learning?"

I'm not talking about the learning of Bible trivia, such as reciting all the names of Israel's tribes, knowing the exact number of Elijah's and Elisha's combined miracles, or explaining the sequence and contents of the "judgment bowls" in Revelation. I am talking about key doctrinal issues we should be teaching our children and our youth—in age-appropriate ways—like the nature of God, the Creation story, and the meaning of the Incarnation. I am also talking about the foundational doctrines of salvation. I am concerned that—for many disciples—we have misunderstood the heart of our faith. We have misrepresented what it means to say yes to Jesus.

What's So Special About Jesus?

This past summer I attended a Habermas reunion, held at a Tennessee state park just north of Nashville. I spent some time talking to my oldest brother, Gary, who is the distinguished professor of apologetics and philosophy at Liberty University, Lynchburg, Virginia. His specialty includes the historical aspects of our Lord's life, particularly the resurrection. Since the topic of salvation centers on Jesus Christ, and since our world is increasingly gripped by relativism ("All religions are basically alike") and universalism ("We'll all eventually get to heaven"), I knew it would be good to hear Gary's expertise, especially regarding how the Son of God compares to the founders of other religions. I remember asking my brother something like: "Tell me what you would say to the person who asked, 'Why does Christianity deserve a place at the table with all other world religions?'"

I don't remember asking Gary too many more questions after that. I do remember taking a lot of notes, though. My brother satisfied my curiosity by providing these amazing facts about the Jesus behind our faith:

- Among all major religions, only Christianity, Judaism, and Islam value a linear-historical view of life. (Gary added this clarifying comment: "In other words, if history matters to you, your options are already narrowed down to these three religions").

- More has been written about Jesus than about any other "religious" person. There's not even a close second. Furthermore, it's quite possible to drop the word "religious" (in the first sentence) and still have a true statement.

- Jesus is the only founder of a major world religion who is both unanimously acknowledged and revered by all world religions. Every other faith, minimally, considers Jesus to be a prophet.

- Jesus is the only founder of a major world religion who made three powerful claims:
    1. that he was God;
    2. that he died for the sins of the world; and
    3. that he rose from the dead.

- Jesus is the only founder of a major world religion who—within the first one hundred years after the founder's death—had both followers and nonfollowers claim he had performed miracles. (By contrast, Gary said, Buddha's followers' claims of miracles surfaced three hundred to five hundred years after Buddha's death, adding, "That's a significant difference in time, when it comes to testing for authenticity.")

In recent years, more and more comparisons have been struck between Christianity and Islam, so Gary also took this opportunity to contrast those two particular religions. He repeated that, in Islam, Jesus was acknowledged as a prophet; for them, Christ is positioned in "second place" behind Muhammad. About one hundred verses of the Koran refer to Jesus, which describe him as: (1) virgin-born, (2) the Messiah, (3) a miracle worker, and (4) a sinless person. Here's the surprising part: None of these four traits is ever tied (in the Koran) to Muhammad![1]

Jesus stands alone. No wonder he is frequently called "incomparable."[2]

In sum, when we talk about the complete message of the cross, it always starts with Jesus. We disciples must regularly celebrate both his unique witness and how that historical testimony still transforms lives today. C. S. Lewis reminded us that—because Jesus did equate Himself with God—every person is left with only a few options for responding to his weighty claim:

> A man who was merely a man and said the sort of things Jesus said would not be a great moral teacher. He would either be a lunatic—on a level with the man who says he is a poached egg—or else he would be the Devil of Hell. You must make your choice. Either this man was, and is, the Son of God: or else a madman or something worse. You can shut him up for a fool, you can spit at him and kill him as a demon; or you can fall at his feet and call him Lord and God. But let us not come with any patronizing nonsense about his being a great human teacher. He has not left that open to us. He did not intend to.[3]

He's the Jesus—the true Son of God—we want others to know.

The Gospel in a Nutshell . . . and More

Sometimes it is dangerous to reduce rich insights to only a few words. At other times, conciseness is a virtue.

When it comes to the Gospel's core meaning, the Apostle Paul met the challenge of conciseness head-on, reducing the Good News to three key beliefs. In 1 Corinthians 15:1-5, he prefaces his summary with "For what I received I passed on to you as of first importance." These are the three historical jewels of our faith:

1. "that Christ died for our sins according to the Scriptures;"
2. "that he was buried"; and
3. "that he was raised on the third day according to the Scriptures."

Believing in Jesus' substitutionary payment for our sins, Jesus' burial, and Jesus' resurrection reduces the "Good News" to its lowest common denominator. Again, it was trusting in these truths that saved the Corinthian believers, and it's what still saves all of us who come to Jesus.

The *Shalom* of God Revisited

If I were forced to choose only one word to describe the Gospel—to come up with a simple term that was largely free from theological jargon—that synonym would be an earlier term I mentioned, "peace." Not only does the word "peace" explain our radical conversion by Christ, but it also addresses many related components of the Good News.[4] It is what the Bible calls "things that accompany salvation."[5] In one sense, those components are inseparable from their core. Yet it is this kind of simplicity—with associative complexity—the church must regain for a complete understanding of the Gospel.

Here are some of Scripture's fantastic descriptions of those "accompanying" features of *shalom*: The "God of peace" was incarnated as the "Prince of Peace." He offered the "peace from God," based upon the "covenant of peace" (which is "an everlasting covenant"), "through the blood of . . . our Lord Jesus." We "peacemakers" (all God's sons and daughters) now proclaim "the good news of peace through Jesus Christ," which covers our feet as God's armor for spiritual warfare. We disciples are also offered God's "perfect peace" to "rule in [our] hearts," enabling us to live "peaceful and quiet lives." This lifelong obligation of peace (to which we are "called") touches our family, fellow believers, and even our enemies. Everyone we meet is to experience God's peace indirectly through us, as much as it is realistically "possible." As Christ's "peace-loving" followers, empowered by God's wisdom, we faithfully walk the "path of peace" throughout our life. We realize that being "a new creation" is "what [really] counts," and it is that mind-set that brings

God's "peace and mercy to all who follow this rule [of life]." Lastly, this committed lifestyle yields the "fruit of the Spirit," including "peace." (The *Supplemental Resource* offers two helps: Sidebar 10.1 illustrates what should not happen when we evangelize, while sidebar 10.2 offers a parable along those same lines.)

Four Principles of God's Peace

Let's go one step further, since that's what the Apostle Paul does. The love of Christ is systematically organized around four symbolic dimensions in Ephesians 3:18: They are labeled the "wide and long and high and deep" dimensions of Jesus' passion. When those same four standards are applied to the previous traits of God's peace, we discover even more about the accompanying principles of *shalom*. As with our Eden legacy of communion, we begin with the only perpendicular measurement.

The Height of *Shalom*

God's peace is the vertical dimension found within this foursome. "Height" says that authentic salvation is intrinsically linked to heaven—to grace alone (Sidebar 10.3 in the *Supplemental Resource* shows the significance of this grace). Again, Christianity is the only world religion whose founder claimed to be God, to die for the world's sins, and to rise from the dead. "Conversion" correlates with those facts, for it occurs when an individual acknowledges his personal sin, repents, and trusts the saving sacrifice of Jesus. (Sidebar 10.4 in the *Supplemental Resource* provides an overview of select Scriptures on salvation, while sidebar 10.5 in the *Supplemental Resource* offers a creative parable about one person's transformed life.)

No wonder Jesus' title as "Prince of Peace" synthesizes his three personal roles from three previous chapters: Last Adam (chapter 6), Great Physician (chapter 7), and Beloved Brother (chapter 8). In other words, his peace reunites us in communion with God.[6] His peace also provides us with holiness (character);[7] supplies us with a godly "respect [for] those who work hard among you" (calling);[8] and encourages us towards harmonious relationships (community).[9] Collectively, this is the Jesus we want others to know.

In short, the supernatural "height" of God's redeeming peace should

- prompt us to say "peace" in our greetings (Luke 10:5-6);[10]
- invite us to serve as peacemakers (Matt. 5:9);
- urge us to actively seek peace (Ps. 34:14; 1 Pet. 3:11);
- cause us to sow peace (Jas. 3:17-18);
- enable us to stand in peace (Rom. 5:1-2); and
- assist us to possess Spirit-led peace (Rom. 8:5-6).

Furthermore, this first dimension reconnects us with Eden and our image. Romans 16:20 announces a very unusual promise, when we compare it with the typical ways we think about *shalom*: "The God of peace will soon crush Satan under your feet." Paul reminded saints that, through Christ, we will partner in the fulfillment of Genesis 3:15. The shameful walk of the first family out of Eden will transform into a triumphant march of God's redeemed family back into the Garden— then on to eternal Jerusalem, the City of Peace.

Most (if not all) of the key points from this first principle are well known in many Christian circles. That's not the case, however, with the last three categories. The width, length, and depth of God's peace will challenge our understanding of biblical discipleship if we listen carefully to his voice.

The Width of *Shalom*

The second principle of divine peace declares that our Maker is thoroughly interested in our entire being, not just part of us. Jesus made this value statement quite clear when he deliberately spoke about "healing the whole man" (John 7:23). His position should officially forbid any compartmentalized views of people (also see Prov. 4:18-22, Matt. 5:22-23, 3 John 2). The hand model from chapter 5 illustrates holistic breadth in all people. *Shalom* plays itself out through this model by initially demonstrating our blamelessness in Christ.[11] This is our "palm." The "fingers" are each linked to peace in this fashion:

- In our physical sphere: God provides "sleep in peace" (Ps. 4:8). Proverbs 14:30 also reminds us that "a heart at peace gives life to the body, but envy rots the bones."
- In our mental domain: "Perfect peace" is the reward for those "whose mind is steadfast," trusting in God (Isa. 26:3; also see Rom. 8:5-6; Phil. 4:8-9).
- In our emotional domain: The "peace of Christ" has the power to "rule [our] hearts" (Col. 3:15), just as God's peace will "guard" our hearts (Phil. 4:7).
- In our social sphere: Believers are directed to live peaceably among many groups, ranging all the way from friends to enemies (Prov. 16:7; Rom. 12:18; 14:19; 2 Cor. 13:11; Titus 3:2; Heb. 12:14).
- In our moral domain: God's children who persist in "doing good" are rewarded with peace (Rom. 2:5-11; also see Ps. 119:165).

The Length of *Shalom*

Dallas Willard has called believers to "do nothing less than engage in a radical rethinking of the Christian conception of salvation."[12] He is especially disturbed that disciples have drifted from their historical roots and their theological words, which are anchored in the Bible's coherent plan of redemption. Willard suggested that, for many, the Christian idea of salvation has shrunk into an overly simplified concept of forgiveness of sins. He deduced that we have become irresponsible in larger duties of faith, most notably the neglect of our bodies.

I share Willard's concern. I extend his instruction here by going beyond our holistic nature (the "width" category) and teaching this "length" principle of our faith. I want to analyze this specific dimension in terms of the chronological aspects of our belief: accepting Jesus as Savior, growing as a disciple, and receiving our eternal reward. The clearest biblical analogy of "length" is this: The Christian life—in terms of its three sequential phases—is best understood by the lifelong commitment of marriage. One reason why this analogy between faith and marriage works is the implied truths found in *imago Dei*.[13]

We often have cheap faith today because we have cheap marriages. Each affects the other, since both require serious and lasting commitments. Some of that cheapness is exposed by our selective language. For example, the theological terms customarily used to describe the three sequential phases of Christian growth are "regeneration," "sanctification," and "glorification." I prefer a simpler and more unified pattern that maintains the label "salvation" for all three segments. There is great value in substituting those three theological terms with the following: "Phase 1, Phase 2, and Phase 3 of our salvation." Through that lone phrase, salvation's persevering "length" stays connected and preserved. We're not as tempted to chop our faith up into discrete units as we are when we use three different terms. Consequently we are not as prone to treat those separate parts as dissimilar.

The following paragraphs draw further analogies to this three-part continuity of both marriage and faith. Marriage commitments of "I do," "I still do," and "I did" are closely matched with the believer's three salvation phases.

"I Do"—Our Past Salvation

Several passages refer to our immediate redemption in Christ, once we say yes to him. We have been saved—instantaneously—whenever we asked Jesus to forgive and ransom us.[14] Phase 1 of our salvation is comparable to our wedding day. It is grounded in a historical event, a point in time. Whether you remember the exact day of your conversion (some believers have trouble because they were so young) is not as important as knowing for sure that you did. (I would never suggest handling our wedding anniversary dates in the same manner!) My favorite verse for this "past" category is John 5:24, "I tell you the truth, whoever hears my word and believes him who sent me has eternal life and will not be condemned; he has crossed over from death to life." (First John 5:13 ranks up there as well.) Think about it: We believers have already "crossed over . . . to life." Praise God!

"I Still Do"—Our Present Salvation

Phase 1 compares to evangelism, while Phase 2 is more like discipleship (also known as sanctification). Several verses identify our state of "being saved," like Romans 10:10, 1 Corinthians 1:18, and 2 Corinthians 2:15; and 6:2. Probably the most remarkable set of verses is Philippians 2:12-13: "Continue to work out your salvation with fear and trembling, for it is God who works in you." These passages remind us of our ongoing salvation process. Phase 2 is the segment of salvation and married life that should get the most attention, because it's where we spend almost all our time and energy. But that rarely happens. Phase 2 (for both faith and marriage) always takes a backseat to Phase 1. To prove my point, speculate what the average dollar-cost-per-hour would run for a typical wedding day (Phase 1). Then compare that figure to all expenses incurred *after* the wedding day, all monies invested to strengthen a marriage throughout the years that follow (Phase 2). Translate your second estimated figure into dollar-cost-per-hour as well. I guarantee there will always be a staggering disparity between your first and second numbers.

Do you see any similarities (in most churches) between the same disparity of dollars spent on evangelism versus discipleship? Less than a decade ago, George Barna validated this discrepancy. He surveyed more than five hundred senior pastors to determine where they were personally investing themselves in ministry. One particular question asked for their top three priorities. Evangelism was cited by 43 percent of senior pastors, but only 11 percent mentioned discipleship![15] That four-to-one ratio is tragically reaping bushels full of immature growth in today's church.

"I Did"—Our Future Salvation

Phase 3 of marriage is usually anticipated in most wedding vows, made in Phase 1. Statements like "I'll love you forever" and "Until death parts us" ideally affirm the couple's lifelong commitments to mutual growth, sacrificial affection, and faithfulness. Several verses, likewise, verify this futuristic faith stage—promising that, one day, we will be saved.[16]

It is critical to recall that all seven churches addressed at the outset of Revelation (chapters 2 and 3) are individually alerted to the significance of perseverance. (The fact that there are no exceptions should keep us as vigilant as the Minutemen in the Revolutionary War.) The comments to the congregation at Laodicea, the last church addressed in Revelation, are an excellent expression of this challenge, since Jesus refers to himself as one who likewise persevered: "To him who overcomes, I will give the right to sit with me on my throne, just as I overcame and sat down with my Father on his throne" (Rev. 3:21). Table 10.1 reviews this three-part analogy between faith and marriage.

The Depth of *Shalom*

This is the final principle of God's peace. It is the most misunderstood of the four, and it is virtually never linked with the Good News. That's a

TABLE 10.1

Parallels of Christian Faith and Marriage

	Christian Faith	Christian Marriage
Phase 1: *Past* **Condition**	Initially saying "I do" to Jesus at the altar of salvation New Identity ("new creation") in Christ (Image reborn) "Count the cost . . . can't serve two masters" Taking Jesus as Savior (with evidence of faith proclaimed)	Initially saying "I do" to spouse at the altar of marriage New Identity ("one flesh") in Christ "Leave (parents) and cleave (to each other)" Taking spouse (and "forsaking all others")
Phase 2: *Present* **Condition**	Daily reiterating "I still do" to Jesus, as Soul Partner in Faith's Journey Idolatry (see parallel sin of Adultery from Jer. 2:32; Mal. 2:10-16) Submitting to Jesus as Lord (with evidence of fruit produced) Image continuously restored so the disciple looks more like Jesus	Daily reiterating "I still do" to spouse, as sole partner in life's journey. Adultery (see parallel sin of Idolatry in 1 Cor. 5:9-11; 10:7-8) Submitting to each other, out of reverence for Christ (Eph. 5:21) Mutual continuous growth, so spouses look more alike in values and habits
Phase 3: *Future* **Condition**	Ultimately testifying "I did" to Jesus, as faithful and loving partner "Persevering to the end" Crowning Jesus as King (with evidence of fidelity preserved) Image fully restored (becoming like Jesus)	Ultimately testifying "I did" to spouse, as a faithful and loving partner "Until death parts us" Honoring Jesus as Creator of marriage (following "this way from the beginning," based upon Matt. 19:1-8) Image fully respected (from esteeming complementary genders in marriage, as in Gen. 1:27 and 2:18-25)

shame. This last category (stated negatively) reminds me of what I call "the Cod Liver Oil View of Faith—If something tastes bad, it must be good for you." The inverse is also true: "If you experience something pleasant, it must be wrong." Don't be too quick to suppose you have never thought this way before. We all think like this, at some level. And we are all healthier when we confess that fact.

Philip Yancey stated this human predicament more philosophically. He made this "aha" discovery, while reminiscing on how G. K. Chesterton influenced his life:

> It struck me, after reading my umpteenth book on the problem of pain, that I have never even seen a book on "the problem of pleasure." . . . It looms as a huge question: the philosophical equivalent, for atheists, to the problem of pain for Christians. On the issue of pleasure, Christians can breathe easier. A good and loving God would naturally want his creatures to experience delight, joy, and personal fulfillment. . . . But should not atheists have an equal obligation to explain the origin of pleasure in a world of randomness and meaninglessness?[17]

The "depth" of salvation can also be called "the problem of pleasure." This depth reaches to our inner soul. It holds the potential to fully satisfy us at the deep level of *shalom*—"the peace that passes understanding." Why do we disciples so quickly forget the many biblical truths about God's pleasurable gifts to us?[18] Why, for instance, do we forget:

- James 1:16-17: "Don't be deceived, my dear brothers. Every good and perfect gift is from above, coming down from the Father of the heavenly lights, who does not change like shifting shadows."
- 1 Timothy 6:17: "Command those who are rich in this present world not to be arrogant nor to put their hope in wealth, which is so uncertain, but to put their hope in God, who richly provides us with everything for our enjoyment."

- Deuteronomy 5:33: "Walk in all the way that the Lord your God has commanded you, so that you may live and prosper and prolong your days in the land that you will possess."
- Isaiah 48:17-18: "This is what the LORD says—your Redeemer, the Holy One of Israel: 'I am the LORD your God, who teaches you what is best for you, who directs you in the way you should go.'"
- Deuteronomy 5:28-29: "The LORD heard you when you spoke to me and the LORD said to me, 'I have heard what this people said to you. Everything they said was good. Oh, that their hearts would be inclined to fear me and keep all my commands always, so that it might go well with them and their children forever!'"

Why do we misunderstand these gratifying provisions from God? Think "cod liver oil." We also dismiss how pleasure is tied to image—we reflect the Creator of pleasure. We misunderstand how God himself experiences pleasure—and how he doesn't. First, the Bible notes our Maker's personal pleasures. Like a loving Parent, God delights in his obedient children: He creates the "Garden of Eden" (literally "a hedging around delight"); also, in his "new heavens and new earth" he promises to again "take delight in my people" (Isa. 65:19). And there are other expressions of divine pleasure (see Deut. 30:9; Ps. 18:19; 149:4; Isa. 5:7; and 62:4).

Second, we must remind ourselves of pleasures God does *not* experience. Ezekiel 33:11 should be memorized by every saint, for it features the real nature of our Creator: "Say to them, 'As surely as I live, declares the Sovereign LORD, I take no pleasure in the death of the wicked, but rather that they turn from their ways and live. Turn! Turn from your evil ways!'" What if we also reflected our Maker's pleasure-free attitude toward the judgment of those who do evil?

Be assured that a pleasure-packed view of salvation does not automatically negate Christ's command to "take up your cross." These are not mutually exclusive charges. A pleasure-packed perspective returns us to Eden and enables us to see this side of God's *shalom* as "the way things are supposed to be."[19] John Piper essentially drew this conclusion when he made these summative statements: "God is most glorified in me when I am most satisfied in him," and "The enjoyment of God and the glorification of God are one. His eternal purpose and our eternal pleasure unite."[20]

We have a good God who gives good gifts to all (Matt. 5:44-45). There is no reason to think this benevolent one withholds additional, special pleasures from individuals who join his family. That's just one more reminder that the Gospel is not limited to forgiveness and deliverance from hell. The Gospel also promises abundant life now. This wonderful promise of deep-seated peace should prompt saints to celebrate the entire Good News. (Sidebar 10.6 in the *Supplemental Resource* summarizes all four principles of God's peace from this section, matching Jesus' names to each category.)

Chapter Ten's contribution to complete discipleship, therefore, may be summarized this way:

Truth 10

God's model for discipleship promotes a comprehensive view of the Good News. When the fullness of the Gospel is believed, holy wholeness results—the thoroughly satisfying *shalom* of God.

Conclusion

Yellowstone National Park, established in 1872, is the oldest of the U.S. national parks, and it was the first park of its kind in the world. It offers breathtaking wonders, from its unequaled beauties of wildlife to its inspiring geysers. The message on the archway at its northern entrance welcomes all who pass through. That message formally reacquaints each traveler with the U.S. Congress's mission for Yellowstone on the first day it opened. It is a purpose statement that saints need to borrow, to express an important component of God's salvation that frequently gets overlooked. The archway simply reads, "For the benefit and the enjoyment of the people."

Like the multifaceted paradox that it is, the Good News of Jesus Christ is simultaneously simpler and more sophisticated than most of us acknowledge. Because of its unpretentious nature, a child may become a child of God. Because of its complexity, a child of God may become a man or woman of God.

I am so thankful for the entire Gospel:

- for its "height," which forever connects us to our Creator.
- for its "width," which reminds us of the complex connectedness within ourselves.
- for its "length," which compares both godly marriage and faith as lifelong journeys.
- for its "depth," which frees us to enjoy our Maker's pleasures.

I am thankful for the *shalom* of God. I am thankful my family is basking in its gracious light. I am thankful my profession is directly associated with its redemptive message. I am thankful *shalom* springs from my heritage in Eden. I am thankful *shalom* is my anticipated Homeland. And I am thankful that *shalom*—by God's restoring image inside me—may graciously surprise me at any second of any day.

It is fitting to end this chapter about the Good News—with accompanying features of redemption, holistic image, perseverance, and pleasure—by quoting from Jewish tradition: "When a man uses a die to stamp out coins, they all come out alike; but God stamped all men with the die of Adam, yet each is different: So everyone has a right to say, 'For my sake was the world created.'"[21]

I would add, "For my sake—and yours—the world was recreated by Christ." His offer of salvation is that personal—and that astounding. He's the Jesus we want others to know.

---

1 I asked Gary what resources (in the introductory fields of comparative world religions and apologetics) he recommended to Christian leaders for further study. He named several—with Edwin M. Yamauchi's "Historical Notes on the (In)Comparable Christ" at the top of his list. This resource was published by *Christianity Today* in its October 22, 1971 (Vol. XVI, No. 2) issue, pp. 7–11. InterVarsity Press later released this same content in a small pamphlet called "Jesus, Zoroaster, Buddha, Socrates, Muhammad."

2 Dr. Gary Habermas' suggestions for further study included Lee Strobel's *The Case for Christ*; Giesler's and Watkins's *Worldview Apart*; Paul Little's trilogy: *Know What You Believe, Know Why You Believe,* and *Know Who You Believe,* as well as his *How to Give Away Your Faith*; and Josh McDowell's books: *More than a Carpenter, Evidence That Demands a Verdict, More Evidence That Demands a Verdict,* and *New Evidence That Demands a Verdict.*

3 *Mere Christianity* (New York: Macmillan, 1979), p. 56.

4 The many verses cited in this summary section on peace include Romans 16:20; 1 Corinthians 14:33; Philippians 4:8-9; Isaiah 9:6a; Romans 1:7; 1 Corinthians 1:3; 2 Corinthians 1:2; Galatians 1:3; Ezekiel 37:26; Hebrews 13:20; Matthew 5:9; Acts 10:36; Ephesians 6:15; Isaiah 26:3; Colossians 3:15; 1 Timothy 2:2; Psalm 34:14b; 1 Peter 3:11; 1 Corinthians 7:15b; Acts 15:33; Romans 14:17-19; Proverbs 16:7; Romans 12:18; 14:19; Hebrews 12:14; James 3:17; Luke 1:79; Galatians 6:15-16; and Galatians 5:22.

5 See some of the corollary items that "accompany" salvation in Hebrews 6:9 and 2 Corinthians 9:13.

6 Psalm 85:8-10 and Micah 5:2-5.

7 Isaiah 26:3 and Colossians 3:15.

8 In Paul's mind, there is a strong bond between hard work (versus idleness) and peaceful relationships, as he notes in 1 Thessalonians 5:12-15 and 2 Thessalonians 3:6-10.

9 See Mark 9:50, 1 Corinthians 7:15, 2 Corinthians 13:11, and 1 Thessalonians 5:13.

10 It is remarkable that eleven (of the thirteen) greetings from the Apostle Paul begin with "peace from God our Father and our Lord Jesus Christ."

11 Psalm 85:8-10; Ephesians 2:13-17; 1 Thessalonians 5:23; Hebrews 12:10-11, 14; and 2 Peter 3:14.

12 *The Spirit of the Disciplines* (San Francisco: Harper San Francisco, 1988), p. 32.

13 When Genesis 1:27 is figuratively placed over Genesis 2:18-25, it becomes apparent that the reason why it was "not good for man to be alone" (even in his sinless condition) is because Adam was incomplete. *Image* of God is plural, both "male and female," according to Genesis 1:27. So the creation of Eve and the inauguration of marriage are complementary. When put together, for the first time, humanity became whole.

14 See Romans 8:24; Ephesians 2:5, 8; Colossians 1:3; and Titus 3:5.

15 Taken from George Barna's *Index of Leading Spiritual Indicators* (Dallas: Word, 1996), p. 36.

16 See passages like Romans 5:9; 10:13; 13:11; 1 Corinthians 3:15; 5:5; and 2 Timothy 4:18.

17 *Soul Survivor* (New York: Doubleday, 2001), pp. 53-54.

18 God "knows our best" is a key principle behind a pleasure-packed view of the Good News. And it's linked with his image, too:

> So there are "rules for life," like the signs of cliff tops, which read: DANGER— KEEP OUT. The signs are there to help not hinder us. God has put them there because to live in this way, according to his rules, is the way for both safety and fulfillment. The God who made us and knows what is for our best good is the same God who gives us his commands. When we break these, it is not only wrong, it is also not for our best good; it is not for our fulfillment as unique persons made in the image of God.

From *Whatever Happened to the Human Race?* by Francis A. Schaeffer and C. Everett Koop (Old Tappen, N.J.: Fleming H. Revell, 1979), p. 155.

Also, Sailhamer, *The Pentateuch as Narrative,* (Grand Rapids, Mich., 1992), pp. 100-01 reminds us that God's early command (in Gen. 2:15) to "work" and "take care" of the Garden is best translated "to worship and obey." Sailhamer closes with these prudent words: "The inference of God's commands in Genesis 2:16-17 is that God alone knows what is good for human beings and God alone knows what is not good for them. To enjoy the 'good' we must trust God and obey him. If we disobey, we will have to decide for ourselves what is good and what is not good. While to modern men and women such a prospect may seem desirable, to the author of Genesis it is the worst fate that could have befallen humanity."

19 From Cornelius Plantinga Jr.'s *Engaging God's World* (Grand Rapids, Mich.: Eerdmans, 2002), p.15.

20 *Desiring God*, (Sisters, Oreg.: Multnomah, 1996), pp. 9, 254. Italics mine.

21 From the TALMUD: *Sanhedrin*, 4:5 (as published in *Leo Rosten's Treasury of Jewish Quotations* [New York: McGraw-Hill, 1972], p. 91).

Chapter Eleven

The Complete Way to Follow Jesus

> "Christ our Example." After "Christ our Redeemer," no words can more deeply stir the Christian heart than these.
>
> — B. B. WARFIELD
>
> The important point in all our imitation [of God] is its deliberate intentionality. We don't just think God's values are good. We embrace them wholly. . . . To embrace is to accept with gusto, to live to the hilt, to choose with extra intentionality and tenacity.
>
> — MARVA DAWN

I can't afford not to think about how people mature.

As a parent of three grown-up daughters, a university professor who has taught biblical studies and discipleship for over twenty years, and an associate pastor-elder who has served for the past ten years, the topic of growth is constantly on my mind. This is particularly true for my local church responsibilities. I need to regularly think through God's image-restoration process for a wide range of people.

Even though our congregation numbers fewer than one hundred, we are quite diverse. So I try to think about this universal need for Christian maturity in case-specific ways—for our elementary-aged kids, blue-collar workers, singles, handicapped, internationals, retirees, parents, teens, college students, and an array of professionals. Whenever the opportunity arises, I try to help each interested person customize his or her answers to this significant inquiry: "What is the complete way to follow Christ?"

Rethinking What It Means to Follow Jesus

As we begin to explore this chapter's topic, recall the building we have assembled so far. Chapters 1 through 10 have provided these building blocks for complete biblical discipleship:

- Following Jesus means breathing together with him. Discipleship that is linked to our Creator's image and breath means we literally join a "conspiracy." We consciously follow the way Jesus deliberately modeled life (chapter 1).

- Following Jesus means returning Home through Eden. Within that place, we remember all that we image bearers once had, so we set out on our new course for heaven's Home (chapter 2).

- Following Jesus means rediscovering our Super Nine gifts from the Garden. These are specific expressions of our Maker's image inside of us. Whenever we reconnect with these gifts we become what the Creator desired for us (chapter 3).

- Following Jesus means recalling our past, specifically our devastating fall through willful disobedience. It also means acknowledging our present, how sin continues to make us unhuman by unraveling our image (chapter 4).

- Following Jesus means embracing God's message to persistently return to our eternal Home with Christ. His full restoration commences at our new birth (when the Holy Spirit breathes new life in us), which rejuvenates his image inside us. God's invitation begins with Eden's promise of hope, it continues at the top of Mount Sinai, and it climaxes at Mount Calvary (chapter 5).

- Following Jesus means valuing the mystery, reality, and majesty of the Incarnation. It is recovering the unedited story of Christmas: God himself became a full, image-reflecting human (chapter 6).

- Following Jesus means recognizing the completeness of Christ's character in his role as the Last Adam. As we understand the entire portrait of Jesus, we see ourselves in a revealing light— we, too, possess the holistic potentials of *imago Dei* (chapter 7).

- Following Jesus means readjusting our views on our Lord's holistic ministry of service and redemption, which he achieved by his Carpenter and Great Physician roles. His principles of calling transfer to our vocations. Complete discipleship includes the cultural, Gospel, and image mandates (chapter 8).

- Following Jesus means reinvesting ourselves in healthy community relationships, as our Beloved Brother did. Moreover, it means understanding and emulating Jesus' example of how people mature—how we "perfect" the image of God in us (chapter 9).

- Following Jesus means trusting in his redemptive offer. That core salvation message is closely associated with "things that accompany salvation," such as experiencing God's peace in our entire being, exhibiting perseverance throughout life, and enjoying our Creator's pleasures from start to end (chapter 10).

Chart 11.1 in the *Supplemental Resource* reviews God's complementary Mandates for his children, discussed earlier in this book.

A Preview of Chapter 11

Let's go back to this chapter's opening question: "What is the complete way to follow Christ?" My standard advice for all believers includes five progressive phases. This design prescriptively matches key biblical directives, while permitting flexibility for each saint to customize a personal plan for her own life. I generally introduce my design (later shown in table 11.3) by saying something like "There are five sequences through which the disciple follows Jesus. Each phase is necessary, paralleling God's natural patterns for human growth. And each phase moves us in the direction of full image restoration."

These five discipleship phases represent specific ways we obey Jesus. Not only do these five periods identify the sequence of our spiritual growth; they also portray our comprehensive human development patterns from infancy to older adulthood. Furthermore, I believe these five categories also indicate the progressive historical periods of the church's collective maturity, from the beginning to the end of the New Testament.

- Discipleship by Observation: The initial phase represents elementary faith commitment. It can be compared to human infancy. In Bible times, this first phase represents the person in the early Gospel chapters who chose to "hang out" with Jesus. Today, this person may "observe" Jesus through cursory Bible readings or by watching how other Christian people live. Remember that the basic meaning for disciple is "learner"—that in Matthew 11:29, Jesus invites followers to "learn from me."

- Discipleship by Continuation: The second phase of following Jesus progresses to an apprentice phase, as the growing disciple more actively assists him. Historically, this time period includes the last half of Jesus' earthly ministry through the transition period of Pentecost, the start of the church age. Just as Jesus continued the work of the Father, so—with the coming of the Holy Spirit—every saint continues her Lord's work. This second phase parallels the human span of childhood.

- Discipleship by Experimentation: Phase three covers the adolescent segment of discipleship. The "followers of the Way"—who identified with Jesus' exclusive "way" claim (both in John 14:6 and throughout the book of Acts)—were maturing, but they were still learning faith basics. Like teenagers, they were testing those concepts out in real life for the first time. An illustration comes from Acts 18:24-28: Apollos (an influential leader of and persuasive orator in the early church) had some of his theology corrected by Priscilla and Aquila. After being shown "the way of God more adequately," Apollos and his ministry yielded even more fruit.

- Discipleship by Imitation: The fourth phase of obeying Christ takes an inside-outside step: The growing disciple consciously chooses to copy godly patterns of living. This progressive movement from personal volition (inside) to corresponding behavior (outside) favorably compares to how young adults mature. Thus, it bears the developmental label of younger adulthood. The simple word "as" frequently accompanies this fourth category, because it links us with the example we must duplicate (e.g., the command in Eph. 4:32 is to forgive "each other, just as in Christ God forgave" us).

- Discipleship by Transformation: The fifth phase conveys more than emulation of godliness. It is the older adulthood phase, whereby mature disciples actually become the ones who are imitated (see 1 Cor. 11:1). There's never a time when we followers reach perfection in this world, but the faithful disciple in this last phase becomes much more like the Lord.

Collectively, these five discipleship phases display several parallel accounts of healthy, growing people. An exceptional verse for this human comparison is Galatians 4:19, where Paul selected the developmental terms "dear children" and "the pains of childbirth." But there's more: The apostle also crafted the brilliant phrase—summarizing the disciple's entire life purpose—"until Christ is formed in you." That's complete discipleship.

More of What It Means to "Follow"

The rest of chapter 11 provides more details about our "followership," as each of these five phases is expanded and explained.

Discipleship by Observation

What did Jesus mean when he commanded disciples to "follow Me"? However we answer that question, we must start with baby steps. This first phase of maturity corresponds with our Lord's "preschool." It is comparable to his initial invitation to the very first disciple: "Come . . . and you will see" (John 1:39). That same simple welcome was given to two other early converts (John 1:46; 4:29). Avoiding any assumption, we begin with some basic building blocks at this elementary level. For instance: There is no doubt Jesus commanded his disciples to "follow" him. (See sidebar 11.1 in the *Supplemental Resource*.)

Discipleship by Continuation

The historical time frame for this second phase begins with the second half of Jesus' public ministry years. The concept of continuation takes prominence in Jesus' Upper Room Discourse (John 14–17) and continues through the subsequent Day of Pentecost. This was a time when Christ transferred his power and purpose to his followers (beginning as early as John 9:4, when the plural word "we" is featured). The Son's mantle was eventually passed to God's sons and daughters. Think of this deliberate perpetuation like this: The work of the first person of the Trinity (since Creation) had been continued by the second person for thirty-three years on earth. Now—at this second discipleship phase—the third person would soon indwell all of God's people, so that this work of the second person would continue. Table 11.1 illustrates these points through all three Garden

TABLE 11.1

Continuation of God's Purposes—by Legacy Goals

(all verses the spoken words of Jesus)

The goals the Father models for the Son . . .	are the same goals Jesus models for the disciples.

	Goal of Communion (with God)	
	"For just as the Father raises the dead and gives them life . . . " (John 5:21a)	" . . . even so the Son gives life to whom he is pleased to give it" (John 5:21b)

Family Name brings . . .	**Goal of Family *Name* (Character)**	
1. Continuation of Divine NURTURE (also John 5:19; 15:5)	"Just as the living Father sent me and I live because of the Father . . ." (John 6:57a)	". . . so the one who feeds on me will live because of me . . . the bread . . . from heaven." (John 6:57b-58a)
2. Continuation of Divine LOVE (from obedience)	". . . just as I have obeyed my Father's commands and remain in his love" (John 15:10b)	"If you obey my commands, you will remain in my love . . . " (John 15:10a)
3. Continuation of Divine PROTECTION (by Father's Name)	". . . I am coming to you. Holy Father, protect them by the power of your name—the name you gave me— . . ." (John 17:11b)	". . . While I was with them and kept them safe by that name you gave me." (John 17:12a)
4. Continuation of Divine TRUTH (John 17:17; 14:10; 15:5)	"For I gave them the words you gave me . . . " (John 17:8a)	". . . and they accepted them." (John 17:8b)

Family Business means . . .	**Goal of Family *Business* (Calling)**	
1. Continuation of Jesus' WORK in the world (see John 9:4; 13:20; 20:21b)	"As you sent me into the world . . ." (John 17:18a)	". . . I have sent them into the world." (John 17:18b)
2. Continuation of Jesus' MIRACLES (see John 5:20)	"Believe me when I say that I am in the Father and the Father is in me; or at least believe on the evidence of the miracles themselves . . . ." (John 14:11)	". . . I tell you the truth, anyone who has faith in me will do what I have been doing. he will do even greater things than these. . . . " (John 14:12)
3. Continuation of Cultural Mandate task of DOMINION (see Luke 22:29-30)	". . . I confer on you a kingdom . . . ." (Luke 22:29b) ". . . just as I overcame and sat down with my Father on his throne" (Rev. 3:21b)	". . . just as my Father conferred [a kingdom] on me . . ." (Luke 22:29a) "To him who overcomes, I will give the right to sit with me on my throne . . . " (Rev. 3:21a)
4. Continuation of the GREAT COMMISSION (Matt. 28:19-20)	"For I did not speak of my own accord, but the Father who sent me commanded me what to say and how to say it . . . his command leads to eternal life. So whatever I say is just what the Father has told me to say." (John 12:49-50) ". . . the world must learn that I love the Father and . . . do exactly what my Father has commanded me." (John 14:31a)	"Therefore go and make disciples of all nations, baptizing them in the name of the Father and of the Son and of the Holy Spirit, and teaching them to obey everything I have commanded you. And surely I am with you always, to the very end of the age." (Matt. 28:19-20)
5. Continuation of GLORIFYING GOD (see John 14:13-14)	"I have brought you glory on earth by completing the work you gave me to do." (John 17:4)	"All I have is yours, and all you have is mine. And glory has come to me through them." (John 17:10; also John 14:13-14)

Family Ties include . . .	**Goal of Family *Ties* (Community)**	
1. Continued Blessings of UNITY (John 14:20; 17:23a, 26)	". . . as we are one" (John 17:11d)	". . . so that they may be one . . . " (John 17:11c)
2. Continued Blessings of WITNESS	". . . the world know that you sent me . . . " (John 17:23c)	"May they be brought to complete unity to let . . . " (John 17:23b)
3. Continued Blessings of LOVE	"As the Father has loved me . . . " (John 15:9a) ". . . as I have loved you" (John 15:12b)	". . . so have I loved you" (John 15:9b) "Love each other . . . " (John 15:12a)

legacies—it presents a complete summary of the disciple's lifelong task to continue Jesus' work through the Garden legacies. The chart reviews the key points first introduced in chapter 3, then updated in chapters 7 through 9, respectively featuring the Garden inheritances of Family Name (character), Family Business (calling), and Family Ties (community).

As table 11.1 and table 11.2 (pp. 254-255) indicate, the modern-day disciple is intrinsically linked to the Garden because her Lord was, too. We continue his work, which continues Adam's work. Obedient followers have no other alternative but to perpetuate the ongoing task of the Cultural Mandate (what some call the Creation Covenant). This second phase resembles an apprenticeship. Unlike the epoch that follows, the disciples in this historical period of the Bible had the benefit of Jesus' physical presence. His leadership in those years compares to the advantages of a mentor relationship today.

Dallas Willard emphasized our Eden bond. He was not hesitant to declare what God's people are still called to do: "So humankind's job description is clearly stated. We were not designed just to live in mystic communion with our Maker, as so often suggested. Rather, we were created to govern the earth with all its living things—and to that specific end we were made in the divine likeness."[1] Willard's challenge grew even stronger as he continued this thought pattern:

> Humans are made to govern—to rule over the zoological realm as God rules over all things. The *imago Dei*, the likeness to God, consists, accordingly, of all those powers and activities required for fulfilling this job description, this rule to which we are appointed. And of course it includes the very rule itself.
>
> But surely this has no bearing on our lives today! Wasn't this just a job description for the first man, Adam? No, it was not. The word "man," or "Adam," is a collective noun, and may be taken as referring

both to the individual, Adam, and to humankind, the community of "governors" over all life higher than the plants. And to accomplish this task, humans were given the abilities appropriate to the task: powers of perception, conceptualization, valuation, and action.[2]

Ruling over all of God's Creation, with loving care, represents the primary activity of our ongoing Eden work. When we follow Jesus (the "Last Adam"), we also continue what our Maker initially directed our first parents to do. In this way, we reaffirm God's image inside us.[3]

Discipleship by Experimentation

The Scripture builds a strong case for discipleship as a lifelong journey. That concept is particularly affirmed by the corresponding first name these early disciples were given. It was a name even more popular than the name "Christian," which they were called only once in the book of Acts (11:26). In John 14:6 our Lord Jesus made a remarkable and unique claim: "I am the way and the truth and the life. No one comes to the Father except through me." Such exclusive claims—whether then or now—usually do not endear the masses. However, Mark 12:13-14 says that even Jesus' critics offered him this commendation: "we know you are a man of integrity. . . . You teach the way of God in accordance with the truth." These remarks led to the first public title attributed to the early disciples.[4] It was a phrase that would be employed at least five times within the book of Acts alone: the followers of the Way.[5]

That descriptive phrase demonstrates our faith's simplicity and sophistication. It describes dynamic and godly living, which necessitates personal experimentation. It was a term so potent that everyone who encountered "the Way" experienced some form of irresistible attraction—out of devotion, curiosity, or hatred. This attraction was never tied to coercion of human will, because one implication of image bearers is

TABLE 11.2

Image, the Super Nine, and Jesus' Names

	Complementary Descriptions of the Super Nine Gifts	Comparable Super Nine Names or Traits for Jesus
1. God-like Physiques	We are *Physical* and *Spiritual*	• A Mere Man (John 10:33) • A Perfect Man (Jas. 3:2) • Appeared in a Body (1 Tim. 3:16) • God with Us (Matt. 1:23) • Immanuel (Isa. 7:14; Matt. 1:23) • Made Like his Brothers in Every Way (Heb. 2:17) • The Child Jesus (Luke 2:27) • The Last Adam (1 Cor. 15:45) • The Son of Man (John 1:51) • Who Died and Came to Life Again (Rev. 2:8)
2. Passionate Thinkers	We are *Emotional* and *Rational* People	• The Light of Knowledge of the Glory of God (2 Cor. 4:6) • The True Light (John 1:9) • The Truth (John 14:6) • The Zeal for God's House (John 2:17) • The Zeal of the LORD Almighty (Isa. 37:32) • Your Light and Your Truth (Ps. 43:3)
3. Sensory Learners	We are *Sensory-Experience* People	• A Fragrant Offering and Sacrifice to God (Eph. 5:2) • Master Teacher of Experiential Education (Luke 24:37-43) • The Bread of Life (John 6:35) • The Spring of Water Welling Up to Eternal Life (John 4:14) • Whose Eyes Are Like Blazing Fire (Rev. 2:18) • Whose Feet Are Like Burnished Bronze (Rev. 2:18) • You Hear Prayer (Ps. 65:2, 5)
4. Kind Rulers	We are *Regal* and *Ecological* People	• Gentle (Matt. 11:29) • Judge of the Living and the Dead (Acts 10:42) • King of Kings (Rev. 19:16) • That Great Shepherd of the Sheep (Heb. 13:20) • The Lord of All the Earth (Josh. 3:11) • The Lord of Peace (2 Thess. 3:16) • The Ruler of God's Creation (Rev. 3:14)
5. Worshipful Workers	We are *Laboring* and *Restfully-Worshiping* People	• Lord of the Sabbath (Mark 2:27-28) • Master-Builder of Firm Foundation (1 Cor. 3:11; Matt. 7:24-25) • One Who faithfully Worshiped (Luke 4:16) • One Who Took Purposeful Time Off (Mark 7:24; 6:30-32) • The Lord of the Harvest (Matt. 9:38) • The Owner of the Vineyard (Matt. 20:8) • Wisdom from God (1 Cor. 1:30)

the moral prohibition of manipulation. As each person was drawn to the followers of the Way, she made a personal choice—like making a purposeful decision at a fork in the road. (Sidebar 11.2 in the *Supplemental Resource* features five references from the book of Acts that use the phrase "the Way.")

TABLE 11.2 CONT'D

Image, the Super Nine, and Jesus' Names

6. Artists & Scientists	We are *Creative* and *Orderly* People	• A Precious Cornerstone (Isa. 28:16) • A Teacher Who Has Come from God (John 3:2) • He Who Created (Rev. 10:6) • Master at Creatively Escaping Entrapment (Matt. 22:22) • One Who Carefully Observed Life (Matt. 6:26-30; Mark 12:41) • One Who Sang Hymns (Matt. 26:30) • Physician (Luke 4:23) • Teacher (Matt. 10:25) • The Carpenter (Mark 6:3) • The Potter (Jer. 18:6)
7. Intimate Families	We are *Individual* and *Relational* People	• Brother of Every Believer (Mark 3:35) • Family Advocate (Matt. 19:1-9) • Not Ashamed to Call Us Brothers (Heb. 2:11-12) • The Bridegroom of the Bride (John 3:29) • The Brother of James, Joseph, Judas, and Simon (Mark 6:3) • The Son of Abraham (Matt. 1:1) • The Son of David (Matt. 1:1) • The Son of Joseph (John 1:45) • The Son of Mary (Mark 6:3) • Who Loves Us (Rev. 1:5)
8. Good Neighbors	We are *Morally-Helpful* People	• A Friend of Tax Collectors and Sinners (Matt. 11:19; Luke 7:34) • A Refuge for the Needy in Distress (Isa. 25:4) • A Refuge for the Poor (Isa. 25:4) • Defender of the Widows (Ps. 68:5) • My Helper (Heb. 13:6) • The Father to the Fatherless (Ps. 68:5) • Who Heals all Your Diseases (Ps. 103:3) • Who Satisfies Your Desires with Good Things (Ps. 103:5) • Wonderful Counselor (Isa. 9:6)
9. Responsible Citizens	We are *Broadly-Cultural* People	• Faithful Citizen of Earth *and* Heaven (Matt. 22:21) • Humble (Matt. 11:29) • Master Communicator (Matt. 7:28-29) • Pure (1 John 3:3) • Servant (Acts 4:27) • Song (Isa. 12:2) • Taxpayer (Matt. 17:24-27) • Tender Mercy (Luke 1:78) • The Lily of the Valleys (SS 2:1)

The adolescent phase of human development parallels this third category. Because of its hands-on experimentation, the church was sometimes characterized by trial-and-error. For instance, the magnificent display of the Spirit's testimony in Barnabas's sacrificial giving (Acts 4) quickly soured in the mockery of Ananias and Sapphira (Acts 5). The heartwarming expression of unity at the Jerusalem council (Acts 15:1-35) was subdued by the sharp disagreement and separation of its two primary leaders, Paul and Barnabas, immediately thereafter (Acts 15:36-41).

Contemporary believers begin to see how radical Jesus' claims and expectations were, by this review of "the Way." Hardly a "Sunday only" faith, historical Christianity soon became an incessant intrusion to those who despised it and a total life cause for all who embraced it. (Sidebars 11.3 and 11.4, from the *Supplemental Resource*, supply further input. The first list provides a summary of all verses in Acts that refer to "the Way," while the second provides additional verses—both positive and negative—on discipleship as a "way of life.") The Gospel call to follow Jesus, then—to actually emulate him—quickly led the early church to earthshaking outcomes. That speaks to the kind of God we serve. Those same earthshaking outcomes may be replicated today, if we trust the Lord to similarly work through us.

Discipleship by Imitation

Simple is often better. This truism is supported in this fourth phase of what Jesus meant by "follow Me," through the two-letter word "as." That simple term provides the contemporary saint with multiple answers to the all-important question, "What am I actually supposed to do if I want to obey Christ?" Several verses remind us of the need for imitation, like these more familiar ones:

- John 13:15: "I have set you an example that you should do as I have done for you."
- Matthew 6:10: "Your kingdom come, your will be done on earth as it is in heaven."
- 1 Corinthians 11:1: "Follow my example, as I follow the example of Christ."
- Ephesians 5:1: "Be imitators of God, therefore, as dearly loved children."

The most underrated verse on imitation, in my mind, is 1 John 2:6: "Whoever claims to live in him must walk as Jesus did." That's exceptionally powerful, as long as we never attempt to analyze, rationalize, or symbolize its straightforward meaning away. (Sidebar 11.5 in the *Supplemental Resource* suggests potential criticisms for *literally* following Christ.)

Sidebar 11.6 in the *Supplemental Resource* gives an overview of these "as" commands throughout the entire New Testament. I have arranged these directives by our three Garden legacies. We speak a lot about modeling or mentoring at this fourth junction of our Christian life, and these simple "as" directives go a long way to provide us with practical strategies for performing these tasks. The imitation of Christ essentially includes a righteous walk, a godly work ethic, and redemptive relationships—each of which expresses forgiveness, mercy, compassion, and empathy. Every entry in sidebar 11.6 connects the disciple with the Lord—either by Christ's direct example, or by that of other godly people living out Christian principles.

Discipleship by Transformation

The concept of the "as" commands is taken one step further in this final phase. I have to confess, when the Holy Spirit helped me to see how simple—and yet profound—all these "as" commands were, I was overwhelmed—overwhelmed by the number of times they appear and overwhelmed by how elementary God's commands are. A high IQ is not required of faithful disciples, but a willing heart is necessary. With a willing heart in place (and faithful obedience as an indicator of that commitment), disciples are eventually transformed to be like their Master. Jesus supported transformation when he described typical student and teacher roles (Matt. 10:24-25). He assumed obedient followers would mature, and that maturity would cause students to "look like" their teacher. That's why transformation is comprehensive and holistic (see Phil. 3:21; 1 Cor. 13:12; Col. 3:5-10). Within this final state of restoration, we share our Master's joy (see Matt. 25:21, 23).

Table 11.3 offers a summary of all five phases of discipleship, from Observation to Transformation. This is what it means to completely "follow Jesus."

Summary of a Pleasurable Process

With all due respect to the richness, mysteries, breadth, controversies, and complexities of Christianity, I offer a one-sentence summary of discipleship.[6] This quotable quote addresses the historical meaning of our Eden heritage, while it also prizes our great potential as image bearers. Perhaps most impressive, it upholds the gusto living that Jesus bequeathed his followers. This summative quote fittingly comes from the Jerusalem Talmud: "When a man faces his Maker, he will have to account for those [God-given] pleasures of life which he failed to enjoy."[7]

This truth may sound quite odd when we compare it to the ways we typically think about our faith. Yet, in our heart of hearts, whenever we recall the pleasurable moments of our life—like being surprised by a rainbow or unexpectedly loved by a friend—most of us would affirm this Talmudic saying. I find that liberating. When we do more research into the Scriptures, we discover some vital Bible passages that pointedly direct us to enjoy life (see sidebar 11.7 in the *Supplemental Resource*).

My favorite verse on this subject of enjoyment comes from 1 Timothy 6:17b. (Though listed in chapter 10, since it's one of my favorites, I will list it again.) The Apostle Paul blessed his spiritual son with a powerful truth. It's one of those mottoes (or bumper-sticker lines) that most of us need to memorize and then daily apply to our lives. Paul told his spiritual son to teach others to "put their trust in God"—then he added, "who richly provides us with everything for our enjoyment." Read

TABLE 11.3
Five Discipleship Phases of "Following" Jesus

Discipleship Phase	Key Concepts (Invitations from Jesus)	Time Line of the New Testament	Related Words and Verses	Challenge for Growth	Life span Developmental Comparison
1. Observation	Come and see My ministry first-hand	The Gospels (beginning of Jesus' ministry)	• "Come and see" (John 1:39) • "Learn from me" (Matt. 11:29)	WATCH Jesus	Infancy
2. Continuation	Wait, then assist Me, by resuming My work	Gospels to Acts (last half of Jesus' ministry up to Pentecost)	• "I am in you" (John 14:20) • "Remain in me" (John 5–8) • "I call you friends" (John 15:15) • "Wait [in Jerusalem]" for the Holy Spirit (Acts 1:4)	ASSIST Jesus	Childhood
3. Experimentation	Witness to the world about Me	The book of Acts	• "Witnesses" (Acts 1:8) • "Follower of the Way" (Acts 24:14-16)	PRACTICE What Jesus Taught	Adolescence
4. Imitation	Recall, then repeat what I did	The Epistles (start of the early church)	• "Follow . . . example of Christ" (1 Cor. 11:1) • Numerous "as" commands (2 John 4, 6; 1 Thess. 4:11-12; Matt. 19:19; Eph. 4:32; Rom. 15:7) • "Walk as Jesus did" (1 John 2:6)	DUPLICATE How Jesus Lived	Younger Adulthood
5. Transformation	Grow daily in Christlikeness; eventually celebrate your complete restoration in heaven	The book of Revelation (start of eternity)	• Becoming like Jesus: *Physically (Phil. 3:21) *Mentally (1 Cor. 13:12) *Emotionally and Socially (Col. 3:5-10) • "Come and share your Master's happiness" (Matt. 25:21, 23)	BECOME Like Jesus	Older Adulthood

259

that carefully. Our loving "God . . . richly provides us with everything for our enjoyment"! In chapter 3 we read how our Creator provides us with "everything we need." That was almost too good to be true. Now we are told to enjoy everything! We are told to take God's gracious provisions and celebrate! Wow!

And (as if Paul had to say more) the apostle added that this mind-set of enjoyment and holy living leads us to "take hold of the life that is truly life." Sounds like a pretty exciting combination to me.

Levels of Life Application

Here's a test: "What relationship, if any, do the following simple pleasures of life have to do with discipleship?"

- Taking a leisurely walk or riding a bike
- Celebrating the completion of a difficult crossword puzzle
- Watching a gorgeous sunset
- Paying a nice compliment to a child or employee
- Organizing a personal calendar for the next week
- Discovering a better way to drive to work—one that's both quicker and more aesthetically pleasing
- Enjoying a satisfying weekend with your spouse
- Participating in a local food drive for the needy
- Taking care of your lawn and garden or learning a new language

How long did it take you to recognize that these are illustrations of our Super Nine gifts, respectively? There are at least three positive ways—different commitment levels, first noted in chapter 3—to approach these daily pleasures:

The person at Level One, Christian or not—whenever she experiences any of these gifts (even unconsciously)—automatically dignifies her humanity. That's because she "opens" a gift-wrapped package from her Maker with her name on it.

At Level Two (someone we might call a "seeker"), the individual is at least conscious of a Higher Being in his life. One way he may express his awareness is by offering thanks for his encounters with any of these gifts.

At Level Three, the Christian disciple deliberately tries to tie his experience to God. His specific aim is that—under his lordship—his image will continue its renewal through that gift he experiences.

Once our Creator's view of enjoyment is established, any growth within these Super Nine categories accomplishes God's will for the believer. Such growth is synonymous with his lifelong purpose of image restoration. Growth includes elementary gains like praising our Maker for an invigorating exercise routine (gift 1) or thanking our Father for the simple pleasures of a delicious pasta meal with homemade garlic-buttered bread (gift 3). At deeper levels, Christian maturity consists of living as people of integrity within our neighborhoods and furthering justice in the lives of those who are powerless to do so (gift 8). These virtues—re-breathed to new life by the redemptive work of Christ—replicate some of the earthshaking qualities of the early church in the book of Acts that "turned the world upside down." Whenever we inch along within these categories of faith and life, God is pleased. We put a smile on our Creator's face.

By God's grace, everyone is given a chance to mature in two categories. First, whenever a person pursues even the smallest details of the Super Nine, he becomes *more human*. He begins to mirror Adam and Eve before the Fall because he reconnects with Creation. Second, whenever a person is transformed by Jesus' sacrifice—then, with God's help, she intentionally pursues the Super Nine—she becomes *more Godlike*. She starts to mirror her Maker from the inside. The former category reminds us how to live; the latter enables us to live again. The former category links us to the Cultural Mandate, while the latter one ties us to the Gospel Mandate. The Cultural Mandate reestablishes our dominion task; the Gospel Mandate reinforces our redemption obliga-tion. (To repeat, these mandates, which indicate how to achieve "the peace of God which transcends all understanding," are featured in chart 11.1 in the *Supplemental Resource*.) Each directive is centered upon the Jesus we want others to know.

To summarize, complete discipleship requires the following:

Truth 11

God's model for discipleship correlates with multiple stages of human development that represent the diversity of disciples worldwide. Every growth phase and every level of discipleship encourages Christlikeness—through daily image restoration.

Conclusion

Mom knew tonight would be no exception—young Jessica always had trouble falling asleep. Her precious, precocious preschooler had formed an alliance with the evening routines known as teeth brushing, bedtime stories, and prayers—each took its turn battling the dreaded "lights-out" foe, prolonging the inevitable darkness. Every night the same combat would rage. You might say it was predestined.

One particular evening, after each routine had successfully extended its time limit beyond even the normal pattern, Mom finally descended the stairs, exhausted, having patiently just logged two more stories and three more choruses than the average night would warrant. Still, she intuitively sensed her evening wasn't yet finished.

Sure enough, just as she was sitting down to read the day's paper, the faint and quick-paced padding of five-year-old bare footsteps skittered across the floor above her. Then—silence. Jessica was up there, at the top of the stairs, waiting.

"Go back to bed, Jessica!" came her perfunctory command, without so much as lowering the paper.

"But Mom, I scared of the dark!" Mom could have mouthed the requisite response in perfect, simultaneous syntax as it was being spoken—the dialogue was well rehearsed.

"Jesus is with you, Jessica. You don't need to be afraid!" came Mom's firm, albeit formulaic reply.

Silence again.

Normally the last rejoinder would have been enough to checkmate the young opponent. But tonight the simple reassurance of Son of God's presence apparently took a bit longer to sink in. But sure enough, the pitter-patter sound finally receded. The subsequent squeaks from a mattress and box springs would cause most inexperienced ears to rest, assured that the child's fearful struggle had ended . . . for this evening.

But Mom knew better.

Sure enough, more quick-paced footsteps approached across the ceiling. Then the silent pause somewhere around the top of the staircase.

"Mom, can you send Dad up? I need someone with skin on him."

The answer to this chapter's opening inquiry—"What is the complete way to follow Christ?"—is located within the question itself. "Follow Jesus" means just exactly that. He is the only One with "skin" on Him—our human skin.

And He has left us with an example to follow. That is why . . . He is the only way.

[1] From Dallas Willard's *The Spirit of the Disciplines* (San Francisco: Harper San Francisco, 1988), p. 48.

[2] Ibid., p. 49.

3 N. H. Belversluis, former professor of education at Calvin College, offered these insights about the saint's synthesized life purpose:

> The missionary mandate of *Matthew* and the cultural mandate of *Genesis* are not two discrete mandates, unrelated, the one pointing to the spiritual and the other to the natural; the one to piety, the other to culture. The missionary mandate is for the sake of covenant and therefore is for the sake of the cultural mandate as restored through Christ.

Taken from Belversluis's "Toward a Theology of Education" (*Occasional Paper* [Vol. 1, No. 1] published by Calvin College, February 1981), p. 27.

[4] The first reference to the followers of "the Way" comes in Acts 9:2, whereas the initial mention of the word "Christians" is found in Acts 11:26.

[5] Besides these five citations, three other less direct usages of this term include Acts 16:17 (regarding the Apostle Paul's teaching on the "the way to be saved") and Acts 18:25 and 26 (where Apollos was described as one instructed in the "way of the Lord" and who, under the tutoring of Priscilla and Aquila, subsequently learned "the way of God more adequately").

[6] I extend my gratitude to my colleague James R. Blankenship for informing me of this Talmudic saying.

[7] From Talmud J.: *Kiddushin*, end (cited in *Leo Rosten's Treasury of Jewish Quotations* [New York: McGraw-Hill, 1972], p. 397).

Section IV

The Jesus We Will Fully Know

Chapter Twelve

---✦---

The Way Home Is Closer than We Think

> *The glory of God is a person fully alive.*
>
> —IRENAEUS
>
> *And for us this is the end of all the stories, and we can most truly say that they all lived happily ever after. But for them it was only the beginning of the real story. All their life in this world and all their adventures in Narnia had only been the cover and the title page; now at last they were beginning Chapter One of the Great Story, which no one on earth has read, which goes on for ever, in which every chapter is better than the one before.*
>
> —C. S. LEWIS

Complete discipleship comes full circle in this last chapter, as the end and the beginning are united. I am invigorated with how the content of these chapters has empowered me to make much more sense out of my own faith. I am also enthused when I consider how our Lord may use this model in his church. God has given me grace to insert the last few pieces into the jigsaw puzzle called biblical discipleship. In my mind, there's more harmony now between the whole, seamless, and perfect picture on the top of the puzzle box (his perspective) and my attempts to recreate that same scene from the interlocking pieces inside. Even though I realize there will always be lines and cracks in my version of his perfect cover portrait, I praise God for his assistance.

Introduction to Coming Attractions from Chapter 12

When you "catch" the contagions of truth, confidence, joy, and peace from the following concepts, you will see why I am so eager to share this chapter's contents:[1]

- Jesus' core message on earth centered upon the excitement of life in heaven;
- Jesus' resurrection validated his teachings about heaven;
- God the Father corroborated his Son's instruction by raising him up;
- Our risen Lord was "Exhibit A" that life after death is real;
- Unlike all other resurrections, Jesus' was immortal—as ours will also be;
- Jesus' disciples were radically changed because they were eyewitnesses of the resurrection—and also because the Holy Spirit helped them put together the puzzle pieces of what Jesus had taught them earlier;
- Jesus' key teachings included the need to start living eternity now. This "outlook on heaven . . . is the most revolutionary idea (next to salvation) ever penned."[2]

Sticking with the principle (cited in this book's introduction) not to repeat what has been said elsewhere, chapter 12 primarily focuses on that last point above. It represents a truth rarely discussed in the church. I plan to align Jesus' command to "store up for yourselves treasures in heaven" (Matt. 6:20a) with the model of image restoration presented throughout this book.

We Are Closer to Our Home

In one sense, Christianity is more simple than we often think. Comprehensive, yes. Multifaceted, absolutely. But our faith is elegantly simple in this sense: The way our first parents were purposefully shaped—in the image of God—set the pattern our Maker chose to use with all people. Not just in Eden, but ever since. Not just now, but also in heaven.

That says a lot about the Jesus we will someday know—one who has been consistent—one who has always wanted the very best for us.

People before the Fall were obviously different than those of us after it. Furthermore, all that we know about our future condition pales beside everything in our lives now. Nobody can deny these contrasts between past and present, as well as between present and future. They are significant in their distinct comparisons, even though they each share common categories. The Creator has chosen to differences work through our humanity—in the Garden, today, and forever. Those common categories have been broadly described by *imago Dei* and specifically detailed as the Super Nine in this book.

A few attractive ideas came to mind when I wrote this chapter's title, "The Way Home (to Heaven) Is Closer Than We Think":

- For those of us who are trusting Jesus as our Savior, eternity has already begun (see John 5:24, 6:47, 1 John 5:13). We occasionally breathe in portions of this celestial air—such as whenever we contemplate the brilliant colors of autumn. Even though we saw those identical breathtaking reds, brilliant yellows, and fabulous oranges less than twelve months earlier, we still marvel. That's because our Creator faithfully goes beyond the call of duty every September and October. He graciously makes his Creation more beautiful, once it dies, than it was when it was alive! God colors outside the lines! The four seasons are one more illustration of the Resurrection's power and the beauty that awaits us "on the other side."

- Heaven's Home is also closer because we are familiar with the categories through which God works—both now and in heaven. The single best indicator of "the now" is the example of our Lord. We have analyzed multiple expressions of these Super Nine categories in Jesus' personal life (chapters 7 through 9), which we are to emulate (chapters 10 and 11). Heaven's ultimate counterpart of this earthly design is presented later in this chapter, through the last vertical column of Table 12.3.

- The final reason to believe heaven is very close—as close as the air we breathe—is that God prompts us to start living eternity now! Yes, we must exercise patience for heaven, since most of our rewards come after we are transported to our celestial residence. But not every reward comes later. Saints do experience eternal life both now and later.[3] This "now-and-not-yet" status means that some of our heavenly blessings can be unwrapped on this temporal side of life.

If you have never asked Jesus to become your personal Savior—the place where every person must start if he wants to go to heaven—I invite you to read table 12.1. Here is an opportunity to start living eternal life now, even before you get to the next paragraph!

The First Day of the Rest of Your Eternal Life

I said I wanted to focus on Jesus' "most revolutionary idea": We disciples can begin to live part of heaven's wonderment today. The thrill of eternity starts when we acknowledge we have already "crossed over from death to life" (John 5:24), then intentionally "store up for [ourselves] treasures in heaven, where moth and rust do not destroy, and where thieves do not break in and steal" (Matt. 6:20).

TABLE 12.1

Accepting Jesus as Your Savior

I want to clarify, in simple terms, what it means to be a Christian. I want to explain how anybody can start enjoying heaven now. Becoming a Christian is like getting married, the way God intended it. Even though Jesus was speaking about the flip-side of marriage (divorce) in Matthew 19:1-9, it is a great place to be reintroduced to the Creator's perspective: our origin and our life purpose to serve him.

Becoming a Christian starts with your personal spiritual need: You realize you can't go it alone. Like desiring a lifetime partner, you must want to partner with Jesus. You must acknowledge that all that you've tried up to this point doesn't work. In fact, what you've tried is wrong, because in setting up your own set of values for how to live (or someone else's)—you have ignored God's plan. This rebellion against God and his Plan is called "sin."

Once you have confessed your personal rebellion—and sincerely have turned from that lifestyle—you must say "Yes" to Jesus. "Yes" that he, as God's perfect Son, came to earth to die for the sins of the world—your sins, my sins, everyone's sins. "Yes" that you trust him—and him alone—as your Savior, just as you would say "Yes" to your new spouse at the altar. "Yes" to him, and absolutely "No" to all competitors—all other faiths, all other ideas or values, even "No" to yourself— "No" to anybody or anything that seduces you with an idea contrary to Jesus' best plans for your life.

Read John 5:24 and 1 John 5:13. Congratulations! You have eternal life! The Apostle John is speaking to you, if you have followed these simple guidelines.

Seek the godly counsel of mature disciples to help you start "living heaven now."

As strange as it might sound, going to heaven is not all that appealing to everyone. There have always been reasons why certain people don't want to go Home (see sidebar 12.1 in the *Supplemental Resource*). For some, it is the specific fear of death (see sidebar 12.2 in the *Supplemental Resource*). For others, the reasons are more clouded—literally. God's Word reminds us that earth is the "shadow," while heaven is the real thing. Earth clouds our thoughts and values so severely we actually prefer this existence, even though it is outrageously inferior to our life beyond the clouds (see sidebar 12.3 in the *Supplemental Resource*).

Thankfully, the Bible discloses extraordinary promises about heaven, promises that can turn all these concerns around. Ten particular promises are featured in table 12.2, and each one reminds us we are that much closer to our true Home. Additional passages specifically challenge each disciple to make heavenly investments now. Gary Habermas and J.P. Moreland[4] identified six of these key texts (four are summarized below). These two scholars described their select passages in terms of what they call a "top-down" perspective: Believers must strengthen their Christian walk by emphasizing God and his eternal truths first, then earthly values second—as these Scriptures detail:

- Matthew 6:19-34—By genuinely "seeking" God and his kingdom first—through stored heavenly "treasures"—obedient disciples have no need to worry about any earthly concern.

- Matthew 10:28 and 16:26—Jesus commanded his disciples to "be afraid of the one who can destroy both soul and body in hell." Correspondingly, he described how foolish it is if someone "gains the whole world, yet forfeits his soul." Heaven's value is much greater than every single earthly possession combined.

- Luke 10:25-37—Jesus answered the question "What must I do to inherit eternal life?" by affirming the two greatest commandments: Love God totally, and radically love your neighbor as yourself (chapter 5 showed how these two laws summarized every law; furthermore, these two directives were explained through *imago Dei*). The Good Samaritan story was, consequently, told as an illustration of these two commands. Jesus' application? "Go and do likewise."

- 2 Corinthians 3:18–5:10[5]—Habermas and Moreland rightly explain Paul's conscious instruction that eternal life supercedes

TABLE 12.2

Ten Promises About Eternal Life We Can Bank On

Contrary to what some may think, the Bible provides several references to eternal life. These are God's promises we can count on—rewards we can bank on. I draw these truths from Chapter 13 in *Beyond Death* by Gary Habermas and J.P. Moreland (Wheaton, IL: Crossway Books, 1998), although I have modified and reorganized some content.

I refer to these facts as "puzzle pieces," since that metaphor not only permits us to "piece eternity together," but it also "pieces together this life, Eden, and our eternal Home." My earlier good-better-best analogy is revisited.

- Piece 1—Eternal life has already begun (John 5:24, 6:47; 1 John 5:13). Occasionally, we "taste" a bit of heaven by the prompting of the Holy Spirit (e.g., an inspirational book or piece of music, or a gorgeous sunset).
- Piece 2—Heaven is a real place. Jesus promised to "prepare a place for us" (John 14:2). We can expect to return to a "real Home."
- Piece 3—We will have real and amazing bodies in heaven. Jesus' body was a real, substantial body—just like ours will be (Phil. 3:21; 1 John. 3:2). But there's more: Jesus' post-resurrection body—just in Luke 24:13-53 alone—tells us that, in heaven, we will be able to think, talk, walk, recall the past, dialogue, use Scriptures, eat, recognize others, and be recognized. We will be "solid" enough to be touched, yet capable of walking through walls. We will have the phenomenal potential of self-transportation, which is imaginable, now, only in sci-fi movies.
- Piece 4—Heaven will be devoid of all negatives (1 Peter 1:3-4; Rev. 7:15-17). There will be no hunger, thirst, or sunburns! Also, no tears, sorrow, spoilage, or death. Wow!
- Piece 5—Healthy benefits of work will be restored in eternity. We will, once again, labor (Isa. 65:21-23) and reign (Rev. 22:5b), as we were originally called to do. Those activities will bring thorough enjoyment (Isa. 65:22b), in terms of literal "fruit," personal fulfillment, and glory to our Maker (Rev. 21:24 and 26). Also, since we are "God's workmanship, created in Christ Jesus to do good works" (Eph. 2:8-10) that fact won't end at the grave. "Good works" are part of our Father's eternal plan for us.
- Piece 6—Justice will consistently reside in our heavenly Home. (Isa. 65:22a; Rev. 21:8, 22:15.) No evil person or activity will be found.
- Piece 7—Fellowship, service, and worship also represent what we will "do" in heaven. (Matt. 26:27-29; John 14:2-3; Rev. 5:10-13, 21:26-27; 22:4.)
- Piece 8—Heaven will be a place where we continue to mature. Eph. 2:6-7 say that "in the coming ages" God will show us "the incomparable riches of his grace," which acknowledges we will grow much more to accommodate this new knowledge.
- Piece 9—Heaven will exhibit a Creation that is, itself, "redeemed." (Isa. 65:17; Rom. 8:19-23; 2 Peter 3:13; Rev. 21:25-27). We are repeatedly reminded that our future heaven and earth will be "new."
- Piece 10—Heaven will be a place of peace, joy, rest, security, and beauty—all rolled into one. God's peace (*shalom*) is prominently featured, both in Jesus' earthly words (John 14:27) and within the promises of eternal life (Rev. 21:22-22:5). The same can be said about joy (John 15:11; 16:22; 17:13; Rev. 21:1-4); rest (Matt. 11:28-30; Heb. 4:1-11); security (John 10:25-30; Rev. 21:3-5); and beauty (John 14:1-4; 2 Peter 3:13; Rev. 21:15-21).

anything in this life, including persecution and death (4:17-18). However, the key point is the verse immediately prior (4:16): "Therefore we do not lose heart. Though outwardly we are wasting away, yet inwardly we are being renewed day by day." Our image restoration—"into his likeness" (see v. 3:18) is paramount, since it is both our Maker's deliberate creation (image) and his preferred strategy (restoration), that accomplish his purposes in us. God's gracious provisions are a bridge in our lives between earth and heaven.

Habermas and Moreland remind us that several other Scriptures could be added to this list, including 1 Timothy 6:17-19, 1 Peter 1:3-9, Hebrews 11, Philippians 2:18-21,[6] and 2 Corinthians 8:1-5. Each of these passages prompts us to invest in heavenly treasures. The next section features the Creator's "portfolio of investment opportunities." It highlights particular ways we may "store up treasures" for heaven, but also begin to savor those pleasures now.

"Treasures in Heaven" Connect with Our Works on Earth

Jesus' call to "store up . . . treasure in heaven" generally relates to investing in any eternal value. Unlike their temporal counterparts, none of these "treasures in heaven" is ever moth-eaten, rusted out, or stolen. Scripture also describes specific kinds of treasures—earthly works based upon the Cultural Mandate. Gift 4 (the task and reward of "Kind Ruler") is the most frequently noted of these treasures, linking earth with heaven. Whether we look at general or specific categories, the important principle to come away with is this: What we do on earth affects heaven. Evangelicals have played down that correlation for too long, fearing repercussions of wrong-minded salvation-by-works, legalism, and the like.

It doesn't need to be that way.

General Principles Worth Noting

Some of the strongest guidelines that connect this world and the next are found in Matthew 25. Verses 14-30 introduce the parable of the talents by saying, "it will be like." "It" stands for "the kingdom of heaven" (v. 1), the subject covering the entire chapter. The first of three principles in Matthew 25 affirms what was noted earlier: "How we live now influences eternity." If this present-to-everlasting linkage is still unconvincing, the parable closes with this solemn warning: Those who are careless and lazy with God's blessings here will eventually be thrown "into the darkness, where there will be weeping and gnashing of teeth" (v. 30b). That's a serious admonition!

The second principle appears two times in this same parable. For obedient disciples, that twice-noted principle (found in vv. 21b and 23b) is this: "You have been faithful with a few things; I will put you in charge of many things." Assurances that the Lord will put faithful disciples "in charge of many things" is a heavenly reality (not an earthly one), for it includes: (1) The fact that this teaching describes the "kingdom of heaven"; (2) Matthew 25:21c and 23c—which represent the eternal opposite of the weeping and teeth gnashing (in v. 30)—are present tense promises: "Come and share your master's happiness!" Faithful followers are immediately ushered into heaven; and (3) the Lord's promise of increased personal responsibility follows this event: "I will put you in charge of many things." So the second principle says: Faithfulness here yields greater benefits and duties there. These "heavenly upgrades" take the fullest advantage of earth's experiences; a tested leader here will be given even greater leadership, and so on.

The third principle follows immediately (in vv. 31-46), emerging from the parable about the sheep and the goats: Storing treasures in heaven is virtually unconscious; it is godly character that has become "second nature." The sheep in this story are genuinely surprised by their rewards (see vv. 37-39)—they were not anticipating recognition for their selfless acts. Notice how this same principle is previously upheld (three times) in Matthew 6:1-18, just prior to the "treasures" reference in Matthew 6:19. Jesus instructs us that godly acts of mercy, prayer, and fasting must be "done in secret"—like unconscious habits.

Building upon these three principles, there are two sides of the coin when it comes to God's evaluation of earthly works. One side is negative and one is positive: judgment and reward.

Coming Judgment of Works

Scripture teaches that a heavenly assessment of earthly behaviors is scheduled for everyone, with no exceptions. This judgment is not the kind that most people suspect. This is how many individuals view our coming judgment: "If my good works outweigh my bad works, I'll go to heaven." The Bible teaches that God's judgment of our works, however, is not associated with salvation. Rather, it prescribes verdicts for every-body—both those in hell (Luke 12:47-48; Matt. 11:23-24) and those in heaven (see following section on "crowns"). How each person arrives at his or her final eternal destination was already determined, based upon how each responded to Jesus' offer of salvation. Note these passages' consistent message on the universal judgment of human works:

- Job 34:11: "[The Almighty] repays a man for what he has done; he brings upon him what his conduct deserves."
- Luke 12:13-21: The parable of the rich fool concludes (v. 21) with "This is how it will be with anyone who stores up things for himself but is not rich toward God."
- Romans 2:6: "God 'will give to each person according to what he has done.'"
- Romans 14:10c; 12: "For we will all stand before God's judgment seat. . . . So then, each of us will give an account of himself to God."

- 2 Corinthians 5:10: "For we must all appear before the judgment seat of Christ, that each one may receive what is due him for the things done while in the body, whether good or bad."
- Revelation 20:13: "The sea gave up the dead that were in it, and death and Hades gave up the dead that were in them, and each person was judged according to what he had done."

Coming Reward for Works

To balance the negative side of works' assessment (judgment), our fair Creator provides the positive side of rewards. Jesus himself promised in Matthew 16:27, "For the Son of Man is going to come in his Father's glory with his angels, and then he will reward each person according to what he has done." Again, this message of justice and reward—independent of salvation—is found throughout the Scriptures:

- Psalm 62:12b: " . . . you, O Lord, are loving. Surely you will reward each person according to what he has done."
- Jeremiah 17:10: "I the LORD search the heart and examine the mind, to reward a man according to his conduct, according to what his deeds deserve."
- 1 Timothy 6:18-19: "Command them to do good, to be rich in good deeds, and to be generous and willing to share. In this way they will lay up treasure for themselves as a firm foundation for the coming age, so that they may take hold of the life that is truly life."
- Revelation 22:12: "'Behold, I am coming soon! My reward is with me, and I will give to everyone according to what he has done.'"

A Combination of Judgment and Reward

Perhaps the most concise passage that reveals not only judgment and reward, but also whether that divine evaluation comes before the grave or after, is 1 Timothy 5:24-25. Consider the Creator-Judge's fairness in these two verses: "The sins of some men are obvious, reaching the place of judgment ahead of them; the sins of others trail behind them. In the same way, good deeds are obvious, and even those that are not cannot be hidden." The Apostle Paul's parallel instruction on this truth arises in 1 Corinthians 3:10-15. Several important details connect the disciple's work on earth with his or her coming experience in heaven:

- The "foundation" of every disciple's work is not in question—it is "already laid" by Jesus Christ (v. 11); again, Paul is not speaking of salvation, but he is stressing subsequent, godly living.

- Each disciple "should be careful how he builds" on that foundation Jesus has already prepared (v. 10b).

- Why "be careful"? Because "The Day [of the Lord] will bring . . . fire [that] will test the quality of each man's work" (v. 13).

- Symbolically, each disciple's work is portrayed by a variety of substances—from greater value to lesser: "gold, silver, costly stones" to "wood, hay or straw" (v. 12).

- The Creator-Judge's ordained fire-testing of these diverse "building" materials causes the valuable substances to remain, while less valuable items go up in smoke (v. 14-15a).

- In the worst scenario, even if every work that a disciple "builds" gets "burned up . . . he will suffer loss." However, "he himself will be saved" (v. 15a). To repeat, salvation is not the issue here; potential rewards from godly living are.

- In a much better scenario, "if what he has built survives, he will receive his reward" (v. 14).

What is this "reward"? God's special grace compensates by allowing the obedient disciple to experience more of heaven. He or she will have greater capacities to serve the Lord and others, along with greater capacities for personal fulfillment.[7] Sidebar 12.4 in the *Supplemental Resource* further demonstrates how gift 4 (Kind Rulers) is linked from earth to heaven.

Making Deposits in the First Eternal Bank of Heaven

Since everything good now was better in Eden—and it will be best in heaven—this next section represents a logical extension of that premise. As we deliberately allow our Maker-Savior-High Priest to restore us, we actively prepare ourselves to better enjoy heaven and to more fully serve God and others eternally. It is investing now for our future. It's like money in the bank—God's bank—with rates that are so good they can't even be advertised. Guaranteed rates that are out of this world! That's the Jesus we will, one day, know fully—the one who wants us to get the best return on our deposits.

I first raised the good-better-best analogy in chapter 2. I wasn't trying to be cute with those words. That is exactly how the Creator shaped our lives and our after-lives. When we are obedient to his Word, God progressively restores his image inside us—working within the standardized, Creator-sculpted categories of human nature and experience. He matures us through the Super Nine classifications we inherited from Eden. Following our salvation, God re-breathes restoration into our many human domains (e.g., our minds, emotions, etc.)—cleansing and expanding those capacities simultaneously—to closer resemble Eden and to prepare us for eternity.

A Family Snapshot

Perhaps a personal analogy is due. As I noted in chapter 2, I thank God for richly blessing me with my family. That includes my dear wife and three special daughters. That also includes my two wonderful parents, my exceptional father-in-law, and his lovely wife. In the following illustration I particularly want to concentrate on my maternal grandparents, Alice Mildred Nix Jarvis (1907–96) and Wilburt Thomas Jarvis (1907–98). They were both precious saints. In chapter 3, I introduced you to my grandmother—one we fondly called "Nin." We grandkids affectionately knew her husband, our grandfather, as "Geep."

I recently wrote a dedication to the both of them in one of my books[8] that went like this:

> Together, they showed me how the three keys
> of godly character,
> industrious and adventurous living,
> and faithfulness to each other
> unlock the secret door to contentment in this life.
> Better still, since both have entered heaven's version of that
> same doorway, they now fully delight in all that the Creator
> intends for every one of his children.
> In our eternal homeland,
> Nin and Geep are glorifying God as they
> "long enjoy the works of their hands" (Isa. 65:22b).

The primary reason why Nin and Geep were such incredible blessings to us and to all who met them is that they found their niche in God's plan by realigning themselves with the Garden. I testified above that they were "industrious and adventurous"—reflecting Eden's Gift 6. Specifically, they were godly "Artists and Scientists." Nin was the gifted artist: a gracious and hospitable cook with admirable skills in sewing and quilting. Geep was the scientist. He was a tool-and-die tradesman and a reliable handyman around the house. He even invented a few tools and gadgets whenever local hardware store employees drew blank stares at his unusual requests. All these accomplishments were achieved with only an eighth-grade education, which Geep received well after he was married.

By finding their niche within the Eden category of Artists and Scientists, Nin and Geep unwittingly experienced a little heaven on earth. And those experiences ushered them through that very "same doorway" to which I referred—the doorway labeled "Fully Restored

Image." It is that same doorway through which "they now fully delight in all that the Creator" still has in store for them, throughout eternity.

I picture Nin now trading secrets of her sewing techniques with Tabitha, who created "robes and other clothing" for widows in the early church (Acts 9:39). I see her sitting down to "talk shop" with the respected Christian businesswoman Lydia, "a dealer in purple cloth" (Acts 16:14). Geep is off to the side, swapping stories with a diverse group that includes Simon the tanner (Acts 9:43).

Once again, the key is restoration of *imago Dei*, since the godly process of rejuvenation connects our past, our present, and our future. That is particularly how image plays itself out through the Cultural Mandate and the Super Nine.[9] Table 12.3 outlines the final summary of the Super Nine, featuring our ultimate restoration within its last vertical column.[10] Sidebar 12.5 in the *Supplemental Resource* looks at gift 9, how culture may be advanced now—to honor our Maker—and how the "best" of culture may be transported into heaven. Sidebar 12.6 in the *Supplemental Resource* provides an acrostic design, applying the concept of image restoration in practical ways.

The twelfth and final truth about complete discipleship is one that should motivate the believer. It is the kind of information that should prompt Christians to be excited about the start of every day. In brief, here is our Creator's amazing promise:

Truth 12

God's model for discipleship assures us as disciples that we are living eternity now. Since eternal life has begun, the daily choices we make store up heavenly treasures, whenever we commit ourselves to image restoration.

TABLE 12.3

A Complete View of the Super Nine: Beginning and Ending

	Complementary Explanations of the Super 9 Gifts	Adam and Eve's Perfect Reflection (from Genesis)	Attributes of God that Adam and Eve Mirrored	Ultimate Image Restoration of the Super Nine in Heaven
1. **God-like Physiques**	We are *Physical* and *Spiritual* People	• (2:7b) People were specially created (from God's breath) to become "living beings" • (2:9c) Trees "good for food" (inferred need for humans to have nutrition and growth)	• The spirituality of God (John 4:24) refers to his immaterial nature; people partially reflect the Maker by their immaterial nature (Gen. 2:7; 1 Thess. 5:23) • Yet God is also something more than spirit – he "breathed" (Gen. 2:7) and walked in Eden (3:8; see 2 Sam. 22:9a, 9b, 10, 14, 16)	• "Our lowly bodies" will one day be "like his glorious body" (Phil. 3:21). • 1 Cor. 15:45-49 also promises our "immortal" bodies
2. **Passionate Thinkers**	We are *Emotional* and *Rational* People	• (2:16-17) There was human potential to discern and to choose • (2:18, 23-25) There was also potential to be lonely and loving • (3:10) Fear resulted from sin	• Intellectual abilities of God (knowledge and wisdom) are seen throughout Creation • God's passion for Adam to have a "helper" (Gen. 2:18); also, God's grief arises from increasing wickedness (Gen. 6:6)	• We will one day "know fully even as [we are] fully known" (1 Cor. 13:12b) • "Delight" and "joy" are restored to God's people (Isa. 65:18, 19) • No more tears in eternity (Isa. 65:19; Rev. 21:4)
3. **Sensory Learners**	We are *Sensory Experience* People	• Garden of Eden meant "hedging around delight" • (2:9b) Trees were created as "pleasing to the eye" (sight) • (2:9c) and "good for food" (taste) • (2:12b) There was "aromatic resin" (smell) • (3:3; 8) Post-sin references are made to touch and to hearing	• Creator "saw" Creation was "good" (Gen. 1:4, 10, 12, 18, 25, 31) • (2 Sam. 22:1-17: esp. v. 7, 9a; 17) Ps. 94:9 Creator God uses some form of senses (cf. Eph. 5:2–Jesus was a "fragrant offering to God")	• "Now we see but a poor reflection as in a mirror; then we shall see face to face" (1 Cor. 13:12a; Rev. 22:4a) • We will continue learning in heaven (Eph. 2:6-7) • Other verses on sensory experiences include: Rev. 21:3, 4, 6, 11, 23; 22:1-3
4. **Kind Rulers**	We are *Regal* and *Ecological* People	• (1:28b) People were commanded to "subdue" and to "rule over" the Garden • (2:15b) People were also commanded to "take care" of the Garden	• *El-Shaddai* values God's power and faithfulness to his people, through his consistent blessings and comfort (see Gen. 17:1; 28:3;Exod. 6:2-3)	• God and his people "will *reign* for ever and ever," fulfilling our original call to be Kind Rulers, now in celestial Eden (Rev. 22:5b)
5. **Worshipful Workers**	We are *Laboring* and *Restfully-Worshiping* People	• (2:2-3) There was an implied command to rest as the Creator did (compare Exod. 20:8-11) • (2:15a) People were commanded to "work" the Garden	• Creator modeled his commendable work pattern throughout his Creation (Gen. 1:1-31)	• Saints will "not toil in vain" but "enjoy the work of their hands" (Isa. 65:22b-23a) • Future eternal rest will soon come (Heb. 4:3-11)

TABLE 12.3
Continued

6. Artists & Scientists	We are **Creative** and **Orderly** People	• (2:19-20) Multiple capacities for curiosity, adventure, and organization for creative problem solving were given to people • (3:1-6) This same potential within people was found in the very first sin	• Creator rested on the seventh day, making it holy (Gen. 2:2) • (Gen. 2:19b) The Creator shows personal "curiosity": He personally "brought [the animals] to the man to see *what* he would name them" –then God made woman (vv. 21-22). In Ps. 147:4 God similarly names the stars • The orderliness of God is displayed in Creation (Gen. 1:1-31; a parallel order is to be found in the church 1 Cor. 14:33, 40)	• God's people will **worship** him (Rev. 5:11-14; 21:22; 22:9) • The **artistic** skills for planting vineyards and the **scientific** accomplishments of building houses are reintroduced in eternity, as godly blessings to enjoy forever (Isa. 65:21-22)
7. Intimate Families	We are **Individual** and **Relational** People	• (1:27) God created people as "male *and* female" • (2:18) it was "not good for the man to be alone" • (2:20-25) The woman was created for man	• The role Yahweh features the Covenant faithfulness of God (Gen. 2:4b; Exod. 3:12-16; 6:2-3) • Relational references to God (plural pronouns "us" and "we") refer to the communitarian (or fellowship) attribute of the Trinity (Gen. 1:26; 3:22)	• God's family will again be "**a people blessed by the Lord**" (Isa. 65:23b) • God will **"live with"** his people as the Bridegroom with his Bride (Rev. 21:3) • "**Family**" is again valued, for the *new definition* of God's "**son**" is reintroduced as those who are perseveringly obedient (Rev. 21:7-8; 22:9)
8. Good Neighbors	We are **Morally-Helpful** People	• (2:9, 17) The "tree of the knowledge of good and evil" implied moral potential for people • (2:20-24) Eve was Adam's "suitable helper" • (3:7-8) Moral shame resulted from the first human choice to sin	• The holiness of God is witnessed in Creation, related to the Sabbath (Gen. 2:2-3) and this quality continues to the end of the Scriptures (Rev. 4:8; 21:2, 27; 22:19) • God's holiness causes him to evict unholy Adam and Eve from the Garden (Gen. 3:22-24)	• Persevering believers will continue **maturing in holiness** (Rev. 22:11b) • Other references to **holiness in eternity** include: Isa. 65:25b; Rev. 21:2, 10, 27; 22:3, 19 • God's people, once again, will experience and enjoy cultural settings **of justice** (Isa. 65:21-22)
9. Responsible Citizens	We are **Broadly-Cultural** People	• (1:28a) God commanded people to "be fruitful and increase ... and subdue" (*Cultural Mandate*) • (3:1-6) The human capacity to communicate and work together was shown, even though it was for evil	• The positive cultural traits of God—modeled by his own attributes of communication and cooperation—are constantly evident within the Trinity (Gen. 1:1-2; 3:22)	• The "**best**" of **culture** will be preserved and redeemed, to glorify the Creator (Rev. 21:24; 26) • There will again be harmony among God's people (Isa. 65:23b; Rev. 21:6b-7, 21, 27; 22:3-4, 8-9, 11b) • There will again be **harmony** among the **animal kingdom** (Isa. 65:25)

Conclusion

Heaven—both our "now" and our "not yet"—simultaneously portrays the finish and the start of our journey. That balance parallels our Lord's concurrent roles as "the Alpha and the Omega,"[11] the beginning and the end.

From time to time we disciples need to reassess the ways we think and talk about heaven. We need to reemphasize our eternal hope, and we need to create "new wineskin" terms for that hope, in fresh, accurate, and alluring ways. Two centuries back, George Macdonald[12] suggested that whenever we teach children about our eternal Home we dare not default to dull, unattractive pictures of heaven like that of "an everlasting prayer-meeting!" His alternative? Use analogies of a child flying his kite on a gorgeous day! What's more, Macdonald added that we should be telling children that "God himself [would be] his playmate, in the blue wind that tossed [the kite] hither and thither in the golden void!"

It also helps when we adults ponder our future from a slightly new angle. So I end this book by suggesting a rather provocative slant on heaven—one that has immediate repercussions for today.

What If the Return of Christ Depended upon You?

There is a fascinating pair of verses in 2 Peter 3:11-12a I want to leave with you. This apostle spent the entire third (and last) chapter of his writings focusing on the triumphant "day of the Lord," which will culminate in "a new heaven and a new earth, the home of righteousness" (v. 13).[13] Read Peter's words from verses 11 and 12a carefully, especially the last phrase: "Since everything will be destroyed in this way, what kind of people ought you be? You ought to live holy and godly lives as you look forward to the day of God and speed its coming." It is one thing to "look forward to" or "to pray for" the Lord's coming—it's a different matter, altogether, to "speed it up"—by living holy lives!

What do these verses mean? One commentary[14] offered this insight:

Peter probably is referring to something more than prayer. There was a strong Jewish tradition based on Isaiah 60:22 (which in the Septuagint[15] uses the same word for "speed" used here) that the coming of Messiah was held back by the sins of the people and that repentance would hasten this day. Peter appears to agree with this. He has talked throughout the letter about holiness. In the verse immediately before this one he has exhorted the people to "holy and godly lives" and two verses later he summarizes with, "Make every effort to be found spotless, blameless and at peace with him." Therefore what is said here is that the holiness of Christians both expresses their expectation of that day and hastens its coming.[16]

I don't want to mix Peter's truthful challenge with the following fictitious legend,[17] but I share this next story because of its narrative appeal. Its realistic portrayal depicts the struggle that many of us have when we think about the return of our Lord:

There's a 19th-century English novel set in a small Welsh town in which every year for the past five hundred years the people all gather in church on Christmas Eve and pray. Shortly before midnight, they light candle lanterns and, singing carols and hymns, they walk down a country path several miles to an old abandoned stone shack. There they set up a crèche scene, complete with manger. And in simple piety, they kneel and pray. Their hymns warm the chilly December air. Everyone in town capable of walking is there.

There is a myth in that town, a belief that if all citizens are present on Christmas Eve, and if all are praying with perfect faith, then and only then, at the stroke of midnight, the Second Coming will be at hand. And for five hundred years they've come to that stone ruin and prayed. Yet the Second Coming has eluded them.

One of the main characters in this novel is asked, 'Do you believe that he will come again on Christmas Eve in our town?'

'No,' he answers, shaking his head sadly, 'no, I don't.'

'Then why do you go each year?' he asked.

'Ah,' he says smiling, 'what if I were the only one who wasn't there when it happened?'

I'm not asking that you quickly buy into the earlier controversial interpretation of the Second Coming from 2 Peter 3:11-12. I am asking—no, urging—you to consider the possibilities, however. Even if there were the slightest chance that this triumphant event will occur, because of your personal revival, what would you do? What if the Creator of the universe placed into your hand the "ultimate remote," allowing you to speed all of us ahead to the end of time—by genuinely confessing your sins and praying "Maranatha"—would you press that fast-forward button?

I admit, it's a scary thought. It's also exhilarating.

The great news about the Good News—however the Creator wants to bring human history to a close—is that we can be totally confident of the ending: God wins. And so do all who choose to move over to his side, through Christ. That's the Jesus we will, one day, know completely. It's complete discipleship.

We can be certain we will, one day, wake up in our heavenly Home.

Can't you feel the certainty of that soon event, in the quiet depths of your heart? Don't you hear our Beloved Brother whisper your secret, personal name along with his personal invitation: "_____, welcome Home. Welcome, good and faithful servant. Welcome to your new, eternal family. We've been waiting for you."

"Let the Party of parties begin!"

1 I express gratitude to my brother Gary for the few, yet potent, conversations we have had on this topic of living eternity now. Much of his helpful input (and more) can be found in the book he coauthored with our friend and colleague J. P. Moreland, *Beyond Death: Exploring the Evidence for Immortality* (Wheaton, Ill.: Crossway, 1998), especially chapters 12, 13, and 15.

2 *Beyond Death*, p. 323. Italics are mine.

3 Notice how the words "will" or "being" are used in Matthew 10:22b, Mark 13:13, 1 Corinthians 1:18, 2 Corinthians 2:15, and Hebrews 9:28.

4 See *Beyond Death*, pp. 324-31.

5 Habermas and Moreland identify this fourth passage as 2 Corinthians 4:7–5:10. But I have deliberately added the seven verses immediately prior, because they provide the significant introduction, grounding these truths upon the image of God.

6 Again, from Philippians 3:18-21, I stress that Paul's main emphasis is image restoration. The word "transform" (v. 21) explicitly refers to this divine process—which eventually results in us having bodies like Jesus ("his glorious body"). Implicitly, verse 17 refers to these partial changes toward that same ultimate end, as the apostle refers to "my example" and the life "pattern we gave you."

7 Habermas and Moreland query: " . . . what if . . . [heavenly] rewards are *capacities* granted by God for greater service and personal growth?" in *Beyond Death*, p. 338.

8 Ronald T. Habermas, *Teaching for Reconciliation* (Eugene, Ore.: Wipf and Stock, 2001).

9 Since our calling legacy—from heaven's vantage point—may require more explanation, consider some provocative ideas from David Bruce Hegeman in sidebar 12.5 in the *Supplemental Resource*.

10 Evangelicals may hold a premillennial view of the end times (Christ will come back, reunite us with Himself, and we will coreign with him for a thousand years, followed by a final judgment, then eternity). Or they may hold an amillennial view (no literal millennium; humanity is ushered into the final days of persecution, then judgment, then eternity). As a case in point, some believers may take passages like Isaiah 65:17-25 to refer to the restoration of Israel on earth, or saved Israel, or to the millennium, or to heaven itself. Whatever position is chosen, the opening verse (Isa. 65:17) must be respected: "new heavens and a new earth" (see Rev. 21:1).

11 Isaiah 41:4, 44:6, 46:10, 48:12 and Revelation 1:8, 1:17, 21:6, and 22:13.

12 "The Inheritance" from Macdonald's *Unspoken Sermons*, Series Three, [Whitethorn, Calif.: Johannesen, (1997 edition)], p. 615.

13 Again, compare that eternal and heavenly phrase with Isaiah 65:17 and Revelation 21:1.

14 Peter H. Davids, *More Hard Sayings of the New Testament* (Downers Grove, Ill.: InterVarsity Press, 1991), pp. 198-99.

15 The Septuagint is the Greek translation of the Old Testament, written (between the third to second centuries B.C.) by Jewish scholars and adopted by Greek-speaking Christians. Many New Testament writers quoted from the Septuagint—rather than the Hebrew Old Testament. For example, all Old Testament references in the book of Hebrews were taken from this Greek translation.

16 A cross-reference (Isa. 60:22) translates this word "speed" as "swiftly." Italics are mine.

17 "Just One More Time" by Hanoch McCarty in *Chicken Soup for the Soul*, eds. Jack Canfield and Mark Victor Hansen (Deerfield Beach, Fla.: Health Communications, 1993), pp. 275-76.